BATTLESHIP
OKLAHOMA

BATTLESHIP
OKLAHOMA
BB-37

Jeff Phister

with

Thomas Hone

and Paul Goodyear

UNIVERSITY OF OKLAHOMA PRESS : NORMAN

Library of Congress Cataloging-in-Publication Data

Phister, Jeff, 1955–
    Battleship Oklahoma, BB-37 / Jeff Phister, with Thomas Hone and Paul
Goodyear.
        p. cm.
    Includes bibliographical references and index.
    ISBN 978-0-8061-3917-3 (hbk. : alk. paper)
    ISBN 978-0-8061-3936-4 (pbk. : alk. paper)
    1. Oklahoma (Battleship)   2. Pearl Harbor (Hawaii), Attack on, 1941.
3. World War, 1939–1945—Personal narratives, American.   I. Hone,
Thomas.   II. Goodyear, Paul.   III. Title.
    VA65.O52P57 2008
    359.3'252—dc22

1   2   3   4   5   6   7   8   9   10

In memory of

Norb Phister,

Ed Raymer,

Jean Goodyear,

and Dorothy Vezey

Contents

Illustrations

Preface

This book is the most complete, true accounting of the USS *Oklahoma* ever placed between two covers. Much of that has to do with the process of engaging the most important component of the book—the survivors of the events that occurred on the *Oklahoma* on the morning of December 7, 1941, at Pearl Harbor.

Most historical accounts of warfare are told through the filter of the author, who in addition to doing archival research interviews battle participants and then paraphrases the story, with perhaps the occasional first-person quotation for emphasis or color. In contrast, the narrative in key portions of this book relies heavily on the personal experiences and remembrances of the men who were there and uses their stories more completely than you might find in other accounts.

As one of those survivors, shipmate to these men, and as a coauthor, I was able to arrange face-to-face meetings or telephone interviews with them and ensure that the taped interviews were properly and accurately transcribed and used as fully as possible. In addition, each man was able to review the text of his interview to ensure his intent, remarks, and information were correct as he conveyed them, and to allow any correction or amplification before the manuscript was sent to the publisher. If a survivor passed away before he had the chance to review his portion, his statement was submitted to his shipmates.

The result is an accounting of one of the most famous U.S. battleships—including her role in the events of those few hours on the "day of infamy"—that includes not just the experiences but the thoughts, words, and emotions of the men on that morning. They are direct from the survivors to you.

Paul Goodyear

Acknowledgments

Ed Raymer and Paul Goodyear—it begins with them. Ed was my god-father. His book, *Descent into Darkness*, the memoirs of his experiences as a salvage diver at Pearl Harbor (1941–1943), first introduced me to the *Oklahoma*. When I decided to write a book about it following his death in 1997, the Internet took me to Paul Goodyear, president of USS *Oklahoma* Family, Inc. Incredibly, he lived only thirty-five miles from my home. Paul graciously granted me an interview, and our journey began. Following our initial meeting in December 2002, we made three sojourns in Southern California to interview more survivors. One by one, they shared their recollections of their ship and of that fateful Hawaiian morning that took the lives of so many of their shipmates. Later Paul invited me to attend their annual reunions, where I met numerous other survivors, as well as their families and friends. I cannot imagine a finer group of people. Paul also allowed me unlimited access to the catalog of written histories that he had collected from his shipmates throughout the years, a catalog that is now the property of the Oklahoma Historical Society. I only wish that Paul and Ed had been able to meet. I have no doubt that they would have experienced the same kind of friendship that Ed had shared with my father, Norbert Phister, a retired U.S. Air Force officer who died in 1981.

On a professional note, I would like to thank Kirk Bjornsgaard, acquisitions editor for the University of Oklahoma Press, for his persistence, patience, and constant support. I want to thank him also for suggesting that I enlist the help of noted author Tom Hone, an expert on the *Nevada* class of battleships. Tom's editing put the book back on course, and his substantial contributions—most of chapters 1 and 2—have given it depth. He's a great man, and it was indeed a privilege to work with him.

I would like to thank distinguished Pearl Harbor historians David Aiken, Paul Stillwell, and Daniel Martinez for their responses to my countless e-mails, and author Eric Hammel for his counsel. I would also like to thank Patrick Osborn for his help at the National Archives and Brian Basore for his help at the Oklahoma Historical Society. Marshall Owens, the former museum curator at the USS *Arizona* Memorial, provided a great deal of information about Ford Island, and Kristin Cheung, Pearl Harbor Naval Shipyard, provided information on the men from Shop 11.

I would also like to give thanks to Oklahoman Kevin King for both his passion and his artistic perspective. Kevin initiated the effort to construct a USS *Oklahoma* memorial at Pearl Harbor when he made a pilgrimage to Pearl Harbor with his son to learn about his state's namesake battleship. When no information was available, King challenged his high school buddy state senator Jim Reynolds to do something about it, which Jim did.

I give particular thanks to my high school buddy John Morgan, for his thorough and insightful edit of the original draft, and to Bob Valley and Ray Emory for the information they provided regarding the journey and current location of *Oklahoma*'s Pearl Harbor casualties. Bob's brother Lowell is one of *Oklahoma*'s 380 Unknowns.

Finally, I would like to thank my wife, Jody; our three incredible daughters, Jessica, Morgan, and Sara; my mother, Rita; my sisters, Brooke and Kimberly; and Marilyn Raymer (Ed's wife) for their unwavering support, particularly when my mind was out to sea . . . on the *Oklahoma*.

Prologue

On April 15, 2004, seven sailors solemnly filed onto the floor of the state senate in the capitol in Oklahoma City. Preceded by Senator Jim Reynolds, they formed a line at the head of the senate chambers. Seated before them was the state legislature. In the gallery above sat their families and friends. Nestled on the bottom of the ocean some four thousand miles to the west lay the USS *Oklahoma*, the battleship that had been their home until a quiet Sunday morning some sixty-three years before. Most had been teenagers then; now the youngest was seventy-nine. They had survived the onslaught of Japanese torpedoes and the horrors of a capsized ship, but 429 of their shipmates had not. Their time to be remembered had finally come, though time was growing short. Barely a hundred and fifty survivors remained, and April had just taken three more.

The seven sailors listened quietly as the resolution was read into the public record. Moments later, a vote was taken. By unanimous consent, the resolution passed. The people of the state of Oklahoma had spoken. Their ship and the proud men who had served aboard her would finally have a memorial along Battleship Row, where she had been moored on December 7, 1941, on the day that Japanese airplanes attacked Pearl Harbor.

This is the story of that remarkable ship and her brave men.

BATTLESHIP
OKLAHOMA

CHAPTER 1

Oklahoma's Genesis

"The President is hereby authorized to have constructed two first-class battleships, each carrying as heavy armor and as powerful armament as any vessel in its class, to have the highest practicable speed and the greatest practicable radius of action, and to cost, exclusive of armor and armament, not to exceed six million dollars each."

—Naval Appropriation Act, March 4, 1911

The war with Spain in 1898 showed that the U.S. Navy was a force to be reckoned with both in the Caribbean and in the far Pacific, where the United States had gained control of the Philippines. To give the navy the muscle it needed to assert American interests in the Pacific and the Caribbean, between 1900 and 1911 Congress authorized the navy to add twenty-two battleships and seven large armored cruisers to the force that had defeated Spain's navy in 1898. Twelve of the newest battleships were of the dreadnought type, with very heavy batteries of 12- and 14-inch guns. USS *Oklahoma* (BB-37) and USS *Nevada* (BB-36) were the newest and most powerful.

The power of *Oklahoma* and *Nevada* came from their batteries of ten 14-inch guns, their great steaming range (eight thousand nautical miles at ten knots' speed), and their heavy armor protection. When launched in the spring and summer of 1914, the two new battleships caused something of a stir among the world's navies. The ships were a sign that the U.S. Navy was technologically and militarily mature— that it could design and build battleships equal to or better than those of any other navy.

Where did these two impressive battleships come from? After all, the U.S. Navy was a Johnny-come-lately on the world stage. Congress did not authorize the navy to build powerful battleships until 1890. In twenty years, the navy had fostered a shipbuilding industry, created a corps of talented engineers and naval architects who could tap the latest developments in technology, and bootstrapped itself from a navy that could never hope to take on the world's best to a force that was capable—finally—of unilaterally enforcing the Monroe Doctrine.

To understand the genesis of *Oklahoma* and *Nevada,* you have to understand the problems that the rapidly growing U.S. Navy faced as it moved from the minor naval leagues to the majors. The basic problem facing the navy's battleship designers was how to pack the most punch into a ship of reasonable size and cost. A battleship was like a prizefighter in the ring. It had to be able to dish out punches as well as take them. It also had to have stamina and employ tactics that would defeat an opponent. Unfortunately for the designers, technological advances had made necessary a tremendous change in tactics.

In 1898, battleships fought at short range. In the Battle of Santiago on July 3, 1898, not one of the 13-inch shells fired by American battleships struck a Spanish ship. Only 13 of the 319 8-inch shells fired by the U.S. ships struck their intended targets. Seven years later, at the Battle of Tsushima between Russian and Japanese fleets, the accuracy of heavy naval guns had not improved much. Japanese gunners were able to hit Russian battleships at 6,000 yards, or less than 3½ miles, but the most severe damage inflicted on the Russian ships came at a range of 4,700 yards, or about 2⅔ miles, and it was not the biggest guns that did the most damage.

The larger navies recognized that the big guns were not accurate at long range, and therefore they built battleships that carried intermediate batteries of 8-inch, 7-inch, and 6-inch guns—as well as many smaller weapons to ward off torpedo boats. But by the time the United States dispatched its Great White Fleet from Hampton Roads, Virginia, on an around-the-world cruise in 1907, a revolution was in the making. The big guns were becoming accurate at long range. They had to. Otherwise, the inexpensive, fast, and highly maneuverable torpedo boats every navy was building would make the battleship obsolete.

But there was still the question: How accurate would the larger (12- and 14-inch) guns be at really long range? When *Texas* and *New York,* the two battleships that preceded *Nevada* and *Oklahoma,* were being designed in the spring of 1910, the designers knew that the ships would carry new and reliable 14-inch guns, but they were also convinced that the ships' gunners could not hit enemy ships at the maximum range of the guns, which was twenty thousand yards, or 11⅓ miles. So they planned for battles at a range of ten thousand yards, or just over 5⅔ miles, where shells approaching a battleship would come in at a shallow angle of fifteen degrees or less. It followed that *Texas* and *New York* would need armor protection mostly on the sides. As it happened, the gunners in every major navy found that with new range-finding equipment, they could hit targets at the maximum range, and the 1,400-pound shells fired from those guns at the maximum range would arc *over* the side armor plating that protected ships such as *Texas* and *New York*.

By the time this was understood, it was too late to change the design of *Texas* and *New York*, but the navy's ship designers understood that they had a problem on their hands for the next class of ship. Their first impulse was to make only incremental changes to the design of *Texas* and *New York*, but the General Board of the Navy, a panel of senior admirals who advised the secretary of the navy, rejected that approach. It was time to take some risks. Otherwise, the navy would not get a battleship that met its needs and was both affordable and not too large for dry docks, anchorages, and the locks of the Panama Canal.

Several innovations developed in 1910 came together to make a new design possible in the spring of 1911: a battleship turret that could carry three guns instead of two, which meant *Oklahoma* and *Nevada* could carry the same number of 14-inch guns (ten) as *Texas* and *New York* but in four turrets instead of five; "all or nothing" armor protection; the shift from coal to oil fuel; and the use of turbine engines.

OKLAHOMA'S ARMOR

In many older battleships, armor on the sides and much thinner armor on one or more decks were like the armor worn by a medieval knight—a burden. The armor provided protection, but at the price of being dead weight. In 1911, however, the navy's ship designers hit on a method to make it an integral part of a battleship's structure.

The method provided the ship with very thick side armor (13½ inches tapering to 8 inches below the waterline) over about two-thirds of her length. Capping this heavy side armor was an armored deck three inches thick. One deck below this one was another, lighter armor deck 1½ inches thick. In essence, the heart of *Oklahoma*, consisting of her engines, her ammunition magazines, and her gunnery and damage-control nerve centers, was inside an armored box—very thick at the sides and ends, and *thick enough* on top. Sticking up out of this armored box were the armored supports for her turrets, a heavily armored conning tower for her captain in battle, and a conical armored foundation for her funnel. Her turrets had faceplates eighteen inches thick, with armor five inches thick on top and nine inches thick on the back.

This form of armor protection was sometimes referred to as "protection where it mattered." As one navy officer reportedly put it, if *Oklahoma* were hit by an enemy shell where it mattered, then it would not matter. Conversely, if the ship were struck by a shell where it did not matter, then that would not matter, either. You can see the difference by comparing the weights of *New York* and *Nevada*:

Ship	Displacement (tons)	Weight of armor (tons)	Weight of weapons (tons)	Year keel laid
New York	27,000	8,965	2,582	1911
Nevada	27,500	11,309	2,586	1912

With just 500 extra tons of displacement, *Nevada*, *Oklahoma*'s sister ship, carried 2,344 additional tons of armor—or about 25 percent more than *New York* or *Texas*. What made this dramatic difference possible was the integration of the heavy side- and deck-protective armor into the ship's structure, where it provided both protection and strength for the hull and for the ship's superstructure. This creative design set the pattern for all U.S. Navy battleships built before the Washington Naval Treaty—halting new battleship construction—was signed in 1922.[1]

OKLAHOMA'S FUEL

The navy had decided in 1910 to fuel all future battleships with oil. Oil fuel was much, much cleaner than coal, which meant less mess when the ship refueled and hardly any residual ash deposits on the burners that heated the boilers. Oil also had more thermal energy per pound than coal, and it took far fewer firemen to tend an oil-fired boiler than a coal-fired one. Oil-fired boilers also did not need pressured fire rooms, which had been required in older battleships to provide sufficient air to burn coal, and oil-fired ships needed fewer smokestacks. It was also easier to take on oil at sea from tankers than coal from colliers, and oil-fired battleships could refuel their own escorting destroyers.

In 1914, fitting *Oklahoma* with oil-fired reciprocating engines was defended because they would use less fuel when the ship cruised at low speeds over long distances. Her engines were also expected to be much easier to maintain because oil under pressure would lubricate their moving parts.

OKLAHOMA'S ENGINES

To make best use of the available energy in coal and oil, the navy experimented with turbines (in *Nevada, Arizona,* and *Pennsylvania*), reciprocating engines (in *Texas, New York,* and *Oklahoma*), and eventually with turbo-electric drive (in *New Mexico, Tennessee,* and *California*). Turbo-electric drive used turbines operating at high speed to spin the armatures in generators, creating direct current that was then used to power separate electric motors. What you see in the battle fleet in the years just before and during World War I is a high degree of experimentation, with navy designers trying out different types of engines, different forms of underwater protection, and even different hull designs. The result was a battle fleet with ships of very different capabilities.

When *Oklahoma* and *Nevada* were designed, the navy decided to equip *Nevada* with steam turbines but *Oklahoma* with reciprocating steam engines. The navy's Bureau of Steam Engineering was not confident that existing steam turbine power plants had the reliability to work consistently well as the battle fleet steamed across the Pacific to meet its likely Japanese opponents. The factors that shaped the choice of reciprocating engines for *Oklahoma* were reliability, fuel efficiency, and ease of upkeep.

Oklahoma's engines were powered by steam produced in boilers. Each of the battleship's two triple-expansion engines was like a huge automobile engine. Attached to a finely balanced crankshaft was a row of four cylinders: a high-pressure cylinder (thirty-five inches in diameter), an intermediate-pressure cylinder (fifty-nine inches in diameter), and two low-pressure cylinders (each seventy-eight inches in diameter). The pistons in the cylinders, like those in an automobile engine, went up and down, through a full stroke of 48 inches in response to 250 pounds of steam pressure from *Oklahoma*'s twelve boilers. The crankshafts converted that up-and-down motion into circular motion, and the circular motion turned the drive shafts that drove the ship's two massive propellers. *Oklahoma*'s boilers and engines weighed just over 1,900 tons, and they generated approximately 22,000 horsepower when she was first commissioned.

But what gave this engine the ability to work both effectively and efficiently? The answer is simple: it used the same steam multiple times. The steam at its hottest and highest pressure was used first to push the piston in the high-pressure cylinder. Once it had done that, the energy-depleted steam was exhausted into the intermediate-pressure cylinder and used to push the piston there. Then, though with less heat and at a lower pressure, it was used yet one more time to displace the pistons in the two large low-pressure cylinders. Finally, the steam, robbed by now of most of its energy, was sent to a condenser, where it was cooled to form water that was filtered and recycled to the boilers.

This is where the reciprocating engines on *Oklahoma* differed from their cousins, the engines that drove steam locomotives. In a steam locomotive, there was only one high-pressure cylinder. Once the steam was used, it was either lost or captured and condensed to water. That was too inefficient a system for a ship that had to operate for weeks at sea without stops for additional fuel. Moreover, the ship had to use distilled seawater in its boilers, and the distilling process used energy, and energy—like ammunition for the big guns—was scarce and therefore precious.

Adding to the reliability of *Oklahoma*'s main engines was her impressive maintenance capability. She carried spare parts for her engines, such as piston rods, piston rings, valve stems, crank pins, bearings, and cylinder head bolts. *Oklahoma* also had spare oil burners, furnace doors, water gauges, condenser tubes, and oil strainers. Her workshops were equipped with machine tools—lathes, drills, milling machines, grinders—and a blacksmith's forge so that her engineering department could repair her main engines and other mechanical devices, such as the pumps that drew in seawater and emptied her bilges. She was even built with a foundry so that her metalsmiths and boilermakers could cast parts in an emergency without having to return to a major base.

In 1911, the weight of her engines was comparable to the weights of existing turbines, and it was easier then to throw a reciprocating engine into reverse. When *Oklahoma* was designed, the basic difference between turbines and reciprocating engines was that the turbines operated more efficiently at high speed than at low speed, while reciprocating engines were more efficient at low speeds. Because the battle fleet did not cruise at high speed, the reciprocating engine was a sensible alternative to turbine propulsion.

Oklahoma's engines were built well. When she was modernized after 1927, she kept her engines but was given six more modern and efficient boilers in place of her original twelve. Her maximum speed dropped below twenty knots because her weight had risen to over thirty-two thousand tons from her original twenty-eight thousand. However, her engineering performance remained impressive. In 1940, for example, at ten knots speed, her boilers burned 752 gallons of fuel per hour, giving her the ability to cruise almost eighteen thousand nautical miles without refueling. At nineteen knots, her maximum speed, fuel consumption jumped to 3,723 gallons per hour, giving her an endurance of only about sixty-nine hundred nautical miles.

Newer battleships did better. *West Virginia,* the last of the battleships built before the 1922 Washington Naval Treaty, had boilers that consumed 521 gallons of oil per hour at ten knots sustained speed. At nineteen knots, *West Virginia's* boilers burned 2,826 gallons of fuel per hour, giving her an endurance of 8,954 nautical miles. But *Oklahoma's* power plant was a good deal for the American taxpayer. When designed, the ship was never intended to serve as long as she did (25 years), yet her engines continued to function effectively throughout her long life— giving her the range and the mechanical reliability she was originally required to have.[2]

OKLAHOMA'S TACTICS AND ARMAMENT

Oklahoma's mission was to destroy or disable any ship that she attacked. Her 14-inch guns were designed to smash through the armor of enemy battleships and cruisers, detonating their powder magazines, wrecking their engines and boilers, or disabling their steering so that they could be picked off later. *Oklahoma's* 5-inch guns were there to repel the attacks of destroyers. In the daytime, enemy destroyers would attack from behind a smoke screen. At night, they would try to overwhelm the ability of *Oklahoma's* 5-inch guns and searchlights to nail them as they dashed at her from the darkness.

But *Oklahoma* was not designed to fight alone. She was meant to serve as one unit in a line of battleships. The goal of battleship tactics in every major navy was the same—to concentrate heavy fire on one part of the enemy's fleet, sinking and disabling one or two divisions of its battleships quickly, and then turning the heavy guns on the rest of the enemy's force. It was essential to find the enemy, strike fast and hard, and keep the enemy from retreating. In May 1916, at the Battle of Jutland, the British battleships hit their German opponents hard, but they allowed the Germans to slip away during the night and were robbed of the victory they had been right on the edge of achieving.

U.S. Navy battleships carried one hundred shells for each heavy gun. *Oklahoma's* turret crews could fire three rounds per gun every two minutes. That meant *Oklahoma* could deal out heavy punches from her 14-inch guns for about an hour or an hour and a half of steady battle. That was not very long. It was therefore important that the battleships maneuver against the enemy in such a way that, when they opened fire, their combined firepower would smash their opponents in minutes.

This might not sound like a difficult problem, but it was. In the mid-1920s, for example, the navy possessed fifteen first-line battleships—each carrying 14- or 16-inch guns. Each ship was about two football fields long, and in battle, they could follow one another at intervals of no less than 600 yards (about ⅓ mile). That meant that the fifteen ships, stretched out in a long column, one behind the other, would cover a distance of at least 11,400 yards, or 6½ miles. If the battleships leading the column were at maximum range from the enemy, then the battleships toward the rear of the column would be out of range and out of the fight.

So battleships practiced maneuvers that would bring their guns to bear on the enemy together. From a long column, the ships would form a line, and then they would practice forming the column again. Then they would practice maneuvering by divisions of battleships. In the 1920s, there were four battleships to a division. In the 1930s, there were three. Repeatedly, the ships would maneuver in a complex choreography that was designed to allow the commander of all the fleet's battleships to concentrate their awesome fire against an enemy, even when the enemy was firing back with everything it had.

It was a duel to the death, and the shells being fired in that duel had incredible force. Each of *Oklahoma*'s 14-inch guns was fifty-three feet six inches long, and weighed sixty-three tons. The shell fired by the gun weighed 1,400 pounds. When the gun was fired, 365 pounds of smokeless powder accelerated the shell to a speed of 1,600 feet per second and gave the shell a force (which is the product of the shell's mass times its acceleration) of over sixty-five thousand foot-tons. That's what each of *Oklahoma*'s guns thundered out to a range of twenty-thousand yards (or about twelve miles) when she first joined the fleet.

Oklahoma could carry two types of shells, armor piercing and bombardment. The armor-piercing shells were ship killers. Though each had an explosive charge weighing only 29½ pounds, the shells' dense metal composition and kinetic energy made them a threat to any ship, even those with heavy armor. These shells were tested against armor plate at the navy's Dahlgren Proving Ground in Virginia, and the tests showed that they could break through foot-thick armor and then detonate behind it. The second type of shell was for use against land targets. It looked the same as the armor-piercing shell, but its explosive filler weighed 105 pounds, and it was manufactured to burst into many splinters when the filler detonated. It was not a ship-killing weapon, but it was very useful in supporting amphibious landings.

Armor-piercing shells could destroy or wreck even heavily armored ships in an incredibly short span of time. On the morning of May 24, 1941, for example, the German battleship *Bismarck* sank the British battle cruiser *Hood* in just five minutes. On November 15, 1942, the American battleship *Washington* wrecked the Japanese battle cruiser *Kirishima* in only seven minutes in a furious night battle. With survival—and victory—a matter of minutes, it was imperative that *Oklahoma* and her sisters be able to find their targets quickly and hit them at long range as rapidly as possible.

But that posed a problem for *Oklahoma*'s designers. To hit at long range, *Oklahoma* needed three things: (1) a range finder, to measure the distance between *Oklahoma* and what she was shooting at; (2) a spotting top, so that her gunners could learn immediately if the shells they fired were "shorts" or "overs"; and (3) a plotter that would predict where the enemy ship would be when *Oklahoma*'s shells got there.

Firing the big guns was like a quarterback throwing a football downfield while pretending to run an option to the outside. The quarterback is moving, and the pass receiver is moving. The quarterback has to throw the ball where the receiver will be when the ball gets there. This is obviously not an easy pass play to execute, but this is precisely what *Oklahoma*'s gunners had to be able to do. In any engagement, their ship would be moving and maneuvering, and their target would be doing the same.

At a range of twenty-one thousand yards (nearly twelve miles), *Oklahoma*'s 14-inch shells would reach their target in about thirty seconds, but in thirty seconds a twenty-knot ship would move about three hundred yards, and shells fired at where the ship was when the range was taken would fall into the sea behind her. So a battleship had to keep a plot of where her target had been and where it was likely to be when her next set of shells reached the vicinity of the target. The plot also had to account for the battleship's own movements. Further, the plotting room itself had to be protected, and it had to be connected securely with the gunners in the turrets and the gunfire spotters at the top of her "cage" masts. *Oklahoma*'s builders protected the plotting room by placing it under the armored deck. The telephone circuits to the top of the cage masts, however, could not be shielded.

The range finders worked by triangulation to calculate the distance from *Oklahoma* to her target, and the calculations were made easier if the base of the triangle was as long as possible. *Oklahoma*'s builders therefore placed her range finders at the back of her turrets, where they were protected and had a long base to ease calculations of range. The spotters atop the high cage masts, 120 feet above the water, were unprotected from shellfire. Their job was to tell the gunners if they had achieved a "straddle," where some of the shells fired in a broadside had landed just beyond the target and others had fallen just short of it. Once that happened, the 14-inch guns were fired as rapidly as possible. To help the spotters, *Oklahoma*'s shells contained a dye that colored the splashes of shells that struck the water.

Photographs of *Oklahoma* early in her career reflect the ship's mission. They show a broad-beamed ship with four large turrets, two towering cage masts, a heavily armored conning tower, one smokestack, and a meager superstructure. There are cranes for the ship's boats and twenty-one 5-inch guns, most of them in single mounts ranged along her main deck. Invisible are two underwater torpedo tubes, one on each side of the ship toward her bow. She is suited for an engagement of battleships and battle cruisers and designed to give and take the heaviest shells then in use by any navy.

After her modernization in 1927–29, *Oklahoma*'s mission remained the same—fighting it out with other battleships at long range. But she received improved fire-control equipment (and new tripod masts to hold that heavier equipment), and the maximum elevation of her 14-inch guns was increased from fifteen to thirty degrees so that she could strike at targets beyond the visual horizon. To spot for her guns at such long range, she also carried three aircraft that could be launched from the ship's two catapults and then recovered from landings in the water alongside the ship.[3]

The navy did not intend for *Oklahoma* to serve for almost a generation. Instead of modernizing her in the late 1920s, the navy would have preferred to replace her with a new battleship, but the Washington Naval Treaty forbade that. As a result, *Oklahoma* sailed on—an old but stout floating fortress due to be retired on May 2, 1942.

CHAPTER 2

Life on the *Oklahoma*

"In the name of the United States of America, I christen thee *Oklahoma!*" trumpeted Lorena Cruce, daughter of Oklahoma governor Lee Cruce, as she smashed a bottle of champagne against the steel-plated bow of the U.S. Navy's newest battleship, the USS *Oklahoma*. The date was March 23, 1914. The location was Camden, New Jersey, home of the New York Shipbuilding Corporation. Moments later the behemoth six-story hull slid majestically into the tranquil waters of the Delaware River. The event, which was witnessed by Secretary of the Navy Josephus Daniels, would signify the dawning of a new era.

The Nevada Class of battleships—the *Oklahoma* and her sister *Nevada,* to be christened some four months later—were the first U.S. battleships powered exclusively by oil, the first to feature three 14-inch-diameter guns in a single turret, and the first to use the "all or nothing" scheme of armor protection.

Both had a top speed of nearly twenty-one knots, displaced 27,500 tons, had a length of 583 feet, and had a beam that measured 95 feet 2½ inches at the waterline. Their armament consisted of ten 14-inch/45-caliber main guns, twenty-one 5-inch/51-caliber broadside guns, and four submerged torpedo tubes. Nevada was commissioned on February 27, 1916; *Oklahoma* on May 2, 1916. *Oklahoma*'s first crew totaled 864 sailors and marines. She was commanded by Captain Roger Welles.

Like her civilian counterpart RMS *Titanic, Oklahoma* was a technological marvel, but as one might expect, the difference in accommodations was pronounced. Her sailors' berthing accoutrements consisted of two items only: a hammock and a twelve-inch-square metal box, called a "dittie box," for their personal belongings. For those who had never enjoyed three square meals a day, the food was considered good. For those who had known better, it was not. You washed your own laundry—in a bucket—and if you wanted your water hot, you stuck it beneath a steam pipe and opened a spigot. The lavatory facilities were a system of metal troughs that ran beneath lines of toilet seats. All the ship's heads were positioned along the side of the hull so that the sewage could drain naturally to the ocean below. Though the ship had evaporators to convert seawater for drinking and cooking, the water in the showers came straight from the sea.

A SAILOR'S EDUCATION

The lives of many sailors on the *Oklahoma* and on other battleships of the era would be improved by the efforts of Josephus Daniels, secretary of the navy from 1913 until 1921. Secretary Daniels was plainspoken but also shrewd and smoothly persuasive. When his appointment as secretary of the navy was approved by the Senate, he set out to change the navy, and change it he did.

As he noted in his official report to President Woodrow Wilson in 1916, the navy was "largely a boy institution," with most sailors enlisting at age seventeen (or even younger for those who could persuade a parent to sign for them). Because so many of these young men had at best an elementary school education, Daniels was committed to making the navy "the greatest educational institution in America." He defended this revolutionary idea by arguing that education was the key to opportunity in a modern society, and that the ideal of opportunity was so deep seated that not using public education to open the door to opportunity was simply un-American.

Daniels was out to change the nature of the navy's enlisted personnel. He wanted native-born, white recruits from the inland areas of the country—boys he thought would be eager to learn a trade and take on the responsibilities that would make them men. To attract them, he supplemented his stress on education with other measures designed to appeal to ambitious young men. For example, he arranged with the U.S. Post Office Department to allow the navy to issue money orders aboard ships so that sailors could send money home to their families. By his order, the cost of enlisted men's uniforms was also reduced, and ships' stores became more like shops ashore in terms of the merchandise they offered.

It is no exaggeration to say that Secretary Daniels revolutionized education for officers and enlisted men in the navy. He persuaded Congress to allow enlisted men to compete for a set number of slots in the Naval Academy in Annapolis, and he ordered the officers serving at the Naval Academy to stop the hazing that was traditional there. He directed ships' officers to conduct classes for newly enlisted personnel, and he ordered senior officers to reward younger officers who demonstrated teaching ability. Daniels also strongly supported postgraduate education for officers at institutions such as the Massachusetts Institute of Technology and at the navy's own War College in Newport, Rhode Island. By 1915, over half of navy enlisted men were taking courses of one sort or another, and enrollment in the residential and correspondence courses offered to officers by the Naval War College had increased dramatically.

Daniels also led the reform of the navy prison system by creating "schools of correction" to separate first offenders from hardened criminals, and he worked to prohibit state and local criminal court judges from offering young law violators a choice between jail and the navy. His methods worked. Navy jails held 1,835 prisoners in April 1914 but only 740 by October 1915. Daniels also persuaded Congress to allow the navy to recruit more chaplains, and he supported the work of the YMCA in cities where that organization assisted young sailors. Finally, in July 1914, to place officers on a par with enlisted personnel, he abolished the officers' wine mess. Officers still condemn him for this move, usually without understanding his very American motive, which was to reduce the status of the officer corps as an untouchable aristocracy.

Fortunately for the navy, the successors to Josephus Daniels retained and furthered his commitment to education for enlisted personnel and officers. They grasped the value of having enlisted men who could master modern equipment. Navy secretary Curtis Wilbur noted in 1926 that "The last 15 years has revolutionized industry in this country by standardization of methods and replacement of manual labor by labor-saving mechanical devices. During the same period a similar revolution has taken place not only in the propulsion and gunnery of naval vessels but in every device which concerns their operation."[1] The navy responded to this increased mechanization with schools ashore and correspondence courses for enlisted sailors at sea.

In 1926, the navy had about eighty-two thousand enlisted personnel of all rates. In that same year, the navy's Bureau of Navigation distributed over fifty-four thousand correspondence courses, some of which were supplemented by training films. But the navy was still an institution of young men. Eleven percent of enlisted sailors were under age twenty, and over 80 percent of all sailors were under the age of thirty. The year before, to provide the younger men with seniors who were both trained and educated, the navy had required candidates for the grade of chief petty officer to pass competitive examinations. To support the demand for materials needed to prepare for the examinations, the Bureau of Navigation had issued more than fifty-seven thousand course books describing what skills new petty officers had to have and how to acquire them.

The onset of the Great Depression after the stock market collapse of 1929, coupled with a strengthening of public education in many states, provided the navy with a wave of better-educated enlistees. In 1930, for example, 12 percent of recruits had not completed elementary school (through the sixth grade). In 1933, that figure had fallen to just 2.5 percent. In 1930, almost 28 percent of enlistees had only finished elementary school. In 1933, the number was just over 9 percent. In 1930, 60 percent of enlistees had completed one year or more of high school. In 1933, over 88 percent had done so. The surge in unemployment during the Great Depression allowed the navy to be very selective all through the mid- to late 1930s. In 1938, for example, the navy took in only 10 percent of those who wanted to enlist.

To deal with all these talented enlisted men, the navy created a system of schools. Class A schools provided basic education and skills training to sailors afloat. Shoreside Class B schools took qualified men from ships and taught them to be cooks and bakers, stenographers, radio operators, fire controlmen, aviation machinist's mates, aviation metalsmiths, and torpedomen. Class C schools were at the top of the heap. Also located ashore, they taught Diesel-engine repair, deep-sea diving, advanced first-aid skills, aerography (or meteorology), photography, echo sounding, aviation pilot training, and other advanced courses. Some courses lasted as little as two weeks. Others were a year long. There was even a six-month prep school for the enlisted personnel selected to attend the Naval Academy.[2]

THE EXPANSION OF ATHLETICS

Athletics had played a role in the life of enlisted sailors even before *Oklahoma* was commissioned in 1916, but athletic competition had been confined to a few forms of competition—mostly boxing and rowing. On March 3, 1917, the sailors of *Oklahoma* invited their counterparts from battleship *Texas* and fleet tug *Ontario* to a "happy hour" of wrestling and boxing matches. The better boxers had managers who helped them train and who arranged matches with men of similar weights from other ships. Betting was not allowed officially, though money changed hands unofficially.

Our Navy, a magazine published for enlisted men, reported on the contests. The December 1916 issue noted, "Battling Frankie Kirk, who as the 'Mare Island Thunderbolt' held the *Our Navy* lightweight belt while in the Service, is a busy guy these days in *Oklahoma.* In the past twelve months, Frank has boxed just twenty times and won every one of the twenty starts. . . . Some of these wise fight managers around New York who make good money out of a bunch of second stringers would do well to send a ticket to *Oklahoma* and bring Frankie Kirk to the big burg. Frank could just about make some of these crack New York lightweights jump over the ropes."[3]

This short article demonstrates both the strength and the weakness of navy enlisted athletics of the time. The strength was that the scheduled formal matches gave enlisted men with talent a chance to show it off and maybe gain the opportunity to contend with professionals in the big time. The weakness was that not enough sailors participated in organized athletics. Navy officers who served with the Royal Navy at Scapa Flow in World War I were impressed with the scale of athletics supported by their British counterparts, and they returned to the United States committed to expanding enlisted participation in inter- and intra-ship athletic contests.

The result was a gradual blossoming of fleet athletics. In World War I, for example, battleship *Nevada* held eight major athletic trophies, but seven of the eight were for winning sailing and rowing competitions. By 1935, the scale of athletic competitions had mushroomed to include baseball, football, competitive shooting, and track and field events, as well as organized boxing, wrestling, sailing, and rowing. There were more sailor athletes than there were athletic fields to play on, and the organization and refereeing of fleet athletic contests took the full time of one lieutenant and a small army of volunteer officials.

To keep the teams from the larger ships from dominating all competitions, the battleships and the large carriers *Saratoga* and *Lexington* were put in a league of their own. The annual rhythm of competition among the teams raised by these ships was extraordinary. The athletic year began with rowing races held in San Francisco and in Puget Sound. While those were taking place, preparations were begun for football season at San Pedro, California. These included readying the fields and training the officials, who were officers who had played football. After football season ended, boxing and wrestling contests began—held usually in the YMCA at San Pedro. Then came the sailing competitions, one of which allowed the crews to use whatever set of sails their small boats could bear, including, according to one witness, "ballooners, spinnakers, genoa jibs and skysails that reached to the heavens."[4] Then there were swimming and basketball contests. All told, there were twenty-seven events for the crews of the battleships and the two big aircraft carriers.

But there was one catch—not enough sailors were competing. The whole point to expanding athletic events was to draw in as many enlisted sailors as possible, but the focus on the major contests between ships' crews had the effect of almost eliminating *intraship* competition. About 20 percent of the sailors made up the regulars of the ship-vs.-ship contests. The other 80 percent were spectators—and bettors. And the bettors wanted sharp referees, umpires, and judges. Too much money rode on these contests to allow a match or game to be lost because the officiating was amateurish, but the navy did not want to hire officials from civilian life.

Some admirals tried to broaden the base of competition. In 1934, for example, Vice Admiral T. T. Craven ordered the major ships, then anchored in Guantanamo Bay, Cuba, to draft almost all their crews into a major rowing and sailing regatta. The results were a social success, if not an athletic one. One of battleship *Mississippi*'s rowing crews dressed as pirates in an effort to spice up their event. Another rowing crew lost control of their boat and plowed straight into the side of *West Virginia*. A witness noted that "the big ship weathered the impact in grand style. Not so the motor launch."[5]

So much for organized athletics. There were other diversions for sailors, including the time-honored games of pinochle and acey-deucey on ship, and pool ashore. After *Oklahoma* and most of the battleships were sent to the West Coast, there was a real need for safe places for sailors to congregate. In the early 1920s, the chief petty officers in the fleet gathered enough contributions for a large club with a gymnasium and dormitory in San Pedro. The YMCA also built its own facility there. Finally, there were dances hosted by the different ships—sometimes aboard ship and sometimes ashore. In the spring of 1922, *Mississippi* hosted almost two thousand revelers for dancing, amateur singing contests, and stage acts.

Several clever names for dances were coined at battleship *Idaho*'s first annual ball, held at the Shrine Auditorium in Los Angeles. One fox trot, in honor of the ship's navigator, was called "She's a B-a-a-d Kitty." The fox trot dedicated to the ship's marines was entitled "First in What? Chow!" while the waltz for the aviation officers was "Never up in the Air." The "Chow Card" carried on the fun, with "Salad à la Sea Gull," "Lettuce Have Peace," "Irish Plums," "Kelp à la Shark," "Ring Buoys," "Ja-Moch," "Red Shellac," "Paralyzed Milk," and "Pipe Down Four to Eight Bells." It was all part of the Roaring Twenties.

BATTLESHIP HEALTH AND SAFETY

Life on the *Oklahoma* was not all fun and games, of course. Infectious diseases were a serious threat to sailors before the development of antibiotics. Influenza killed six *Oklahoma* crewmen during World War I and struck the ship in a major way again in July 1932. But influenza was not the only killer that stalked *Oklahoma*'s crew. Spinal meningitis, scarlet fever, mumps, measles, and diphtheria also threatened ships because they were so contagious. Sailors stricken with these diseases had to be identified and isolated quickly, before the illness could spread. Americans do not quarantine the victims of most infectious diseases today, but public health officials during World War I and after had few other weapons against rapidly spreading diseases.

Routine work aboard ship could also be hazardous. There was always the danger of being swept overboard or knocked down by heavy seas. Ships are also notoriously hard, even big and steady ones like *Oklahoma*. If you didn't crack your head going through a watertight door, you ran the risk of barking your shin. And there was worse than that—sometimes much worse. On August 16, 1925, a sailor was killed when a 14-inch gun in turret 1 slid back into the gun pit when all three guns were elevated. The gun was supposed to have been held in place by its counter-recoil hydraulics, but a leak in the hydraulic line caused the sixty-three-ton gun to crush one of the gunners and severely injure another.

In January 1926, there was another gun accident. As navy secretary Curtis Wilbur stated in his annual report, one of *Oklahoma*'s 3-inch anti-aircraft guns had misfired. The gun captain opened the breech of the gun "without waiting for further attempts to be made to fire the gun or for the 30 minutes required by the safety regulations."[6] The cartridge case then exploded, severely injuring two members of the gun crew. Gun crews also had no official protection for their ears—even against the great blast wave created by the firing of the 14-inch main guns.

The navy tried to reduce injuries aboard ship. In 1926, for example, folding bunks were fitted on an experimental basis to *Oklahoma* and *California* in an effort to determine if the men using them slept better and were less likely to fall out of them than out of the standard hammocks. Navy physicians also worried about diet, and about how to best to serve food fresh and hot. Experiments with cafeterias started in 1918, though what was called a "cafeteria system" was not widespread in the fleet until the late 1930s.

A well-meaning Congress often did not help. Early in the twentieth century, Congress had encouraged the navy to serve sailors "Irish potatoes." As a result, the navy required that almost three-fourths of all fresh vegetables served onboard be Irish potatoes. As the navy's surgeon general pointed out in 1926, that meant sailors were not getting enough green vegetables. They were also not receiving adequate amounts of milk and fruit. But they *were* wolfing down the calories—over 4,600 per day per man aboard ship. For many sailors, this high-calorie ration was necessary. Some were still growing boys. Many had strenuous physical work to perform.

The medical problems that got the most attention were the venereal diseases, especially gonorrhea and syphilis. The prevalence of venereal disease was not talked about openly until the 1920s, but it was a serious matter. In 1926, for example, more than 12 percent of all navy personnel were diagnosed as having a venereal disease. Battleship *Maryland*'s medical officer reported that the primary source of venereal infections on his ship was the area around the Puget Sound

Navy Yard, including the notorious Boston Club in Seattle. Other medical officers pointed to San Francisco as the liberty port where sailors most frequently became infected.

As the navy's surgeon general reported, "the venereal disease admission rate in 1931 was 136.79 per 1,000 of total personnel. A total of 15,425 admissions and 217,535 sick days were reported" for a force of 79,700 men in the navy.[7] It was hard for sailors—especially young sailors—to avoid coming into contact with infected females. Desperate and poor prostitutes waited for sailors in every major liberty port. In San Diego, for example, the lifting of Prohibition allowed what had been an underground trade in alcohol to flourish openly, from places like the Fleet Café and the Bay City Grill on Broadway to Big Boy's Bohemian Grill along Third Street. The shore patrol was there to break up fights and calm down young men who could not manage the nickel beer they drank, but sailors with enough money could usually find a girl who wanted it—with the all-too-often inevitable result. Yet the prime killer of young sailors after 1930 was not disease or drowning at sea; it was the automobile combined with alcohol, a devastating combination even today. The life of a U.S. Navy sailor could be more dangerous on land than at sea.[8]

CHAPTER 3

Oklahoma's First Mission

In February 1917 Germany adopted a policy of unrestricted submarine warfare on the British Isles. Under this policy, any ship found in British waters, regardless of its nationality, would be subject to attack. Shortly thereafter, British intelligence intercepted a telegram authored by Arthur Zimmermann, the German foreign secretary. Intended for the German ambassador to Mexico, Count Johann Heinrich von Bernstorff, the telegram proposed that Mexico join Germany in a war against the United States. If U.S. troops were engaged in the defense of her southern border, there would be fewer troops to send to Europe to fight. In return, Mexico was promised the lands she had lost to the United States in the Mexican War of 1846–48: Arizona, California, and New Mexico. Primarily as a result of these two events, the United States declared war on Germany on April 6, 1917, providing Britain and France with a long-needed ally.

Unfortunately, there would be no immediate avenue of participation for *Oklahoma*. The British could not accommodate the new oil-burning U.S. battleships because their oil supply had dwindled due to the successes of German submarines in the Mediterranean. Only the older, coal-burning battleships were sent abroad. *Oklahoma* would spend the ensuing months at various navy yards while the three other oil-burning battleships, *Nevada, Arizona,* and *Pennsylvania,* spent the period as training platforms along the eastern seaboard.

Oklahoma would also undergo her first refit. Because Germany was becoming increasingly dependent on airships and seaplanes for naval reconnaissance, a pair of 3-inch/50-caliber antiaircraft (AA) guns were installed in the *Oklahoma*'s superstructure just forward of the main-mast. In addition, nine of the ship's 5-inch/51-caliber broadside guns were removed because of positioning problems. While the two forward guns were eliminated because they were prone to flooding, the seven guns aft, including the "stinger" in the stern, were removed due to limited fields of fire as a result of their positioning near the waterline. Two of the 5-inch/51-caliber guns were remounted on the deck alongside the conning tower.

IRELAND

In the summer of 1918, *Oklahoma* was finally dispatched to Europe along with *Nevada* and *Utah*. The three composed Battleship Division Six (BatDivSix), commanded by Rear Admiral Thomas S. Rodgers. *Oklahoma* and *Nevada* departed together on August 13. Ten days later, they rendezvoused with destroyers *Balch, Conyngham, Downes, Kimberly, Allen,* and *Sampson* approximately 275 miles west of Ireland. Racing east at twenty knots, the ships dropped anchor in Berehaven Harbor, located on the northern shore of Bantry Bay. It would be another eighteen days before *Utah* arrived.

Though the division's mission was to protect U.S. convoys from attack by German cruisers, it spent most of its time at anchorage. Only once during the eighty days *Oklahoma* was in the war zone did she venture out of the harbor. Under the command of Captain Charles B. McVay, Jr., she departed on October 14 with *Nevada* and *Utah* to escort troop ships into England, a mission that would last only two days. The majority of the time was spent drilling. With the exception of a gunnery exercise conducted in Bantry Bay, the *Oklahoma*'s drills were conducted while the ship was still at anchor. As one might expect, boredom ran rampant. In an effort to combat it, recreational parties were sent ashore to Bere Island, where a YMCA was being constructed, and to neighboring Castletown. Athletics was another form of recreation, particularly football and sailing. The *Oklahoma*'s sailing team defeated the *Nevada* and *Utah* teams on September 18, and the crowning moment of the football season was a 7–6 win over *Utah* on November 19.

As it turned out, the division's greatest foe would be disease. During the fall of 1918, more than 21 million people would succumb to a worldwide flu virus. BatDivSix was equally hard hit. Between October 21 and November 2, *Oklahoma* would lose six crewmembers, including Commander Gardner L. Caskey, a gunnery officer who had graduated at the top of his class from the Naval Academy in 1907. A memorial service was conducted for each on *Oklahoma*'s quarterdeck. To honor the men, the flags of the ships in the harbor were lowered to half-mast for thirty minutes. Following each service, the shrouded body was taken to the U.S. naval hospital at Queenstown for eventual transportation to the United States. The cause of death was generally listed as pneumonia.[1]

At approximately 9:00 in the morning on November 11, 1918, *Oklahoma* received a radio broadcast announcing that the Allies and Germany had agreed to an armistice, and that the war would officially end at 11:00 A.M. the same day. Ten days later, the British Grand Fleet accepted the surrender of the German High Seas Fleet. Aligned in two parallel columns, each nearly ten miles long, the British fleet surrounded the German fleet in the North Sea. The German warships were then escorted to the eastern coast of Scotland, where they were anchored in captivity at the Firth of Forth.

Though the Americans in Bantry Bay greeted the news of the German defeat with great exuberance, it had quite the opposite effect among the members of Sinn Fein, an Irish political faction that advocated independence from England—a cause that would probably have been advanced if the Germans had won. Because the Americans had been allied with the English, the American sailors were not well received as their postwar liberty excursions extended eastward into the county of Cork. In one particular incident, a gang of Sinn Feiners challenged a group of *Oklahoma* sailors going ashore for liberty. As the sailors disembarked onto a dock, the gang attacked them. The onslaught backed the unsuspecting sailors toward the end of the dock, where several fell off and nearly drowned in the frigid waters.

Later the same day, a second altercation occurred in the city of Cork. In a melee that took place in a restaurant, the sailors took vengeance with their fists. Though no one was killed, the restaurant was nearly destroyed. When Admiral Rodgers learned of the incident, he ordered his sailors to pass a hat. After a sufficient amount of money was gathered, the admiral presented the funds to the mayor as compensation. Fortunately, there were no further incidents.

END OF THE GREAT WAR

On November 26, *Oklahoma* departed for Portland, England, with the *Utah.* She would be joined there by *Arizona* on November 30, *Nevada* on December 4, and by the five BatDivNine battleships on

December 5. A week later the entire contingent departed Portland for a rendezvous in the English Channel with the battleship *Pennsylvania* and the transport ship *George Washington*. Sighting the two ships on the morning of December 13, *Oklahoma*'s crew manned the railings to greet the *George Washington*'s esteemed passenger, President Woodrow Wilson. Following a twenty-one-gun salute, the president was escorted to Brest, France, where he disembarked to participate in the Paris Peace Conference. The following day, *Oklahoma* departed for the United States. Arriving in New York City on December 26, the sailors were greeted as conquering heroes and quickly took advantage of their newfound celebrity.

The fate of the German sailors would be quite the opposite. Transferred to Scapa Flow from the Firth of Forth, they remained interred on their ships until the conclusion of the Paris Peace Conference. When it was decreed that their ships would be divided among the victorious Allies, the German sailors decided to scuttle them. In a final act of defiance, they literally pulled the plugs from the bottoms of their ships, sinking over four hundred thousand tons of modern warships.

Ironically, Japan, who would be Germany's ally in World War II, benefited greatly from the treaty. Fighting alongside the British because of their 1902 alliance, Japanese ships had escorted Australian troop ships across the Pacific and patrolled the Mediterranean, while Japanese troops captured the German bastion at Tsingtao, China. As a result, Japan received Germany's Pacific Ocean possessions: the Marshall, Caroline, Mariana, and Palau Islands.

Japan's ascension as a Far East power would be prompted further by the publication of a political manifesto in 1923 Written by Japanese revolutionary Ikki Kita, *An Outline Plan for the Reorganization of Japan* proposed a Japanese hegemony of the Far East that would eventually lead to *hakko ichiu*, the hegemony of the world. Though the Japanese government tried to suppress it, it received widespread circulation. Ten years later, its doctrines would have a marked influence on the officer corps of the Japanese military, particularly its youngest members, starting a decade of increasingly military-dominated rule that would come to be known as a "government by assassination."

CHAPTER 4

The Great Cruise and Modernization

In the spring of 1919, the U.S. Fleet was divided to form two autonomous units. While *Oklahoma, Nevada, Pennsylvania,* and *Arizona* remained on the East Coast with the Atlantic Fleet, the newly commissioned battleships *Mississippi, New Mexico,* and *Idaho* would form the nucleus of a new Pacific Fleet. Commanded by Admiral Hugh Rodham, the Pacific Fleet battleships would be based in San Pedro, California.

That same year *Oklahoma* was equipped with flying-off platforms atop turrets 2 and 3. Though the biplanes they launched would give the ship newfound reconnaissance capabilities, the set-up was rather awkward because the planes could be launched but not retrieved. During another refit in 1921, six more 3-inch/50-caliber AA guns were added, bringing the ship's total complement to eight. When the refit was completed, *Oklahoma* transited the Panama Canal to join the Pacific Fleet for exercises. Officially transferred to the fleet a short time later, she would subsequently undergo a West Coast refit at the Puget Sound Navy Yard in Bremerton, Washington. She would emerge in 1922 with a true air arm. Replacing her obsolescent flying-off platforms and one-way biplanes was a quarterdeck-mounted compressed-air catapult, a Vought VE-7H seaplane, and a crane to retrieve it. The question was, would she remain in commission long enough to use them?

WASHINGTON NAVAL TREATY

Though the world was officially at peace, it was a thinly veiled veneer. The Great War in Europe, penned as "the war to end all wars," had resulted in quite the opposite. Instead of vying for peace, the world's five major powers—the United States, Britain, France, Japan, and

Italy—were embarking on a massive arms race. As a result, when Warren G. Harding became president in March 1921, he did so with a mandate. With a pledge to return the world to normalcy, he tasked his secretary of state, Charles Evan Hughes, to convene an international conference with the purpose of disarming the world's major navies. The conference was indeed convened, resulting in the Washington Naval Treaty of 1922. Signed by France, Britain, Italy, Japan, and the United States, the treaty placed a ten-year ban on the construction of new battleships and established a ceiling for those that existed, requiring that a great many be removed from service.

The effect on the U.S. battleship roster was dramatic—at least numerically. Of the forty-five battleships on the U.S. Naval Vessel Register, seventeen were scrapped, one became a crane ship, one became a museum, one became a floating barracks, one was decommissioned, two were sold to Greece, and six became target ships. Of the nine U.S. battleships either under construction or planned for construction, only two would be completed—*Colorado* and *West Virginia*. When they were commissioned, the battleship roster would consist of twelve oil-powered battleships and six coal-powered battleships. Fortunately, the eighteen were considerably more powerful than the ships that were lost, resulting in minimal change to the overall firepower of the battleship force.

In general, the United States benefited a great deal from the treaty, because monies previously allocated for operation and maintenance could now be invested in aviation and submarines.[1] Japan had a totally different perspective, however, because of the inequity of the 5:5:3 tonnage ratios assigned respectively to the United States, Britain, and Japan. It was not until the United States agreed not to further fortify her Pacific bases west of Hawaii, and Britain agreed to the same for her bases east of Singapore, that the Japanese government finally capitulated—much to the disdain of her military, who felt the disproportionate ratio was just another example of Anglo ethnocentricity.[2] The U.S. Immigration Act of 1924 heightened that belief. Signed into law by Calvin Coolidge, the act effectively barred the Japanese from immigrating into the United States. The discriminatory fervor the law created was so intense that the Japanese government declared May 26, 1924—the date the law became effective—as a Day of National Humiliation.

THE GREAT CRUISE

By 1925 sixteen of the eighteen U.S. battleships were assigned to the Pacific Fleet. Their primary duties consisted of maneuvers off the coastal islands of southern California and "flower show" forays to various ports along the western seaboard. Conceived as public relations venues, allowing civilians a hands-on view of the fleet's ships, the shows were a rousing success. Resplendent with tours and assorted mixers, they did a great deal to enhance the public's perception of its navy. In April 1925 the show was taken abroad.

Similar in scope to the voyage of the Great White Fleet in 1907, the intent of the Great Cruise of 1925 was to display the long-range capabilities of the U.S. Navy. Comprising three battleship divisions and supporting cruisers and destroyers, the cruise garnered considerable goodwill in the southwest Pacific in addition to providing a broad scope of experiences.

After rendezvousing in San Francisco, twelve battleships set sail on April 15, 1925. Arriving in the Hawaiian Islands twelve days later, they conducted war games until July 1, when they departed for Samoa. Following the departure of *Arizona* for the mainland in June, the battleship contingent was set at eleven: *Oklahoma, Nevada, Pennsylvania, Colorado, Maryland, West Virginia, New Mexico, Idaho, Mississippi, Tennessee,* and *California,* which served as the battle force flagship. Commanding the fleet was Admiral Robert E. Coontz. His flagship was the cruiser *Seattle.* Following an age-old tradition, the fleet came to a standstill on July 6, when it crossed the Equator. It was time to initiate the pollywogs—those who had never crossed before.

According to the *Oklahoma*'s deck logs, His Majesty Neptunus Rex, his consort, and his court were sighted a thousand yards dead ahead at 7:55 A.M. Ten minutes later, the engines were stopped and His Majesty came aboard. At 8:07 A.M. Captain Willis McDowell relinquished his command.

Keeping with tradition, King Neptune convened his court, and the hapless pollywogs were tried—for being pollywogs. Attired in the appropriate garb—whatever was handy—King Neptune and his judges read the charges and dispensed a unanimous verdict: Guilty. The pollywogs would be punished. A makeshift swimming pool and canvas tunnel had been constructed. Because the pollywogs were already seated alongside pool, the transition from trial to punishment was immediate. Their faces were smeared with grease; then they were tipped over backwards into the pool. Awaiting them were bears—veterans of prior equator crossings—who clubbed them with cloth mallets as they attempted to escape. Once free of the pool, the pollywogs were greeted by the devil, a bear with a blunt-tipped pitchfork that was electrically charged with a hand-cranked generator. After being zapped in the buttocks, they were forced into a three-foot-diameter canvas tunnel filled a concoction of flour and mashed potatoes. Their initiation was not complete until they reached the tunnel's end, which generally took a while. The festivities consumed the better part of a day—the cleanup, a little longer.

After arriving in Samoa on July 10, the fleet anchored at the U.S. Navy fueling facility in Pago Pago. Samoa would prove an interesting cultural experience for *Oklahoma*'s sailors because there was no currency, and the women went topless. The island was void of any venereal diseases, so any sailor being treated for a sexual malady was confined to the ship.

Instead of currency, the island's commerce was based on bartering. The items most coveted by the sailors were Samoan war clubs and grass skirts, while those most coveted by the natives were navy-issue undergarments. Trading was rigorous and without bias because there was no requirement for proof of ownership. In fact, one sailor was welcomed ashore by a woman wearing one of his shirts.

Following its departure for Australia, the fleet split up on July 21. While most of the fleet voyaged to Sydney, *Oklahoma, Nevada, Pennsylvania,* and the cruiser *Seattle* traveled to Melbourne. The merriment began soon after the ships docked at Princess Pier. Because the population of young Australian males had been severely depleted during the Great War in Europe, the civilian populace was abundantly female. The sailors disembarking onto the pier were greeted not only by an incredible array of women, but also by fathers seeking suitors for their daughters. It was quite the gala event despite it occurring in the middle of the Australian winter. A luncheon held for local dignitaries aboard the *Pennsylvania* lasted well into the evening because the attendees enjoyed the respite from the cold provided by the ship's central heating system.

For the sailors, there was a different sort of warmth. America was in the midst of Prohibition, so the Melbourne pubs provided many

Oklahoma crewmen their first experiences with alcohol. Selection was quite easy for the novices because the pub walls sported picture advertisements for the pub's concoctions. For those enjoying the new adventure, assorted schemes were devised to smuggle some of the bottled versions aboard ship.

Because the Australians were such gracious and fun-loving hosts, Admiral Coontz decided to reward them with a farewell party. Conceived as an invitation-only dance with a specific allotment of tickets, the event, which was well publicized, quickly escalated into much more. Though local policemen were positioned as ticket takers alongside each ship, they could do little to quell the throngs of partygoers, particularly the many without tickets. Navy personnel made further attempts to stop them as they raced up the gangways, but their numbers were simply overwhelming.

Needless to say, the party was a rousing success. When the music ended at midnight, the guests, both invited and uninvited, milled gratefully toward the gangways. The following day, *Oklahoma* was the talk of the town.

OVERHAUL

Following a foray to New Zealand, the fleet headed east for home. In early 1927 *Oklahoma* transited the Panama Canal to join the Scouting Fleet on the East Coast. In September she entered the Philadelphia Naval Yard for a two-year modernization. The changes would be dramatic.

Gone were the cage masts. Replacing them were tripod masts with three-story fire-control tops. The upper deck was extended aft to the mainmast, and a deckhouse was built atop it. The deckhouse had five casemates along both sides with a galley in between. Lined with teakwood planking, the top of the deckhouse became the superstructure deck. Because the ship's boats were stored there, it was commonly known as the boat deck.

When the deckhouse was completed, the 5-inch/51-caliber broadside guns were removed from the hull. Ten were reinstalled inside the deckhouse casemates, and four were mounted forward on the boat deck. Also removed were the ship's four torpedo tubes and the eight 3-inch/50-caliber AA guns, which were replaced with eight 5-inch/25-caliber

AA guns and a new aiming device called a director, an electromechanical device that took into account such variables as wind speed and direction of travel to determine where the guns should be pointed.

The guns were installed on the boat deck, the director at the rear of the range-finder platform. For short-range AA defense, eight .50-caliber machine guns were mounted in gun tubs atop the masts, four in the foremast and four in the mainmast. To increase the range of the 14-inch/45-caliber main guns, their maximum elevation was raised from 15 to 30 degrees. In addition, two inches of special treatment steel was overlaid on the armor deck, and a catapult was installed atop turret 3.

Perhaps the most startling change was the addition of antitorpedo blisters. Forming an extended hull along most of the ship's length, the blisters provided added protection to each side of the ship from the second deck down. Welded to the hull where it turned inward toward the keel, each blister was six feet six inches wide below the waterline, tapering to about a three-foot width at the third deck level. From there it rose vertically to the level of the second deck, where it was capped, creating a three-foot-wide ledge along its length.

The purpose of the blisters was to absorb the energy of a torpedo explosion. When a torpedo hit the blister, the energy of the explosion could vent itself in the open spaces between the blister's wall and the hull, which in theory would minimize the damage to the hull itself. To isolate the zone of destruction of a potential torpedo hit, the blister was constructed as a matrix of four-foot-wide compartments. A side benefit was the enlargement of the ship's waterplane area, which increased her stability. For cleaning and maintenance, the blisters could be accessed via manholes in the ledge.

When her modernization was completed, *Oklahoma* became the widest ship in the navy, with a beam of nearly 108 feet, still narrow enough to allow passage through the locks of the Panama Canal. The associated increase in weight reduced her top speed from 20.5 knots to 19.68 knots. She departed Philadelphia in August 1929, venturing south into the Caribbean for a shakedown cruise. In June 1930 she rejoined the Pacific Fleet in San Pedro, where she was assigned to BatDivOne along with *Nevada* and *Texas*.

On July 11, 1931, the *Oklahoma*'s officers' roster would be augmented by the arrival of one of the youngest ensigns of the modern era, twenty-year-old John Sidney McCain, Jr. Fresh out of the Naval Academy, young McCain would eventually become a four-star admiral, as would his father, John Sidney McCain, Sr. They would be the first father and son admirals in the history of the U.S. Navy.[3] McCain, Jr., and other sailors on the *Oklahoma* would find their careers put on hold because of an event that left much of the nation destitute— including the government itself.

CHAPTER 5

Earthquakes, Refugees, and War

In 1929 the United States was a primary importer of Japanese goods. But when the United States curtailed its imports following the Wall Street crash in October, the Japanese yen plummeted, creating a state of economic ruin that undermined the civilian-controlled government and allowed the militarists a toehold. Trumpeting the Great Depression as a natural by-product of capitalism, the Japanese militarists sought an economic solution based on expansion. Following the explosion of an alleged bomb beneath the tracks of the South Manchurian Railway, which Japan had received as an indemnity at the conclusion of the Russo-Japanese War of 1904–1905, a Japanese army invaded Manchuria in the fall of 1931. Following an official condemnation by the League of Nations in 1932, Japan withdrew from the league and, in effect, the international community. The military's ascension to power would be further solidified on May 15, 1932, when a group of young naval officers and army cadets assassinated two of the most influential members of the civilian government, Prime Minister Tsuyoshi Inukai and Finance Minister Junnosuke Inouye.

OKLAHOMA TO THE RESCUE

While the Great Depression gave impetus to the Japanese military, it had the opposite effect on the military of the United States. Because of a lack of funds for maintenance and operations, U.S. warships spent an inordinate amount of time in port. As a result, *Oklahoma* was in San Pedro when a series of earthquakes struck Southern California on March 10, 1933. The effects were most pronounced in nearby Long Beach, where fifty-one people were killed.

Though no major buildings toppled, there was a great deal of damage. Businesses with broken storefronts soon became the targets of looters. With the fall of darkness, the looting became so widespread that local police could not control it. Fortunately, the navy was available to help. Unsolicited, Admiral Richard H. Leigh, the commander of the Pacific Fleet, dispatched his men to render aid. Within hours, several thousand marines and sailors were en route, including 107 from the *Oklahoma*. Their presence stemmed the flow of looting almost immediately. Subsequently, they relieved local fire, police, and medical personnel, enabling them to perform the more intimate details of their duties.

The ships also became refuges for the fleet's navy and marine dependents living ashore. Making their way to the Pico Street Navy Landing, the wives and children of the fleet were ferried to the appropriate ships for safekeeping. Soon, washings were hung out to dry, and shipboard sailors became proficient in mixing baby formulas and babysitting while their shipmates were ashore rendering aid. The navy maintained patrols for twelve days. Crewmen from the *Oklahoma* would aid the public again in August. While dry-docked in Bremerton, Washington, fifty members of her fire and rescue crew were dispatched into the city to help extinguish a fire at the Loftus Lumber Company.

On February 11, 1935, *Oklahoma* departed San Pedro with nine other battleships to conduct a series of tactics while en route to San Francisco. The following afternoon, the ships received word that the airship USS *Macon* had gone down off Point Sur. Within an hour, the battleships were at the presumed crash site. After searching for nearly seven hours without result, the ships resumed their voyage. Later, word was received that eighty-one members of *Macon*'s crew had been rescued, and that two had perished.[1] Among the survivors was the airship's executive officer, Lieutenant Commander Jesse L. Kenworthy, Jr. Reassigned to the *Oklahoma* some five years later, he would be in command of the ship on the morning of December 7, 1941.[2]

CONFLICT IN EUROPE

In the autumn of 1935, Japan withdrew from the 1922 Washington Treaty system when her demands for battleship parity were denied at a disarmament conference held in London. The ratio system was abandoned, and rearmament began anew. The world was gearing up for a new conflict, and it would start in Europe.

In 1936 *Oklahoma* was selected for the Naval Academy's Midshipmen Cruise along with *Wyoming* and *Arkansas*. In June, she embarked 234 "middies," two of whom would later become crewmembers, First Classman D. L. Johnson and Third Classman W. K. Yarnall. The three ships were in Cherbourg, France, when the Spanish Civil War broke out in mid-July. The war, which began as a Spanish social uprising, quickly escalated into a European conflict when Germany and Italy sided with the Nationalists under Francisco Franco, and Russia and France sided with the pro-Communist Republicans. The conflict would provide a proving ground for weaponry that would be used on a much broader scale just three years later.

The U.S. government's immediate concern was for the safety of its citizens who were in Spain on business or vacation. When the U.S. consulate at the besieged city of Bilbao requested that warships be sent to rescue them, the State Department immediately contacted the Navy Department. Because Cherbourg was fewer than six hundred miles from Bilbao, the logical choice was to send one of the three "cruise" ships. *Oklahoma* was selected because she was the largest. However, her departure was delayed because several crewmen were still on leave in Paris. The French were notified, and within a short period, Parisian police were scouring the streets for American sailors and marines. It would take three days to round them up.

After transferring the midshipmen to the *Wyoming*, *Oklahoma* departed Cherbourg on July 23. She arrived at Bilbao the following night, anchoring in the outer harbor. Shortly after midnight, the American consul came aboard with the captain of the port. Later the same morning, *Oklahoma* embarked thirty passengers, only sixteen of whom were American. The youngest was a one-month-old British girl. Carrying only what they could carry, the refugees were berthed in the ship's junior officer and warrant officer quarters.

On July 25, *Oklahoma* departed for Santander, Spain. Following a five-hour voyage, she embarked ten more passengers, including A. C. Vasquez, a professor at the U.S. Naval Academy. After departing Santander early the next morning, *Oklahoma* cruised to Bayonne, France, where the refugees were put ashore. Five hours later, she was back in Bilbao embarking refugees. Because of a heavy ground swell, the refugees were brought aboard in a boatswain's chair suspended from the stern crane.

During the following two weeks, *Oklahoma* would make another stop at Bilbao, and one at Vigo, a village near the Portuguese border. A provocative incident would occur at La Coruna, a town just north of Vigo. Americans Martha and Robert L. Odom were missionaries in La Coruna for the Seventh-Day Adventist church. The couple had a six-year-old son, and Martha was nine months pregnant. When the fighting began, Robert left the family to check on church members in the surrounding villages. While he was gone, an officer from the *Oklahoma* came by to evacuate the family. Not willing to leave without her husband, Martha refused. The officer returned some three hours later, but Robert was still gone, so Martha's response was the same.

Shortly after Robert returned, the family was awakened in the middle of the night by a knock at the door. Robert had already been arrested several times, and he and Martha feared that the Fascists were after him again because the family had failed to display a Fascist flag on their balcony. Martha convinced her husband that it would be best for her to answer, and she was ordered to display the flag immediately. She agreed without argument, and the soldiers departed. Fortunately, the soldiers never looked back, because the Odoms did not have a flag—or the intent to get one. The following morning, their balcony was the only one on the street without a flag. Fearing retribution, which could cost him his life, Robert hastened to the American consulate in Vigo. He returned with a huge American flag, a gift the consul had received from the *Oklahoma*'s captain, and immediately draped it over the railing of the balcony. Never again would there be a knock at the door in the middle of the night.[3]

In general, the stops along the northern coast of Spain would occur without incident. It would be quite a different story in the Spanish seaports that bordered the Mediterranean. Malaga, located on the Mediterranean side of Gibraltar, was the site of a major battle. The harbor was so littered with bodies that *Oklahoma* sailors had to push them away from the bottom of the gangways to bring refugees aboard. Later, crewmembers watched in disbelief as captured Republican soldiers were chained to the deck of a submarine, then taken out to sea and drowned. In another incident, *Oklahoma* sailor Howard C. French watched a biplane drop a handheld bomb on the German pocket battleship *Deutschland.* The following morning the *Deutschland* departed. French learned later that the warship had bombarded a nearby city in retribution.

In total, *Oklahoma* made six trips at eight different cities over a thirty-four-day period, embarking 179 evacuees—including one pregnant woman. For the first time in documented history, a baby was born aboard an American battleship.

FROM CELEBRATION TO THE BEGINNINGS OF WORLD WAR

In May 1937 Oklahoma was dispatched to San Francisco to participate in the events celebrating the opening of the Golden Gate Bridge. The festivities commenced at noon on May 28 when President Franklin D. Roosevelt pressed a telegraph key in the White House, announcing the event to the world. Following a ribbon-cutting ceremony, a number of Oklahoma's sailors marched in a celebratory parade that terminated on Market Street—the site of a huge party. The gala event, attended by tens of thousands, including a throng of celebrities, was the crowning event of the day. It was particularly memorable for many of the Oklahoma's less inhibited sailors, of which there were many, because it afforded them the opportunity to dance with Gypsy Rose Lee, the notorious cabaret stripper.

Throughout much of the world, the mood was anything but celebratory. In July 1937, China and Japan became embroiled in a full-scale war following an altercation at the Marco Polo Bridge in Beijing, China. Japan would use the incident as a pretext for occupying Beijing, and subsequently the entire country. This event, which the League of Nations condemned, prompted President Roosevelt to send military aid to the Chinese Nationalist Army, despite the fact that America was indirectly supporting the Japanese by providing them with oil. When Roosevelt's efforts became public, the U.S. Senate demanded that the aid be revoked under the dictums of the Neutrality Act, which prohibited the delivery of arms to belligerents regardless of the circumstances. Yet nothing was done to alter America's export policies out of fear that depriving Japan of U.S. oil would lead to a direct confrontation. Instead, the U.S. focused its efforts on diplomacy by offering to negotiate an agreement between China and Japan, an offer the Japanese refused.

On December 12, 1937, the United States became physically involved in the conflict when the USS *Panay* was attacked by Japanese warplanes while escorting three Standard Oil barges along the Yangtze River north of Nanking. The unprovoked attack claimed the lives of three American sailors, wounded forty-three sailors and five civilian passengers, set two of the barges ablaze, and sank *Panay*. Lieutenant Shigeharu Murata spearheaded the *Panay* attack with a flight of high-level bombers. Four years later, Murata would lead the torpedo assault on Pearl Harbor.

In March 1938, the U.S. Fleet conducted its annual exercises in Hawaii. Designated as Fleet Problem XIX, the exercises had provocative results. Evading the segment of the fleet defending Hawaii, the aircraft carrier *Saratoga* was able to sweep in undetected from the northwest to launch her planes in a mock bombing raid on Pearl Harbor. Because the attacking force had utilized a weather front to conceal its advance, the significance of the event was not trumpeted as loudly as it might have been otherwise. Hitler's advances into Austria on March 12 overshadowed it as well. The year would end with Japan and China involved in an undeclared war, and with Germany firmly entrenched in the Sudetenland of Czechoslovakia.

By August 1939, Russia and Japan were embroiled in a vicious battle at Nomonhan, a village on the Siberia-Manchuria border, and Germany was massing an army along its border with Poland. By September 1, Russia had secured a victory—ending Japan's hopes of northern expansion—and Hitler was invading Poland, effectively beginning the Second World War. In compliance with their treaty agreements with Poland, Britain and France declared war on Germany two days later. Russia, Germany's ally of less than a week, invaded Poland on September 17, and then Finland on November 30. Following Germany's invasion of France in June 1940, Italy, another German ally, declared war on France and England.

The invasion of France had a profound effect on the midshipmen of the U.S. Naval Academy. Due to the international uncertainty that resulted, the first-class midshipmen's summer, fall, and Christmas leaves were canceled so that they could complete their coursework early and join the fleet. They would graduate in February instead of June 1941. Among the early graduates were future *Oklahoma* ensigns Joseph C. Spitler, Paul H. Backus, Lewis B. Pride, Jr., Adam W. De Mers, John B. Davenport, and Waldron M. McLellon. All but one would be aboard the *Oklahoma* during the attack on Pearl Harbor.

Left to right: Elizabeth Ames, Madeline Cottingham, and Lorena Cruce at the USS *Oklahoma*'s christening ceremony at Camden, New Jersey, March 23, 1914. Courtesy Oklahoma Historical Society.

U.S. government delegation to USS *Oklahoma* christening ceremony, March 23, 1914. Representing the U.S. Navy is Secretary of the Navy Daniels (standing in front of white door, left) and Assistant Secretary of the Navy Franklin Delano Roosevelt (standing to Daniels's right). Courtesy Oklahoma Historical Society.

Preliminary trials, January 15, 1916. Courtesy National Archives.

At anchor in Berehaven, Ireland, 1918. Courtesy Navy Historical Center.

Cruising the Culebra cut, Panama Canal, January 1921. (Navy Historical Center. Courtesy USS *Oklahoma* Association, Elmer R. Sykora Collection.

Firing her 14-inch/45-caliber main guns in the 1920s. In the rear is her sister ship, *Nevada*. Courtesy National Archives.

Above: The *Oklahoma* prior to her modernization in 1927. Courtesy National Archives. *Below:* After her modernization was completed in 1929. Courtesy National Archives. Note that tripod masts that have replaced the old cage masts. The casemates containing the broadside guns have been sealed, and the guns have been relocated on the newly constructed upper deck. Also note the three-story towers above each mast and the floatplane catapult above turret 3.

Oklahoma with her main guns trained to starboard following her 1927 modernization. Courtesy National Archives.

Oklahoma in Portsmouth, England, June 1936, during the 1936 Midshipmen Cruise. *Above:* view from stern. *Below:* starboard side view. Courtesy Thomas C. Hone Collection, copyright by Wright and Logan, 20 Queen Street, Portsea, London.

On December 7, 1941, the twenty-four "Kate" torpedo planes from the Japanese carriers *Akagi* and *Kaga* approached from the upper left and turned toward Battleship Row and Ford Island. The four planes from the *Hiryu* and the one from the *Soryu* approached from the far right, flew over Hickam Field, and then turned to join the attack on the battleships. Courtesy National Archives.

CHAPTER 6

Countdown to Pearl Harbor

In May 1940 the U.S. Fleet conducted its annual exercises in Hawaii. At their conclusion, the fleet was ordered to remain in Hawaiian waters indefinitely. The deployment, controversial from the onset, was a mitigated response to British prime minister Winston Churchill. Fearful that the Japanese would take advantage of Britain's preoccupation with Germany to attack the British-held bastion at Singapore, Churchill asked Roosevelt to dispatch a battleship force to protect it. Roosevelt believed that a battleship presence in Hawaii would be sufficient to deter the perceived invasion, and he converted the belief into policy—much to the disdain of Churchill as well as the U.S. Fleet commander in chief, Admiral James O. Richardson, who believed that the fleet could better prepare for war using the training and logistical facilities available on the West Coast.

CAPTAIN FOY AND THE BARGE ENCOUNTER

In the late spring, *Oklahoma* journeyed east to Puget Sound Navy Yard for her annual overhaul. She also received a new skipper, Captain Edward J. Foy, replacing Captain Emmanuel A. Lofquist, who had been reassigned to the Naval War College in Newport, Rhode Island. Foy's tour began officially on June 24, while *Oklahoma* was still in the yard. His sea duties would begin rather precipitously some three months later.

On the morning of September 19, *Oklahoma* departed the navy yard for postrepair trials. She was cruising at four knots when a fog closed in from the north. Suddenly a foghorn sounded off to port—three long blasts, followed by two short ones. Positioned in the conning tower, Captain Foy immediately issued the order to stop all engines.

Moments later, a tugboat appeared off the port bow. It was one hundred yards ahead and angling toward their path. Realizing that the two vessels were on a collision course, Foy ordered full speed astern. The maneuver worked, allowing the tug to cross in front of them unscathed. Unfortunately, it was towing a barge. The *Oklahoma* collided with the tow chain, swinging the barge inward against the *Oklahoma's* port side. The barge was carrying railroad freight cars. When the two ships collided, one of the cars dumped into the water. Fortunately, it was loaded with lumber and stayed afloat. *Oklahoma* dropped anchor immediately and put in a call to the navy yard. The freight car was subsequently retrieved, and *Oklahoma* returned to the yard for minor repairs.

WARNINGS

In October Admiral Richardson traveled to Washington to discuss the Hawaiian deployment with President Roosevelt. During the meeting, the president held fast to his belief that the fleet should remain in Hawaii as a deterrent to the Japanese. Richardson emphatically disagreed with the premise, adding that a fleet at Pearl Harbor was "disadvantageously disposed" to prepare for war. The meeting might well have ended there had not Richardson verbalized his own personal opinion. "Mr. President, I feel that I must tell you that the senior officers of the Navy do not have the trust and confidence in the civilian leadership of this country that is essential for the successful prosecution of a war in the Pacific."[1]

He would be relieved fewer than three months later.

On November 11, 1940, British torpedo planes launched from the Royal Navy aircraft carrier *Illustrious* crippled the Italian Battle Fleet based at Taranto, Italy. Because some of the British torpedoes had been launched in water shallower than seventy feet, the successes they achieved were considered fantastic; it was previously believed that torpedoes needed at least one hundred feet of depth to operate successfully. Despite the waters of Pearl Harbor being some thirty feet shallower than those at Taranto, Japanese admiral Isoruku Yamamoto drafted a nine-page outline two months later proposing a similar attack on Pearl Harbor, to prevent the Pacific Fleet from interfering with the planned invasion of Southeast Asia, known as the Southern Operation.

Though the contents of the outline were supposed to be secret, they were leaked. On January 27, 1941, the information was received by Ricardo Rivera Schreiber, the Peruvian envoy in Japan, who immediately relayed it to First Secretary Edward S. Rocker of the American embassy, who in turned passed it on to his boss, Ambassador Joseph C. Grew. Grew sent the following dispatch to the State Department: "The Peruvian Minister has informed a member of my staff that he has heard from many sources, including a Japanese source, that in the event of trouble breaking out between the United States and Japan, the Japanese intend to make a surprise attack against Pearl Harbor with all their strength and employing all of their equipment. The Peruvian Minister considered the rumors fantastic. Nevertheless, he considered them of sufficient importance to convey this information to a member of my staff." The dispatch was forwarded to the Division of Naval Intelligence, where it was ignored for lack of credence.[2]

On February 1, 1941, the man who would oppose the attack, Admiral Husband E. Kimmel, was given command of the U.S. Fleet. Previously the commander of the fleet's battle force cruisers, Kimmel would not inherit the same fleet that Richardson had commanded because the U.S. Fleet had been divided in two. While Admiral Ernest J. King would command the Atlantic Fleet, Kimmel would command its counterpart in the Pacific. Admiral Thomas C. Hart retained command of the diminutive Asiatic Fleet. The realignment had little effect on *Oklahoma,* because all twelve of the modern U.S. battleships remained in the Pacific. Two weeks into his new command, Kimmel received a letter from Admiral Harold R. Stark, the chief of naval operations, informing him of the impracticality of using antitorpedo baffles (nets) at Pearl Harbor. The ramifications of Kimmel's agreement would be ill omened.[3]

PRELUDE TO WAR WITH JAPAN

On February 13, *Oklahoma* returned to Puget Sound Navy Yard. She would depart with two new 3-inch/50-caliber AA guns mounted on the quarterdeck (these would augment the two 3-inch/50-caliber guns that had replaced the two 5-inch/51-caliber guns on the boat deck in a prior refit); waist-high armor shields on all her 3-inch/50-caliber and 5-inch/25-caliber AA guns, and a .50-caliber machine-gun platform in the mainmast. An antiaircraft fire-control station was added as well as two autonomous AA directors (Ford Mark 19s), one for the port side battery and another for the starboard side battery. While the fire-control station was perched atop the pilothouse, each director was housed in an armored cabin perched atop a tower mast on either side of the pilot-house.

In March Congress approved the Lend-Lease Act and appropriated $7 billion for the aid of friendly nations; the act permitted direct military aid to Britain and prompted Hitler to extend his U-boat area of operations far into the western Atlantic. In response, the United States instituted a naval force to protect the British ships ferrying U.S.-provided war materials to Europe. BatDivThree (*Idaho, New Mexico, and Mississippi*) was slated for transfer to the Atlantic along with the aircraft carrier *Yorktown,* four light cruisers, seventeen destroyers, three oil tankers, three transports, and ten auxiliaries—in all, nearly a quarter of the Pacific Fleet.[4]

In April, Japan signed a nonaggression pact with Russia. Though the two countries were longtime adversaries, Russia needed the pact to secure its southeastern flank in anticipation of an expected invasion from Germany. The pact was advantageous to the Japanese because it secured their northern flank, allowing them to pursue their interests in Southeast Asia.

Following the departure of BatDivThree in May, the Pacific Fleet was restructured into three task forces. Task Force I, commanded by Vice Admiral William S. Pye, consisted of BatDivTwo (*Pennsylvania, California, Tennessee*), BatDivFour (*Maryland, Colorado, West Virginia*), aircraft carrier *Saratoga,* five light cruisers, eighteen destroyers, and five mine vessels. Task Force II, commanded by Vice Admiral William F. Halsey, consisted of BatDivOne (*Arizona, Nevada, Oklahoma*), aircraft carrier *Enterprise,* four heavy cruisers, eighteen destroyers, and four mine vessels. Task Force III, commanded by Vice Admiral Wilson Brown, consisted of aircraft carrier *Lexington,* eight heavy cruisers, nine destroyers, thirteen mine vessels, and six attack transports. The fleet had an operational directive stating that at least two of the task forces must remain at sea at all times.[5]

On June 13, 1941, Admiral Kimmel received a memorandum from Rear Admiral Royal E. Ingersoll, Admiral Stark's deputy. It stated that "while no minimum depth of water in which naval vessels may be anchored can arbitrarily be assumed as providing safety from torpedo plane attack, it may be assumed that depth of water will be one of the factors considered by any attacking force, and an attack in relatively deep water (10 fathoms or more) is more likely." (One fathom equals six feet.) It went on to say, "the torpedoes launched by the British at Taranto were, in general, in thirteen to fifteen fathoms of water, although several torpedoes may have been launched in eleven or twelve fathoms."[6]

Prior to Taranto, it had been generally accepted that air-launched torpedoes required one hundred feet of depth, because they would sink almost that deep when launched. Using their own power, they would then climb to an attack depth of twenty feet. The average depth of Pearl Harbor was only forty feet, a substantial enough differential for Kimmel to view the information as inapplicable.[7]

What Kimmel had no way of knowing was that the Japanese had been experimenting with shallow-depth aerial torpedoes since 1939. By attaching a wooden fin that broke off when the torpedo struck the water, thereby reducing the depth of sinkage, the Japanese Navy had already narrowed the operational depth to forty feet by 1940. Tests to reduce the sinkage further were continuous. By varying the plane's air-speed, and the elevation at which the torpedo was a dropped, Japanese torpedo plane pilots were experimenting to find the perfect blending of the two at Japan's Kagoshima Bay, a location that mimicked Pearl Harbor. In July, Japan signed an accord with Vichy France, a faction of the French government sympathetic to Germany, which allowed the Japanese to occupy French Indochina.

The intent was clear.

Using airfields in Saigon, Japanese warplanes would be within bombing distance of Singapore. It was the final straw. The following day, President Roosevelt issued an executive order freezing Japanese assets in the United States, a move that was seconded by Great Britain and the Netherlands. Five days later, Roosevelt placed an embargo on all high-octane gasoline, in addition to crude oil. Though Japan would continue to obtain oil from the Netherlands East Indies, it would now have to pay for it with cash, a process that was extremely difficult because most of its cash was frozen in American banks. As a result, Japanese tankers were tied up in East Indies ports for weeks awaiting the arrival of funds. Though the Japanese had been building storage tanks at an acceler-ated rate, and stockpiling oil for several years, they had enough accumulated for only one more year of war. If Japan wanted to continue its conquest of Southeast Asia, it would have to find oil elsewhere, which meant that the Southern Operation had to become a reality, as well as the related preemptive strike on Pearl Harbor.

Though negotiations would continue, for all intents and purposes, the U.S. war with Japan began that very day: July 25, 1941.

WEATHERING THE STORMS

On August 22, *Oklahoma* departed Pearl Harbor for San Pedro. En route she encountered a massive storm. In the process of installing gun shutters in the casemates of the 5-inch/51-caliber broadside guns, three men were injured by waves washing onto the upper deck, and another turned up missing. When a search of the ship by the master-at-arms and the Fifth Division petty officers failed to locate him, it was assumed that the missing sailor, Seaman First Class C. E. Suttee, had been washed overboard. Another crewman would be knocked off his feet the following afternoon. Fortunately, he was able to secure a handhold and survive.

At 9:55 the next morning, an entry in *Oklahoma*'s deck log entry recorded a "heavy vibration throughout the ship." At 9:57 the starboard engine was stopped, followed by the portside engine ten minutes later. At 10:54 a motor launch was lowered with divers aboard. The ensuing investigation disclosed a broken outboard coupling on the starboard shaft.

After crewmen had secured the shaft with cables, the port side engine was restarted. With the destroyers *McDonough* and *Dewey* screening ahead, and *Nevada* bringing up the rear, *Oklahoma* headed northeast at twelve knots. Because San Pedro did not have adequate dry-dock facilities, *Oklahoma* was redirected to San Francisco, where the navy had a repair yard at Hunter's Point. She entered San Francisco Bay on August 28, shifting to Hunter's Point the following day.

Her stay would be a long one. Though the crew received extended leaves as a result, many would be greeted with some disconcerting news when they returned. Due to the deteriorating international situation, the army draft had been extended at the end of September. Fearing that navy enlistments would be extended as well, sailors formed an OHIO club—Over the Hill in October. When October ended without change, the club was disbanded.

Three days later, *Oklahoma* departed for Pearl Harbor. She was en route when "strictly secret" message 83 was deciphered. Intercepted on September 24 by U.S. Army Intelligence, the dispatch known historically as the "bomb plot" message, requested that Hawaiian-based Japanese spies prepare a grid of Pearl Harbor, pinpointing the exact location of American warships in five specific areas. For the most part, the message generated only casual interest within the U.S. intelligence community because similar general information requests had been intercepted for other U.S. military installations. However, the information requested in message 83 was much more specific than in prior intercepts. Unfortunately, the man who could have best judged the message's merits, Admiral Kimmel, was never given the opportunity to do so.[8]

On October 22 *Oklahoma* was on maneuvers with *Arizona* and *Nevada* in the fleet training area southwest of Oahu as a member of Task Force II. The weather was bad, with low-hanging clouds and intermittent rainsqualls. Due to the poor visibility, the *Arizona,* the acting guide ship, would occasionally bounce her searchlight off the clouds to mark her location for the others. At 5:35 P.M. the three were aligned in a column under "darkened ship" conditions. *Arizona* was in the lead, with *Nevada* behind her, and *Oklahoma* bringing up the rear. At 5:42, on the signal of the officer in tactical command, *Nevada* and *Oklahoma* sheered out of formation to take up station on the *Arizona*'s port quarter. Within a short period, the *Arizona* was out of sight. It was not until 6:05 P.M. that *Oklahoma*'s watch noticed her searchlight some five thousand yards away. She wasn't seen again until she turned on her reference light at approximately 6:15. By then she was closing on a perpendicular course some six hundred yards to starboard.

Captain Foy was standing on the starboard wing of the bridge when *Arizona* suddenly appeared. Realizing that the ships were on a collision course—at the same moment that he heard the junior officer of the deck give the order to maintain a steady heading—Captain Foy raced into the pilothouse to man the conn. Ordering the ship hard left and the engines into full reverse, he sounded three blasts on the ship's whistle, another on the siren, and then turned on the running lights. Despite his efforts, *Oklahoma* struck *Arizona* a glancing blow amidships, slicing a V-shaped hole in her port blister and tearing off a garbage chute, which landed on *Oklahoma*'s bow. Though both ships would complete their scheduled exercises, the event would prompt an investigation when they returned to Pearl Harbor on October 26.[9] Two days later, a board of inquiry convened on the *Tennessee*. Pending the outcome, Captain Foy was confined to port.[10]

On October 31, the Pacific Fleet received a new operational directive. Conveyed by Pacific Fleet Confidential Letter No. 14CL-41, it stipulated that only one task force be kept at sea, instead of two, because of a rapidly depleting fuel supply. However, the new directive was not strictly adhered to; on two occasions the following month, the eight battleships were in port simultaneously: November 17 and November 19–21.

On November 1, Captain Howard D. Bode became *Oklahoma*'s new commanding officer. His first challenge as a battleship captain occurred on the evening of November 10. As part of an attack exercise being conducted by Task Force II, *Oklahoma* was in formation with the aircraft carrier *Enterprise*. When a referee declared that destroyers had sunk the carrier, *Enterprise* was ordered to retire, subsequently turning to port. However, the ships were operating in darkened conditions, and her quartermaster did not realize that he had turned into the path of the *Oklahoma*, which was approaching off the port quarter. What followed was almost comedic. While *Oklahoma* maintained her speed and course, the *Enterprise* sent her engines back full emergency. As a result, *Oklahoma*'s public address (PA) system kept moving the expected point of impact farther aft, causing what Ensign Joseph C. Spitler described as a "track meet down below," as sailors raced away from the designated impact areas. Fortunately, there was no collision. The only damage was a bent flagstaff on *Oklahoma*'s fantail, which had been hit by the overhang of the *Enterprise*'s flight deck when she passed astern. On November 13, *Oklahoma* entered dry dock, presumably to have the damage repaired from her collision with *Arizona*, which had departed the same dry dock the day before. *Oklahoma* would remain there for sixteen days.

DISPATCHES AND SUB SIGHTINGS

On November 22, BatDivTwo and BatDivFour departed Pearl Harbor for the fleet training area. Two days later Admiral Kimmel received the following message from Admiral Stark, the chief of naval operations: "Chances of favorable outcome of negotiation with Japan very doubtful. This situation coupled with statements of Japanese Government and movements of their naval and military forces indicate in our opinion that a surprise aggressive movement in any direction including attack on Philippines or Guam is a possibility."

That same day, the Japanese Malaya invasion force departed Hashirajima, Japan. Two days later, the Pearl Harbor Air Fleet departed Japan's Kurile Islands, and the southern Philippine invasion force departed Sasebo. On November 27, Admiral Kimmel received another message, this one from the Navy Department: "This dispatch is to be considered a war warning. Negotiations with Japan looking toward stabilization of conditions in the Pacific have ceased and an aggressive move by Japan is expected within the next few days. The number and equipment of Japanese troops and the organization of the naval task forces indicates an amphibious expedition against either the Philippines, Thai or Kra Peninsula or possibly Borneo." Of the potential invasion sites mentioned in the two dispatches, the closest one to Hawaii was Guam, located some 3,800 miles to the west. The only location the dispatches had in common was the Philippine Islands, 5,300 miles southwest of Hawaii.

On November 28, *Nevada* and *Arizona* departed Pearl Harbor with *Enterprise* and a destroyer escort. Vice Admiral Halsey commanded the group (Task Force II less *Oklahoma*). Once it reached the open sea, Halsey dispatched the battleships and a destroyer escort to the training area southeast of Oahu. He then turned *Enterprise* west, proceeding to Wake Island to offload a squadron of marine F4F fighter planes. Departing with the battleships had been a ruse to maintain the pretense of a routine mission, because it was believed that the Japanese had a well-established spy network in Honolulu. Leaving the other ships behind was a tactical measure, because Halsey had no desire to be reined in by his slow-moving battleships.

That same morning BatDivTwo and BatDivFour returned to the harbor. By noon *California* was at her standard F-3 mooring, *Maryland* at F-5, and *Tennessee* at F-6. A short time later, *West Virginia* pulled in alongside the *Tennessee*. The *Pennsylvania* would also return, berthing alongside the 1010 dock at B-2. The following day *Oklahoma* shifted out of dry dock 1 to pull in behind her at B-3. Two days later, *Pennsylvania* entered dry dock 1. Berthed ahead of her were the destroyers *Cassin* and *Downes*.

In the early morning hours of Sunday, November 30, *Oklahoma* departed Pearl Harbor, rendezvousing with *Nevada* and *Arizona* in the fleet training area at 7:15 A.M. The following morning, *Arizona* departed the formation in the company of a destroyer. Two hours later, *Oklahoma* departed for short-range battle practice, striking out on her own when the drill was completed. That night, while operating under darkened conditions, her watch spotted a submarine. Because no American submarines were scheduled to be operating in the area, the sighting caused considerable concern.

The next morning, *Oklahoma's* gunnery department officers were summoned to the wardroom by the ship's executive officer, Commander Jesse L. Kenworthy, Jr. When they arrived, they were informed that the gunnery exercise scheduled for that night had been canceled, because the task force destroyers, including the one scheduled to tow a target for *Oklahoma,* had been dispatched to find the sub.

Later in the week, *Arizona* reported a sighting. Supposedly, her commanding officer, Captain Franklin Van Valkenburgh, responded by proposing that *Oklahoma* and *Nevada* return to Pearl Harbor while the Arizona remain at sea as a decoy. Believing that the submarine would pursue a single battleship, he hoped to lure it into an attack where his destroyers could sink it.

Assuming that the proposal was relayed to Admiral Kimmel, it was obviously denied, because the entire task force was ordered back to port on December 4. Though the submarine was never found, there is little doubt that Japanese submarines were in the vicinity. During the first week of December, twenty-five Japanese submarines would go on station in the Hawaiian Islands. While four approached from the northwest, twenty-one would approach from the west and southwest, the same area where the task force was operating. However, the sighting seemed to have a pronounced effect on the disposition of the fleet. Contrary to the dictates of Pacific Confidential Letter No. 14CL-41, no task force was sent out to replace the one coming in.

Nonetheless, the channel entrance to Ford Island had already been busy when BatDivOne approached on the morning of December 5.[11] The heavy cruiser *Indianapolis* had departed for Johnston Island with four destroyers, while the aircraft carrier *Lexington* and heavy cruisers *Astoria, Chicago,* and *Portland* had departed for Midway with five destroyers.

Arizona would be the first to enter the channel, at 8:12 A.M. Proceeding up the inland waterway, she turned left at the southern tip of Ford Island, then circled clockwise around the island for a northerly approach to Battleship Row.[12] With her starboard side to the island, she was nudged alongside the F-7 quays with the help of harbor tugs. Positioned directly ahead of her was the *Tennessee*. Alongside the *Tennessee* was the *West Virginia*. Ahead of the *Tennessee* was the *Maryland*. The *Colorado*, sister ship to the *Maryland* and the *West Virginia*, was at the Puget Sound Naval Yard.

At 8:30 A.M. *Oklahoma* started in. Because *Nevada* had been scheduled to offload her 14-inch/45-caliber projectiles and powder bags the following day, she was preassigned to the F-8 mooring because it had open water on both sides, allowing a maneuvering area for the ammunition barges that would be tethered alongside her. *Arizona* needed to have her port side clear because the repair ship *Vestal* was scheduled to moor alongside her on Saturday to perform some construction work. Therefore, *Oklahoma* was forced to moor alongside *Maryland* at F-5 because it was the only slot available. Ironically, it was the only time in 1941 that *Oklahoma* would moor at F-5.

Once *Oklahoma* was secured, preparations began in earnest for an inspection to be held on Monday. Because it was a materiel inspection, it would endure the highest degree of scrutiny, particularly since it would be Captain Bode's first. The work would include the time-honored polishing of decks and bright work, cleaning of work and living areas, and the securing of battle stations, in particular the 5-inch/25-caliber AA guns. Not only would the mounts be thoroughly scoured and grease free, the firing mechanisms would be taken to the ship's armory for cleaning. In addition, the ammunition would be taken four decks below for storage.

To allow the inspection team access to each of the ship's compartments, all the deck and bulkhead hatches were opened. The order was also given to remove the manhole lids from the torpedo blisters to allow them to vent. Although all three BatDivOne battleships were scheduled for an inspection on December 8, only *Oklahoma* opened her blister manholes, possibly out of caution after *Oklahoma* sailor G. W. Gross, on October 26, suffered "anoxmea fume poisoning and lost consciousness" while opening the hatch to lower blister A-158-LB.[13] Though the incident occurred while Captain Foy was still in command, it is possible that it was relayed to Captain Bode when he assumed command on November 1. If so, it is also possible that the event contributed to Bode's decision to vent the blisters on December 5 and 6.

On Saturday, Lieutenant Commander Harry Henderson, *Oklahoma*'s gunnery officer, met with Captain Bode to voice his concern about the ship's lack of defensive readiness. When Henderson proposed that at least a portion of the antiaircraft guns be manned, Captain Bode denied the request, maintaining that the inspection took precedence. That same day, Admiral Kimmel received a dispatch from Admiral Thomas C. Hart, commander of the Asiatic Fleet, reporting that two Japanese convoys were believed headed for Kohtron, and that another thirty-ship convoy was sighted at anchor in Cam Ranh Bay in Indochina, seemingly validating the message Admiral Kimmel had received on November 27.

At the conclusion of Saturday's workday, approximately half of the crew went ashore for liberty. While many made a beeline for Honolulu and its big-city nightlife enticements, others attended the Battle of the Bands at the navy's Bloch Recreation Center, including *Oklahoma* sailor Francis R. Parkinson, who attended with his brother Clayton, also assigned to the *Oklahoma,* and *Arizona* Seaman First Class Charles E. Swisher, a high school buddy from Vista, California.[14]

Ensign Joseph C. Spitler watched a movie on the *Oklahoma*'s fantail, as did Gunner's Mate Second Class Leon C. Kolb. The movie would be a welcome reprieve for Kolb, who had spent the prior evening on shore patrol duty in Honolulu. Assigned to a street corner, he'd been summoned into a bar to break up a fight involving some forty to fifty drunken patrons, most of them wearing uniforms.

Fireman First Class R. M. Bentley also remained aboard. Having purchased a Harley-Davidson Model 61 motorcycle with shipmate Fireman First Class Leonard Geller on Friday, he spent Saturday evening planning their itinerary for a Sunday excursion.

He would never see Geller, or the motorcycle, again.[15]

CHAPTER 7

A Quiet Sunday Morning

Designated the First Air Fleet, the Japanese Pearl Harbor Strike Force consisted of six aircraft carriers, two battleships, two heavy cruisers, one light cruiser, nine destroyers, three picket submarines, and eight tankers.

At 1:50 A.M. Commander Minoru Genda, the Japanese tactical planner for the attack on Pearl Harbor, received the results of a telegram sent by a Japanese spy in Hawaii. Genda was not pleased. Relayed to the *Akagi* by the naval general staff, the message compounded the discouraging news he'd received previously from a Japanese submarine at Lahaina Roads. It had been his utmost hope that the fleet would be found there instead of at Pearl Harbor, because the moorings were in open water, and the water was fifty feet deeper: open water meant easy maneuvering for his torpedo-plane pilots, and deep water would prevent the ships from being raised. A second report confirmed the first: the battleships were at Pearl Harbor. Neither message could confirm the whereabouts of the three American aircraft carriers.[1] A report received at 2:00 A.M. was more encouraging: there were no barrage balloons above the harbor, and no antitorpedo nets protecting the battleships.

By the early morning hours of December 7, 1941, the Japanese Pearl Harbor Strike Force had nearly completed its prestrike positioning. Approaching from the northeast, the primary force consisted of thirty-one ships of which six were aircraft carriers. The subsurface Advance Expeditionary Force featured twenty-five submarines. Of these, five were deployed to the north of the islands to intercept reinforcement ships; thirteen were deployed around Oahu to attack any ships escaping the harbor; two were positioned west of Oahu to rescue downed pilots; and five were positioned at the mouth of the channel entrance. The latter, fleet submarines I-16, I-18, I-20, I-22, and I-24, were mother subs, with eighty-foot-long midget submarines piggybacked on them. The midgets, featuring a conning tower, a two-man crew, and two torpedoes stacked one above the other, were six-foot-diameter vessels positioned atop cradles on the mother sub's rear decks, with their noses pointed aft. The first of the five was released from its mother at approximately 1:00 A.M.[2]

At 5:30 that morning, floatplanes from the cruisers *Chikuma* and *Tone* were catapulted aloft for a preattack reconnaissance of both Pearl Harbor and Lahaina Roads. Two hours later, they would report that the there were nine battleships at Pearl Harbor and that Lahaina Roads was empty. The *Tone* floatplane would also scout the area south of Oahu in an effort to locate the U.S. Fleets' aircraft carriers. The search would be in vain.

Positioned 230 miles northeast of Oahu, the carriers began launching their planes at 6:15 A.M. Within fifteen minutes, 183 aircraft were aloft. Of the total, 49 were horizontal bombers, 51 were dive bombers, 43 were fighters, and 40 were Nakajima B5N2 torpedo bombers. Codenamed "Kate" by the Allies, each B5N2 had a three-man crew, a rear-firing 7.7 mm machine gun, and an eighteen-foot-long torpedo suspended from the fuselage. Packing a warhead containing 452 pounds of explosive, the eighteen-inch-diameter torpedoes had been modified for shallow running with detachable wooden fins that broke off when the torpedo entered the water.

While the overall commander of the air fleet was Commander Mitsuo Fuchida, Lieutenant Shigeharu Murata commanded the torpedo planes. Of the forty in his command, twelve were launched from the carrier *Akagi*, twelve from the *Kaga*, eight from the *Hiryu*, and eight from the *Soryu*. After assembling in a spiral above their respective carriers, the planes headed south at 6:30. Homing in on a beacon from a Honolulu radio station, they arrived off Kahuku Point at 7:40, approximately the same time that Captain Bode was being ferried ashore for liberty. Commanding *Oklahoma* in his absence was Commander Kenworthy.

At 7:45 *Oklahoma* ensign Irving J. Davenport relieved Lieutenant (junior grade, or j.g) William T. Ingram as the officer of the deck. In preparation for the eight o'clock hour, he sent the quartermaster of the watch aft to hoist the colors, and the boatswain's mate forward to strike eight bells.

At 7:50 the tanker Neosho, berthed at the F-4 gas dock just forward of the Maryland and the Oklahoma, completed its discharge of aviation fuel to the storage tanks on Ford Island. Moments later, the Oklahoma's band began congregating on the fantail. At precisely 7:55, a blue-and-white prep flag would be hoisted aloft to signal that the colors would be raised in five minutes.

If the Japanese Air Fleet reached Oahu undetected, Murata's torpedo bombers would spearhead the attack. If not, the fighters and dive bombers would go first to neutralize any resistance. Flares would be used to signal the order of attack. A single flare meant that surprise had been achieved. Two would indicate that it hadn't. When Fuchida looked south and saw that the skies above the harbor were empty, he opened his cockpit and fired a single flare.

Seeing the signal, the dive bombers climbed to 12,000 feet, the horizontal bombers moved to 9,800 feet, and the torpedo bombers descended to sea level. However, the commander of the high-flying fighters missed the signal. Seeing that the fighters were not moving to their proper position, Fuchida fired a second flare. Though it was aimed toward the fighters, the commander of the dive bombers also saw it. Interpreting it as a second flare, he prepared to take the lead. Murata did not see the second flare, so his torpedo bombers continued their descent in the belief that they would be leading. Fuchida realized his mistake, but there was nothing he could do. Because silence was essential, using his radio was not an option.

Shadowing the western foothills of the Waianae Mountains, Murata guided the torpedo bombers south. With the mountains behind them, the group divided approximately six miles west of Pearl Harbor. While the sixteen Hiryu and Soryu planes headed due east, the twenty-four from Akagi and Kaga angled southeast to approach the harbor from the south.

The attack on Pearl Harbor began at 7:55 when nine dive bombers descended on the naval air station at Ford Island. After sweeping in from the north, they banked right over the navy yard, approaching Ford Island from the south. Their attack was focused on the massive seaplane hangar at the island's southern end. Following two near-misses, a third bomb penetrated the hangar's roof and exploded inside. Within minutes the entire structure was engulfed in flames.

Marine bugler Private Joe Lawter had just sounded first call aboard *Oklahoma* when he noticed the planes. Recognizing the Rising Sun insignias, he informed the corporal of the guard that the planes were Japanese. The guard's response was not what he'd expected. "Lawter, you're paid to blow, not to think."

Lieutenant Commander Logan C. Ramsey, duty officer of Patrol Wing Two, witnessed the explosion from the Ford Island command center. Racing across the hall to the radio room, he instructed the radiomen to hammer out the following message posthaste: AIR RAID, PEARL HARBOR. THIS IS NOT A DRILL!

At 7:56 eighteen dive bombers descended on the army's Hickam Field. Most of the Hawaiian Air Force's B-17, B-18, and A-20 bombers were clustered in the middle of the airfield—easy targets for the strafing planes. Moments later the torpedo attack began when the sixteen torpedo bombers from *Hiryu* and *Soryu* descended on the harbor from the west. Dividing into two battle groups, six targeted the ships on the northwest side of Ford Island while the others angled for the 1010 dock.

There were four ships on the northwest side of Ford Island, the cruisers *Raleigh* and *Detroit,* the seaplane tender *Tangier,* and the *Utah,* a battleship that had been converted into a target ship in 1930, then a gunnery training ship in 1941. *Utah* would be the first ship attacked. Struck by two torpedoes, she began to capsize. Of the four remaining planes, only one launched its torpedoes successfully, striking *Raleigh.* Though the others launched, none of their torpedoes struck a ship. Two torpedoes would become embedded in Ford Island, while the third remains unaccounted for.

Meanwhile, the ten planes that composed the second group angled for the 1010 dock. The burning seaplane hangar on Ford Island was centered in the line of attack, so the group's leader had to fly through a billowing cloud of smoke to make his approach. Because of the narrow width of water between the hangar and dock, he had to launch the instant his plane emerged into the clear. Moored near the center of the dock was the light cruiser *Helena.* Alongside her was the minesweeper *Oglala,* flagship of Rear Admiral William R. Furlong's minecraft battle force. The leader's torpedo passed beneath the shallow-draft *Oglala* and detonated against the *Helena*'s starboard quarter. The resulting concussion tore open *Oglala*'s hull as well.

There were four more launchings aimed at the 1010 dock, none of which hit a ship. The five remaining planes, four from *Hiryu* and one from *Soryu,* aborted to seek better targets on Battleship Row, intermixing with Murata's twenty-four-plane group, which was approaching from the southeast.

Oklahoma at the Puget Sound Navy Yard, September 28, 1940. Though the ship would undergo some minor changes in February 1941, the picture provides a good approximation of her appearance on the morning of December 7, 1941. Courtesy Oklahoma Historical Society, Petrovic Collection.

The Nakajima B5N2 "Kate" had a three-man crew and could carry either a torpedo or an armor-piercing bomb. The machine gun at the rear of the cockpit was responsible for most of the strafing that occurred on Battleship Row. Courtesy National Archives.

Japanese photo taken shortly before 8:00 a.m., December 7, 1941, by the navigator of Lt. Heita Matsumura's torpedo plane. Note the shock waves from torpedo explosions. Courtesy National Archives.

Japanese photo of attack on Pearl Harbor. Note the waterspout erupting along-side *Oklahoma* from a torpedo hit (*Oklahoma* is the ship on the left of the two ships paired together at the top of the photo). Also note the explosion on the aft section, starboard side, of *Arizona* (inboard; third pair from the top). A clock found in this vicinity had stopped at 8:06. The blackened areas along the port sides of *Oklahoma* and *West Virginia* (ship directly behind *Oklahoma*) are oil from their violated fuel bunkers. Courtesy National Archives.

Overturned hull of *Oklahoma*, with *Maryland* in the background. Courtesy National Archives.

Frontal view of overturned *Oklahoma* alongside *Maryland*. Courtesy National Archives.

Rear view of overturned *Oklahoma* alongside *Maryland*. Courtesy National Archives.

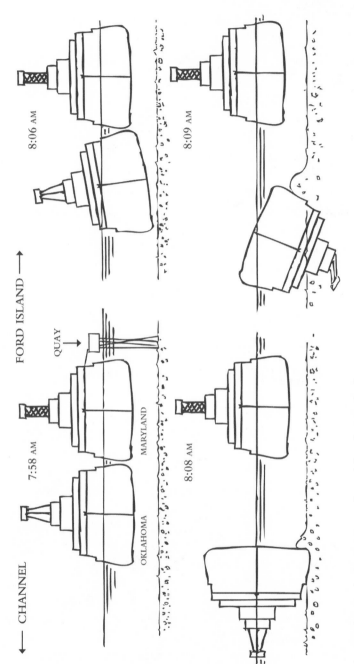

— CHANNEL

FORD ISLAND →

7:58 AM

QUAY →

OKLAHOMA   MARYLAND

8:06 AM

8:08 AM

8:09 AM

Approximate time sequence of capsizing (stern view).

CHAPTER 8

Damn the Torpedoes

On the morning of December 7, 1941, Oklahoma*'s AA defenses consisted of eight 5-inch/25-caliber guns, four 3-inch/50-caliber guns, and eight .50-caliber machine guns. Because of the inspection scheduled for the following day, none of them had firing mechanisms or ammunition.*

As Murata's columns approached Hickam Field from the south, they were shocked to find it was already under attack by dive bombers from the *Shokaku,* the result of Fuchida's botched signal. Realizing he'd lost the element of surprise, but wanting to reach the battleships before they could mount a defense, Murata decided on a shortcut to Battleship Row. Dropping to 150 feet, he led the two columns along the eastern perimeter of the stricken airfield.

Six planes from *Akagi* would initiate the torpedo assault on Battleship Row. Flying at 160 knots, they attacked in parallel columns of three planes each. Murata would lead one column while Lieutenant Jinichi Goto led the other. The tail-to-nose spacing between the planes in the columns was about a third of a mile. The reason for the clustered grouping was twofold: (1) If antitorpedo nets were deployed, the lead planes would attempt to breach them. (2) If nets were not deployed, the close tail-to-nose spacing would allow all three planes to launch and depart before the first torpedo hit, thus avoiding the massive debris-laden waterspout that would follow.

Banking left over Merry Point, the columns descended on the southeast loch. Dropping to an altitude of sixty-five feet, Murata immediately aligned on *West Virginia.* His flight path would take him along the perimeter of the submarine base, then over the Kuahua Peninsula to the main channel. Two hundred yards to his left, Goto aligned his column on the *Oklahoma*. His path would be entirely over water.

When Murata realized there were no antitorpedo nets, he initiated the attack, launching on the *West Virginia* at approximately 7:57. Seconds later Goto launched on *Oklahoma*. Because the distance from the launch point to the outboard battleships was approximately a third of a mile, and the speed of the torpedoes was forty miles per hour, the time from launching to impact was approximately twenty-eight seconds. Given the close spacing of the planes in each column, a torpedo would arrive at their target approximately every six seconds.

By the time the last torpedo reached Battleship Row, the six planes had already departed the harbor. Of the six, two had launched on *Oklahoma*, two had launched on *West Virginia*, one had jettisoned its torpedo, and one had flown over the *Oklahoma* with its torpedo still attached.

But another six were behind them. Though these were also from the *Akagi*, their alignment was different from the first groups. Instead of being clustered in two parallel columns, they were positioned in a single line. To avoid the waterspouts that would result from the explosions of prior torpedo launches, they were spaced more than a mile apart.

Approaching Battleship Row, the first three planes angled left for the *California*. Two of the planes launched on the *California*. The third one switched targets, launching on *West Virginia* instead. The last three targeted *Oklahoma*. Flying in among them were the five planes that had aborted their attacks on the 1010 dock. Of these, it is believed that two launched on the *Oklahoma* and three on the *West Virginia*.[1]

Trailing the *Akagi* planes by nearly three miles was the twelve-plane group from the *Kaga*. Using the same alignment as the second *Akagi* group, the planes formed a line more than eleven miles long. Leading the group was Lieutenant Ichiro Kitajima, who launched on the *West Virginia* at approximately 8:01. Of the twelve planes Kitajima commanded, six would target the *Oklahoma*, the last one launching around 8:05.

While the torpedo attack on Battleship Row can be divided into two separate launching phases, the same distinction could be made for the U.S. ships' AA defenses. Although the planes from the *Akagi*, *Hiryu*, and *Soryu* received very little AA fire, the planes from the *Kaga* flew into a virtual gauntlet of machine-gun fire. The three minutes that had elapsed since the torpedo assault began—the two minutes that the *Akagi-Hiryu-Soryu* assault lasted followed by the one-minute lull before the *Kaga* planes arrived—allowed most of the AA crews the time needed to man their guns. There were seven ships berthed along the southeast loch at the submarine base and eleven at the navy yard—fifteen including the four PT boats lashed to the deck of the oiler *Ramapo*. Though the planes were flying too low for the ships to use their 3-inch/50-caliber and 5-inch/25-caliber AA guns, all the ships had machine guns, and several had many. As a result, the *Kaga* planes were fired on during the entire duration of their flight across the loch. Four were shot down before they could launch, a fifth right after. It is believed that three of the five were targeting the *Oklahoma*.

Though there were some reports to the contrary, the Japanese machine-gun fire that occurred during the torpedo assault on Battleship Row came from the torpedo plane tail gunners, who generally opened fire the moment their planes passed over the battleships after making their launching runs. Because the torpedo planes were not armed for strafing, they did not return to the battle area after launching. Instead, they headed to a rendezvous area southwest of Oahu.

Though fighters were still strafing Ford Island and Hickam Field, and a small flight of dive bombers attacked Battleship Row from the northeast, the air space above Battleship Row and the southeast loch was relatively barren of Japanese planes for most of the torpedo attack. During the assault of the *Kaga* planes, only one plane flew over the combined length of the southeast loch and main channel (approximately one mile) at any given time. Contrary to popular belief, there were no fighter planes swooping in among the battleships.

At approximately 7:56, Ensign Herbert F. Rommel was finishing his breakfast in the *Oklahoma*'s wardroom. Hearing explosions on Ford Island, followed almost immediately by the general alarm, he rushed up a ladder to the forecastle. Exiting through a hatch, he glanced left toward the sound of an approaching engine. The source was a low-flying plane headed straight toward the ship from the southeast loch. Seeing it launch its torpedo, he immediately headed aft. Racing down the port side toward his battle station in turret 4, he recalled an incident about an incinerator fire and a quick-thinking boatswain who had spurred his crew into action with an expletive. Believing that the crew would interpret the alarm as just another drill, Rommel decided to use the same tactic. Stopping abreast an intercom for the ship's PA system, he depressed the lever.

"This is a real air raid! This is no shit!"

Moments later, the torpedo struck amidships, a muffled *whompf* followed by a tremendous explosion that shot a column of water and debris more than a thousand feet high. The impact was some twenty feet below the waterline between the smokestack and the mainmast, and the explosion blew away a large section of the antitorpedo blister and heaved the ship upward. The resulting shock waves sent oil gushing upward through the adjacent fuel bunkers' sounding tubes, blowing the caps off on the third deck level. The effect of the second torpedo, which hit approximately six seconds later, was similar. Neither would penetrate the hull.

Though few of the crew were aware of cause, the explosions dispelled any notions that the alarm was for a drill. With a profound sense of urgency, they raced for their battle stations. Nearly eighty would head topside to man the AA guns. But their efforts would be useless because the firing locks were in the armory.

The majority of the crew headed down.

Though many were responsible for hatch and porthole closures on the main and second decks, the bulk of the men had battle stations below the waterline. Those without specific battle station duties, primarily those assigned to the ship's assorted deck divisions, sought the protective confines of the third deck because the overhead (second deck) was armored. This was protocol for an aerial attack, a measure designed to safeguard the sailors and marines not engaged in fighting off aircraft. Because dive bombers had initiated the attack by bombing Ford Island, it was assumed that the explosions were due to bombs, not torpedoes. Another battle station protocol was that you go up and forward on the starboard side of the ship, down and aft on the port side. When the attack began, most of the crew were in their living areas, the majority of which were amidships on the main and second decks. Awakened from their sleep, many just rushed to the nearest ladder, regardless of where it was located. Many of the ladders became clogged, particularly those on the third deck.

At approximately 8:00, *Oklahoma* was struck amidships near frame 65. The result was devastating. Following the same course that the first torpedo had taken, which had blown away the antitorpedo blister, this third torpedo penetrated the hull. The ensuing explosion destroyed the adjacent fuel bunkers and void spaces on the second platform deck and ruptured the access trunks to the two forward boiler rooms as well as the transverse bulkhead to the aft boiler room. Damage to the first platform deck, located directly above the second platform deck, was nearly as serious. The explosions tore off the remains of the antitorpedo blister, destroyed the adjacent fuel bunkers and void spaces, and then buckled the longitudinal bulkhead of the two forward fire rooms. With water pouring in through a gaping hole, the list increased, straining the hawsers that secured the ship to the *Maryland*. Believing that *Oklahoma* would pin the *Maryland* against the starboard quays if she sank, making it impossible for her to get under way, officers issued an order aboard *Maryland* to sever all lines. While *Maryland* sailors went to work with fire axes, the *Oklahoma* was hit again.

Commander Kenworthy experienced the explosion while climbing to the conning tower. Believing that the resulting damage would be fatal, he retreated to the boat deck. Informed by some crewman that the lower decks were flooding, he conferred with Lieutenant Commander William M. Hobby, Jr., the ship's damage control officer. When Hobby agreed that the situation was untenable, the word was passed to abandon ship.

Barely two minutes had elapsed since the first torpedo hit.

The blast from the next one, the fifth, would shear the hawsers to the *Maryland* that were not already cut. Absent its constraints, *Oklahoma*'s list became pronounced. There would be at least one more hit, possibly three, before the *Kaga* planes arrived. By then most of the *Oklahoma* crewmen who would survive had already escaped to the upper decks or had entered the water. Many had swum to the *Maryland*. Though it is believed that *Oklahoma* would absorb three more hits from the *Kaga* planes, the mortal damage had already been done. By 8:08 the *Oklahoma* was lying on her side.

She had already capsized when the *Arizona* exploded a minute or two later.[2] Two-thirds of BatDivOne would be sitting on the bottom when its final member, *Nevada*, sortied at 8:42. By midmorning, *Nevada* would be on the bottom as well.[3]

Battleship Row on December 10, 1941. Left to right: *Arizona*, *Tennessee* with *West Virginia* outboard, *Maryland* with overturned *Oklahoma* outboard. Courtesy Naval Historical Center.

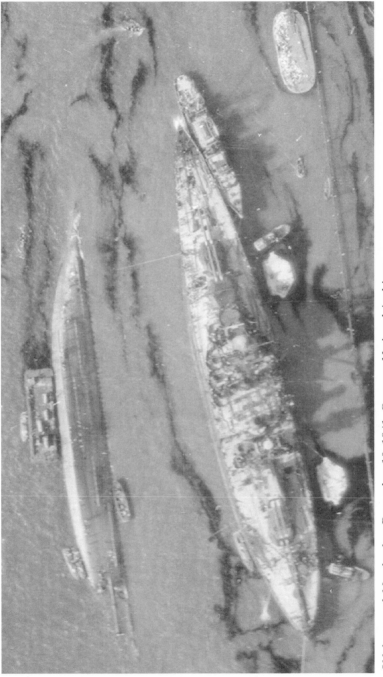

Oklahoma and *Maryland* on December 10, 1941. Courtesy National Archives.

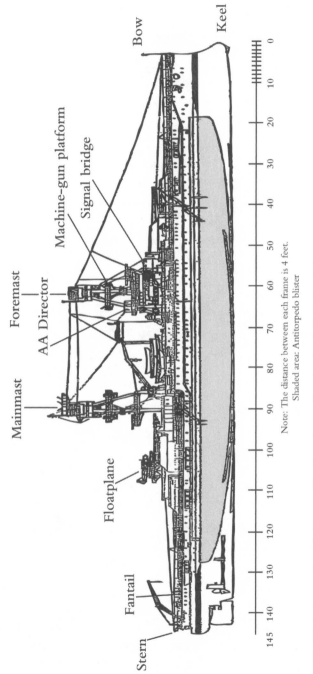

Bow

Keel

Machine-gun platform

Signal bridge

Foremast

AA Director

Mainmast

Floatplane

Fantail

Stern

145 140 130 120 110 100 90 80 70 60 50 40 30 20 10 0

Note: The distance between each frame is 4 feet.
Shaded area: Antitorpedo blister

USS *Oklahoma*, starboard side profile. Based on a drawing by A. D. Baker III.

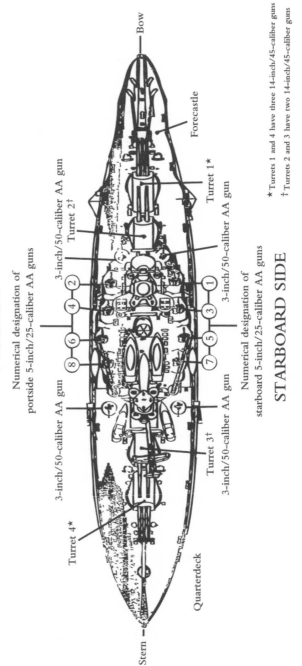

PORTSIDE

Numerical designation of
portside 5-inch/25-caliber AA guns

3-inch/50-caliber AA gun

Turret 2†

3-inch/50-caliber AA gun

Turret 1★

Forecastle

Bow

★ Turrets 1 and 4 have three 14-inch/45-caliber guns
† Turrets 2 and 3 have two 14-inch/45-caliber guns

Numerical designation of
starboard 5-inch/25-caliber AA guns

STARBOARD SIDE

3-inch/50-caliber AA gun

Turret 4★

3-inch/50-caliber AA gun

Turret 3†

Quarterdeck

Stern

USS *Oklahoma*, plan view. Based on a drawing by A. D. Baker III.

79

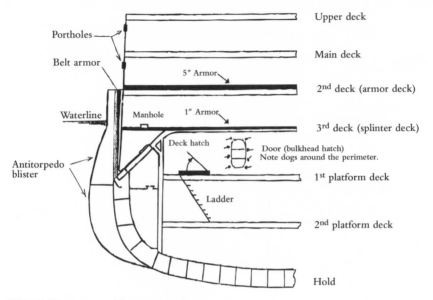

USS *Oklahoma*, portside cutaway view.

CHAPTER 9

Topside—7:55 A.M.

"Though there are many tales and stories, each and every one took place in a period of less than fifteen minutes, and in a square limited to six hundred feet on either side of the ship."

—*Oklahoma* sailor Paul A. Goodyear

When the attack began, few crewmen were above decks: the signal watch, the deck watch, the ship's band, the Marine Color Guard, and a few others simply enjoying the morning.

At 7:55 Signalman Third Class Paul A. Goodyear had just relieved the watch on the signal bridge when he saw a line of planes approaching Ford Island from the southwest. It wasn't unusual for U.S. Navy pilots to approach the Ford Island airstrip from that direction, particularly when on bombing maneuvers. Sand Island, located at Waipio Point, was a barren spit of land where the pilots would drop their unused sand bombs prior to landing. But it was strange that the planes had their landing gear down when it was obvious by their altitude that they weren't attempting to land. Plus their wheels had pronounced fairings, much different from U.S. Navy planes. Goodyear's concern was cemented when he saw the lead plane drop a bomb after it had passed over Sand Island.

The bomb whistled downward toward the southwest end of Ford Island. He raised his binoculars and focused on the plane. Painted on the fuselage was a large red "meatball."

"It's the goddamned Japs!" he exclaimed.

He saw the second plane drop a bomb that failed to explode. The bomb from the third plane penetrated the roof of the massive seaplane hangar. An instant later, a ball of flame some two hundred to three hundred feet in diameter erupted into the sky.

Goodyear witnessed the explosion and the fiery inferno that ensued. A few moments later Seaman First Class Richard N. Luttrell and Seaman First Class Robert D. Ryburn joined him. While Luttrell stared at the devastation, Ryburn attempted to contact the officer of the deck on the sound-powered phone. While he waited for a response, which never came, a torpedo plane zoomed overhead.

Crossing over the ship from port to starboard, the plane banked hard left toward the harbor entrance. Surprised that it had come from a different direction than the others, Goodyear and Luttrell headed aft for a better vantage because their portside view was obstructed. They had just turned into a lateral passageway when they saw a "fish" (torpedo) descending from the belly of a low-flying plane that was headed straight toward the ship, with another one right behind it. Reaching the end of the passageway, located directly above the No. 4 5-inch/25-caliber AA gun, they were stunned to see that the AA gunners were oblivious to what was happening. In fact, the gun captain had his back to the channel.

Goodyear knew the man and yelled at him to fire. Thinking it was just another of Goodyear's pranks, the man put his hands on his hips and stated, "Flags, you've had too much to drink!" It wasn't until Goodyear pointed out the torpedo wakes that the gun captain took his words to heart. By then it was too late.

They stood transfixed and awaited the inevitable.

There was a *whompf,* an explosion, and then a towering column of water. Seconds later the second torpedo hit. Whereas the initial impact had left Goodyear momentarily paralyzed, the second one prompted him to action. Grasping Luttrell by the shoulder, he gestured toward the bridge. By the time they'd returned, Ryburn was gone, having left for the battle signal station on the second deck.

Goodyear looked across the channel to the navy yard. His eyes riveted on the signal tower, he saw a Baker flag racing up the halyard. Generally, the flag was raised halfway up as a signal to prepare to fire, then the rest of the way to signal to commence firing. But there was no hesitation this time. The flag went straight up.

Goodyear turned to relay the message to the bridge. He then relayed the same message to the battle signal station. Ryburn received and confirmed it, removed an identical Baker flag from the signal bag, attached it to the halyard, and sent it aloft.

By 8:00 at least four torpedoes had hit the ship. With an increasing list, *Oklahoma* was obviously going to sink. When the ship's telescope, which was mounted on a sliding track, slid all the way to port, Goodyear knew it was time to go. He gestured to Luttrell, and they left.

Midway down the ladder to the boat deck, Goodyear recalled that he had left the signal book, which was marked "Secret," on his desk in the signal office. Because he had signed for it when he'd taken the watch, he'd have to retrieve it or face the consequences. Though his basic instincts told him otherwise, he retreated up the ladder.

After turning right at the bridge, Goodyear hastened up the sloping passageway to the starboard side, then hustled forward alongside the signal office. Stepping inside, he grabbed the book then retraced his steps to the ladders, which he descended with some difficulty because they were canted due to the list. By the time he reached the bottom, he was totally spent. He sat down for a short rest. The war would have to wait, if only for a minute.

Gathering his breath, he saw a flight of planes approaching Battleship Row from the northeast. The planes had fixed landing gear, the same type he'd seen attacking the airfield on Ford Island. Suddenly they began to dive. Moments later he saw a bomb descend from the belly of the lead plane. He followed the bomb's trajectory along its entire path. Looking down the long chasm between the *Tennessee* and the *West Virginia,* he saw it hit the port side of the *Arizona*'s main deck just aft of turret 2. The bomb bounced, then disappeared, seemingly without exploding.[1]

Rising to his feet, Goodyear tucked the codebook under his arm and headed aft along the boat deck to a metal container filled with life jackets. It was large, nearly half the width of the ship, with the life jackets held inside by a canvas tarp. Goodyear helped another sailor cut the rope lashings securing the tarp to the container, and within moments, several hundred life jackets had plummeted into the water. Unfortunately, the men's efforts were in vain. Due to aging and a lack of maintenance, barely a dozen jackets remained afloat. Not willing to trust his life to those that did, Goodyear descended a ladder to the main deck, passed through the lifelines, then made his way down the side of the ship. Arriving at the turn of the hull, he ran into

Commander Kenworthy. Presenting him with the codebook, Goodyear asked him what to do with it. To Goodyear's surprise the commander told him to toss it.

Goodyear did as he was told, and with a bit of defiance jumped right in after it, plummeting some fifty feet to the water below. Fighting his way to the surface, he found oil everywhere. He avoided it where he could and swam to the *Maryland*. By the time he arrived, he was exhausted. Fortunately, a sailor aboard the *Maryland* saw him and tossed him a line. Goodyear grabbed it and was wrapping it around his arm when a line of jagged circles appeared on the hull directly above his head.

It took a moment for him to realize they were bullet holes.

Scared that more attacks would follow, he released his grip and dropped into the water. He took a moment to regain his composure, then scanned the sky and tried again. This time there were no bullets. After reaching the blister ledge, he climbed over it, then pushed himself to his feet. He followed the ledge to the nearest ladder, which he scaled to the *Maryland*'s main deck. He then joined a detail of sailors passing ammunition to the *Maryland*'s AA battery; a bomb hit had rendered her electrically powered hoists inoperative. He would remain there until ordered off when the attack ended.[2]

When the attack began, Ship's Cook Third Class Jesse T. Kalman was emptying a trashcan on the port side; he noticed a low-flying plane approaching from the southeast loch. Seeing it launch its torpedo, he rushed back to the galley to warn his buddy Ship's Cook Second Class Archie West. With no time to waste, Kalman went straight to the point. "Let's haul ass—a fish is about to hit us!"

At seventeen, Seaman Second Class George H. Smith, Jr., was the youngest of the ship's crewmen. After hearing the first explosion, he hustled portside to his battle station at the No. 4 5-inch/51-caliber broadside gun. When the second torpedo exploded below him, Smith and another sailor dove out through the gun port.

At approximately 7:30, Seaman First Class John A. Cole, Jr., went topside to the boat deck. His battle station was the No. 8 gun on the portside 5-inch/25-caliber AA battery. Because Rear Admiral Isaac C. Kidd's materiel inspection was the following morning, he was anxious to clean his equipment.

Arriving at the gun, he removed a wire brush and a section of canvas from his toolbox. He spread the canvas beneath the trainer's station foot rests, then kneeled and began to clean. It was a typical Hawaiian morning: sunny, with light clouds and a slight breeze.

At 7:55 he heard the ship's PA system sound the bugle for first call to colors. While he continued working, a contingent of marines assembled on the fantail.

"Look at those crazy bastards dropping practice bombs on Hickam Field!" quipped a nearby sailor. Cole straightened up for a look. Across the channel, beyond the 1010 dock and the adjacent navy yard, a column of smoke was rising above Hickam Field. In amazement, Cole pondered the cause. Suddenly there was an explosion off to his right on Ford Island. It appeared to be near the seaplane hanger. Then an anxious voice resounded over the ship's PA.

"Man the antiaircraft batteries, man the antiaircraft batteries!"

"General quarters! General quarters!"

"All hands, man your battle stations! All hands, man your battle stations!"

The klaxon sounded the general alarm. *Bong-bong, bong-bong!*

Then more explosions, one from the west side of Ford Island, others from the island's airfield, still another from the 1010 dock. Automatically, he cleared the gun for action. His mind was racing. Someone would have to get the firing lock from the armory, and then the ammunition from down below. The inspection couldn't have happened at a worse time.

Suddenly Cole heard the distinctive whine of an airplane engine, followed almost immediately by the distinctive bark of an American .50-caliber machine gun. Turning toward the southeast loch, he saw a low-flying plane zooming skyward in a hard left turn. On the underside of each wing was a large red ball. Though he immediately discerned that the plane was Japanese, he didn't realize it was a torpedo bomber until a few seconds later, when he noticed an identical plane—aligned directly behind the first one—with a torpedo slung beneath its fuselage.

Cole stood mesmerized, his feet rooted to the gun platform. Moments later, the plane's torpedo, which was the size of a small telephone pole, descended into the water. Gauging its line of travel, Cole surmised that it would strike the ship forward of his position. Convincing himself that he was sufficiently removed from the point of impact to survive the resulting explosion, he refocused his efforts on his gun. In the process, he heard Ensign Rommel's warning on the ship's PA system—and the continuing sound of machine-gun fire from behind him.

Then he heard another plane, this one directly above him. Looking skyward, he saw it cross over the width of the ship. As it flew over the *Maryland,* he noticed that it was still carrying its torpedo. He found little consolation in the knowledge because he knew that one had already made it into the water and was on its way toward the ship. He didn't know about the one that had preceded it, which struck amidships a few moments later.

There was a muffled explosion, followed by a towering geyser of water as the ship heaved upward. Positioned only twenty yards from the point of impact, Cole was awed by the enormity of the geyser's column; so voluminous, it seemed an aberration. He was too close to see it crest, but he saw debris, a great deal of it. Realizing that it would soon be raining down, he dove beneath a boat positioned bottom side up on chocks just behind him. While he lay coiled beneath it, a second torpedo hit, sending another massive geyser exploding upward. Soon the deck was inundated with falling steel and water. Cole would spend nearly a minute waiting it out. Though the sound was deafening, the wait allowed him time to think. Deciding he would go to the armory to retrieve the firing lock for his gun, he started forward at a dead run the moment the maelstrom stopped. His dash was interrupted when a third torpedo hit. Knowing what would follow, he took shelter beneath an overhang.

His wait would be extended by a fourth torpedo hit. He studied the deck ahead. It was sloping to port. Water and oil were everywhere. He'd have to be careful to keep from slipping. He glanced at the transverse passageway leading to the armory. Fortunately, it wasn't far.

When the second maelstrom ended, he inched his way forward. Turning blindly into the passageway, he stumbled over a body, then stared at the lifeless form—he recognized the face. Terrified, he scrambled to his feet, took a final look, and then headed for the armory.

He had barely stepped inside when two petty officers arrived. Both were members of the 5-inch/25-caliber AA crew. They were there for the same reason. Together they gathered the firing locks. They had just started for the door when another torpedo hit, forcing them back inside. When they finally exited, they realized that the pronounced list had made the portside guns useless. Following a hasty discussion, they headed to starboard with the firing locks.

After arriving at the No. 1 5-inch/25-caliber AA gun, they inserted a firing lock in the breech and attached the electrical cable. When another torpedo hit, they were forced to seek shelter again. After the ensuing deluge ended, they made their way aft to the No. 3 5-inch/25-caliber AA gun. They were in the process of installing the firing lock when Commander Kenworthy descended from the bridge.

Grimly, he passed the word to abandon ship.

Deciding to depart from the forward part of the ship, Cole retraced his steps to the No. 1 5-inch/25-caliber AA gun. He passed it, then descended a ladder to the forecastle, where he climbed upward along the sloping deck to the starboard lifelines. After stepping through the lines, he slid down the side of the ship on his rear end. His descent ended at the blister ledge, where he quickly removed his shoes. His mode of escape had obviously been shared—at least a hundred pairs of shoes already lined the ledge. On either side of him, hosts of shoeless crewmen were sliding down the bottom of the ship, including Commander Kenworthy. Cole found himself somewhat amused as he watched the ship's rather dignified executive officer go sailing out over the bilge keel, the tails of his unbuttoned jacket streaming behind him.

While removing his socks, Cole noticed that the smaller six-inch and eight-inch mooring lines that tethered the *Oklahoma* to the *Maryland* were rapidly shrinking in size. Reaching their shearing point, they parted in a shower of sparks. Absent its final constraints, the ship lurched, and then slowly began to roll.

Cole was about to jump into the water when he noticed a forty-foot motor launch tethered to the aft boat boom, a thirty-five-foot pole that protruded horizontally from the side of the ship. Because the boom was moving toward vertical with the roll of the ship, it was dragging the boat attached to it up along the hull. Preferring a dry boat to oily water, Cole scurried aft. He pulled the pin that secured the mooring line to the boat's king post. Fortunately, the slime that had accumulated on the hull acted as a lubricant, allowing him to push the boat into the water by himself.

As the boat's momentum carried it into the ever-widening void between the two ships, Cole heard a chorus of shouting from sailors on the *Maryland*'s quarterdeck. They were pointing at the sky. Looking up, he saw a cluster of bombs descending from a V-shaped group of planes, seemingly straight toward him. Terrified, he jumped into the water. After shooting to the surface, he realized he had misjudged their trajectory. Missing the cluster of four battleships at the F-5 and F-6 quays, the bombs descended on F-7, where *Arizona* and *Vestal* were moored. Moments later, a horrific explosion rocked the entire harbor. Within seconds, the *Arizona* was a mass of flames.

Cole watched the massive tripod foremast slump forward, then, in shock, he swam to the boat and slowly pulled himself aboard. A short time later, he glanced at his watch. It had stopped at 8:08, apparently when he had jumped into the water. That time, and the demise of the *Arizona,* would be forever linked in his memory.[3]

Seaman First Class Jacob F. Chassereau, Jr., was cleaning one of the ship's portside 5-inch/25-caliber AA guns when he was interrupted by the chattering of machine-gun fire. Jumping behind the gun shield, he saw a Japanese plane banking left into a climb, its tail gunner strafing the ship.

Gunner's Mate First Class Charles F. McBeth was placing a firing lock in a portside 5-inch/25-caliber AA gun when the first torpedo exploded. In horror, he saw the shrapnel decapitate a shipmate.

Seaman First Class Theodore G. "Ted" Woodward was at his battle station at the No. 7 5-inch/25-caliber AA gun on the starboard side when he heard the call to move to the *Maryland.* He never did hear the call to abandon ship.

Coxswain Raymond L. Bowden was a member of *Oklahoma*'s Eighth Division. The division was responsible for maintaining the third deck and operating the No. 3 motor launch, of which he was the coxswain. He had boarded the *Oklahoma* in March 1939. Two years later, his younger brother Tom had joined him. On the night of December 6, 1941, the two went ashore on liberty together.

The following morning, Ray awakened early and had breakfast, because the No. 3 launch was a designated duty boat. As such, the fifty-foot launch had to be ready to board passengers at 8:00 A.M. Because it was Sunday, most of the passengers would be churchgoers. Though all the fleet's ships had chaplains who conducted services for all denominations while the ship was at sea, *Oklahoma* specialized in Catholic services while in port because her chaplain was an ordained Catholic priest. The launches provided transport to ships conducting services in the other major faiths, or to services being conducted ashore.

At 7:45 Bowden assembled his three-man crew on the starboard side of the quarterdeck. Tuning their instruments in the center of the quarterdeck was the ship's band. Mustering along the fantail was the *Oklahoma*'s color guard. A stone's throw away, similar preparations were being made on the quarterdeck of the *Maryland.* Aboard the *West Virginia,* moored directly aft, sailors were congregating on the bow to raise the Union Jack.

Shortly before 7:50, Bowden gestured his men toward the boat boom. Grasping the support line that extended from the end of the boom to a stanchion on the ship, they shuffled sideways across the boom to a Jacob's ladder, made of rope with wooden rungs, that descended into the launch. Looking ahead through the grottolike cavern formed by the hulls of the *Oklahoma* and the *Maryland,* Bowden could see the stern of the *Neosho,* a tanker berthed at the F-4 gas dock that had just finished discharging aviation gas to the storage tanks on Ford Island.

Once aboard the launch, Bowden cleaned the fantail while his crew wiped the dew from the seats. At 7:55 the bugler sounded first call on the ship's PA system, and the prep flag was raised. While Bowden and the others continued with their cleaning, the ship's band began marching aft toward the flagstaff.

A minute later, Bowden heard airplane engines over Ford Island but thought nothing of it until he heard the distinctive hammering of .50-caliber machine-gun fire from atop the *Maryland,* followed by an explosion at the southern end of the island. A moment later, he heard a voice on the *West Virginia*'s PA system summoning the ship's fire and rescue team. While he puzzled over its meaning, a plane flew overhead from the direction of Ford Island. Seeing a red ball on the underside of each wing, he immediately ordered his men to their battle stations. One after another, they scampered up the Jacob's ladder. Bowden was the last to go.

After climbing the ladder to the boom, he grabbed hold of the support line, and then shuffled sideways along the length of the boom to the side of the ship. By the time he'd secured a foothold on the teakwood deck, his men had already dispersed—as had the band and the color guard. Racing forward along the quarterdeck, he heard a resounding explosion on the port side of the *West Virginia,* followed by a similar explosion alongside the *Oklahoma.*

Though the resulting tremor did nothing to impede his speed—the explosion had occurred well forward, and on the opposite side of the ship—it definitely heightened his sense of urgency. When he reached the break of the quarterdeck, he raced up a ladder to the upper deck, and then up another to the boat deck. Starting forward, he saw a low-flying plane headed toward the ship from the southeast loch. Seeing it drop its torpedo, he accelerated into a sprint. As he raced alongside the four 5-inch/25-caliber AA gun mounts on the starboard side of the ship, he heard the pinging of bullets careening off the gun shields and ready boxes. At the forward end of the boat deck, he scaled the double ladders to the signal bridge, then started up another ladder to the navigation bridge—only to be rocked by a second explosion, as another torpedo struck amidships. Barely avoiding the geyser that followed, he raced up another ladder to the pilothouse top, where the AA directors were located.

Stepping through the door of the starboard side director, he was surprised to find that only one other crewmate had preceded him, Fireman First Class Robert "Bobbie" Jones. They'd barely had time to acknowledge each other when Bowden saw a torpedo plane headed for the *California,* and still another angling for the *Oklahoma.*

Bowden positioned himself behind the telescopic sight on the port side of the director, endeavoring to align it on a target when he realized there wasn't any power. Without electricity, the director was useless. A moment later, the telescope would be useless as well. Bowden recoiled as the eyepiece was jerked from his face when the telescope was struck by some projectile.

Staring at the tubular casing in disbelief, he realized that he was utterly defenseless. He steadied himself on the tilting deck and prepared for the explosions he knew were forthcoming. His wait would be short. Moments later, Bowden heard the directive to abandon ship from a nearby PA speaker, which fortunately was on a different circuit than the director.

"Let's get the hell out of here!" he shouted to Jones. Bowden unlatched the portside door. Because of the ship's portside list, it swung open without prompting. Looking below, Bowden could see sailors already beginning to leave. Off to his right, sailors aboard the *Maryland* were using axes to cut the hawsers that tethered the two ships together.

Deciding to leave on the starboard side, he descended a ladder to the wing of the navigation bridge and was about to descend another when he noticed the body of a sailor in an adjacent scupper. Bowden recognized the man's face. It was West, one of his men from the motor launch.

Upon reaching the signal bridge, Bowden descended the double ladders to the boat deck, turned to starboard, and walked up along the sloping deck about fifteen feet. Grasping the aft portion of the waist-high gun shield that encircled the No. 5 5-inch/25-caliber AA gun, he pulled himself up to the edge of the deck. After climbing through the lifelines, Bowden slid down the front of an exterior bulkhead to the upper deck. Yet he still had to cross a section of deck to reach the side of the ship. He wasn't sure he could make it. The ship was now listing more than 45 degrees. He was close to six feet tall, but the lifelines were a good eight to ten feet away. He couldn't reach them by jumping. Instead, he would have to crawl. Dropping to his knees, he crabbed his way upward. After pulling himself through the lines, he stood up and started walking.

Though he was initially walking at a decline, the slope had been reduced to almost nothing by the time he'd reached the blister ledge—which was now nearly vertical. Scaling it, he glanced down to survey the ship's bottom. After finding a route that was clear of protruding pump intakes, he had just sat down when he saw a tremendous plume of smoke erupting to his right. He realized that it was the *Arizona*. An instant later, it exploded into a fiery inferno.

He took a final look and then pushed himself off. When he reached the turn of the keel, he shot off into the air, arcing outward before dropping some eight feet to the water below. Surfacing, he swam toward the *Maryland*, now some fifty feet away. He started toward a cane fender suspended from her blister. Though he encountered oil along the way, he was able to avoid it by splashing it from his trail. Reaching the fender, he shimmied up the rope to the blister ledge. Fortunately, two *Maryland* sailors hustled over to help him aboard. As they pulled him up, Bowden noticed another group of sailors just a few feet to his right helping someone else aboard. Glancing toward them as he gathered his breath, he realized it was his brother, Tom.

Incredibly relieved, he gathered his younger sibling in a massive bear hug. Following a few quick words, Tom asked Ray what he should do next. Ray answered that he should report to his regular battle station. As Tom hustled off, Ray heeded his own advice, proceeding to the bridge to see if he could be utilized on the AA director.

A gunnery officer instructed him to post himself on the flying bridge as a lookout for targets. During the second wave of the attack, Bowden was struck in the chest by a piece of shrapnel, the result of 250-pound bomb blast on the *Maryland*'s forecastle. The man standing to his left was wounded in the leg. An officer standing to his right was killed.

Seaman First Class James A. Ehlert was perched in the foremast on a painting stage when the attack began. Seeing a Japanese plane zoom over the ship, he tossed a hand towel over a hawser, creating a zip-line that he used to descend to the boat deck. When word was passed to abandon ship, he shimmied upside down across another hawser to the *Maryland*.

Marine Private Charles M. Risher was on the fantail when machine-gun bullets began splintering the deck around him. Seconds later, he was blown off the ship when the first torpedo hit.

Seaman First Class Charles R. Curtis was in the cab of one of the ship's cranes when the attack began. When the ship rolled over, he rode the cab downward, jumping out a moment before it hit the water.

Positioned high in the mainmast when the second torpedo hit, Seaman First Class Harry L. Scott, Jr., was catapulted into the air when the resulting explosion side-whipped the masthead. Incredibly, he landed on the *Maryland*. He survived because an awning broke his fall. A bomb blast some ten minutes later would blow him off the Maryland, and he would survive that fall as well.

When the attack began, Private First Class Jimmy D. Black was in the marine quarters on the second deck aft, port side. He had just finished the four-to-eight watch and was enjoying a cigarette and a cup of coffee. After the colors were raised at 8:00, he planned on enjoying a leisurely breakfast.

He hadn't heard the general alarm before the first torpedo hit. Along with Private First Class Elmer E. Drefahl, he scrambled for the nearest ladder. Because their battle station was located high in the foremast, they'd have to hustle to get there. While they were en route, the second torpedo hit.

When they reached a ladder on the starboard side of the turret 4 barbette, they scaled it to the quarterdeck. Seeing bullets splintering the deck as they exited the hatch, they immediately jumped back through it, barely avoiding some others who had started up the ladder behind them. They quickly headed forward to climb aloft through the ship's superstructure.

Arriving amidships, they scaled a ladder to the main deck, another to the upper deck, and then a third that took them to the boat deck. Hustling forward, they scaled the starboard leg of the foremast to their battle station in the ship's secondary AA battery. Located above the range finder, the area was a large platform surrounded by a waist-high shield, featuring four air-cooled .50-caliber machine guns. Because the gun's firing locks had been stowed for Monday's inspection, none of the guns was operative.

A moment later the third torpedo hit, and shortly thereafter a fourth one. With the resulting geysers spouting up along the port side, Black stared in disbelief at the torpedo planes closing in on Battleship Row from the southeast loch. Powerless to do anything but watch, he saw the lead plane angle south toward the *California*. Knowing what lay ahead, he had no desire to watch it happen. Instead, he turned his thoughts to their escape.

Because the ship was listing, he knew that if they didn't leave the foremast soon, they would eventually be thrown out. If that happened, they could be sucked under when the ship keeled over. He decided they should jump but wanted to wait until the platform was canted over the water. When Black relayed his plan to Drefahl, Drefahl refused, despite Black's contention that they would drown if they didn't. Black didn't pursue the matter further. Glancing across the channel, he saw another torpedo plane coming in over the southeast loch. After a few more seconds, he decided it was time to go. Stepping over the port side of the gun shield, he stared down at the water. The platform was usually about eighty-five feet above the waterline. With the ship listing, it was somewhat less. Either way, it was a long drop. Though he could see men in the water, none were directly below him.

He took a moment to prepare himself. At the final instant, he decided to dive instead of jump. Incredibly, it would be his first diving attempt ever, from any height. He fortunately had the foresight to position his hands above his head as he departed the platform.

Several seconds had elapsed by the time he reached the water. He pierced the surface and continued down. Though he was stunned and had the wind knocked out of him, he had the presence of mind to propel himself upward. Finally, he breached the surface and began to swim. It wasn't until he was sufficiently clear of the ship that he stopped to catch his breath. He rolled over onto his back and used his legs to stay afloat. Having absorbed the brunt of his impact, his arms felt like they'd been torn from their sockets.

Though the torpedo attack was still in process, Black's battle was over. He had never felt so exhausted or alone in his life. The *Oklahoma*'s list was increasing, and there was no doubt that she would soon be on her side. His only duty now was to survive. Turning toward the channel entrance, he kicked his feet to propel himself forward, aided by an occasional flutter from his arms. Moving parallel to the *Oklahoma* until he drew even with her bow, Black then angled toward the *Maryland,* which he bypassed in favor of a landfall on Ford Island. Finally, he touched bottom. When the water was waist deep, he realized he had lost his uniform. All that remained were his skivvies, his socks, and a single shoe.

CHAPTER 10

Chaos Below

The Oklahoma *had four deck hatches on the quarterdeck, three on the forecastle, and five on the boat deck. Each of the four turrets had an escape hatch on the underside of the overhang.*

Gunner's Mate Second Class Leon C. Kolb was the gun captain of the center gun in turret 1. When the attack began, he was relaxing in the turret's lower shell deck. He had just returned from breakfast. The first indication that something was amiss was a thud that sent a quiver through the deck. For some reason, his initial reaction was to check the time on an old alarm clock that was hanging by a string from the overhead. It was 7:55.

Seconds later, there was an explosion, this one within the ship. The deck heaved upward a good foot and fell, a sensation similar to a rising elevator stopping suddenly. He couldn't imagine how something could raise a battleship. Following a second explosion, sailors began streaming down onto the shell deck from the turret's upper levels. When one informed him "the enemy is off Diamond Head attacking us," Kolb assumed that a German battleship was shelling Battleship Row. Climbing a series of ladders, he ascended the equivalent of four decks to his battle station in the gunroom. After stowing his army cot (the gunroom was also where he slept), Kolb formulated a plan of action. A seasoned veteran—he'd served on the battleship *Texas* prior to *Oklahoma*—he knew that in order to return fire, the turret's centering pin would have to be removed to allow the turret to rotate. He also wanted to close the turret's ventilation system to prevent any smoke entering from outside.

Needing approval to do both, he descended to the shell deck to find his supervisor, Gunner's Mate First Class William G. Silva, whom he'd seen there earlier. When he found him, Silva answered no to both his proposals, saying he would take care of them himself. He told Kolb to return to his battle station. Before Kolb could leave, another torpedo hit. He grabbed hold of a towel bar to keep his feet. Then another one hit. The alarm clock was swinging like a pendulum. When the swinging started to slow, he started up the ladder.

In the gunroom, he could do nothing but wait. He still had no idea what was happening outside. Neither the division officer nor his assistant had arrived, nor the chief petty officer. He'd heard Rommel's warning on the PA but nothing since. Why weren't the guns being trained? If there was an enemy ship off Diamond Head, the turret should be rotated to port. It didn't make sense. Consumed with frustration, he ducked out through the hatch in the overhang to find out. Hearing the *ping, ping, ping* of ricocheting bullets, he immediately glanced to his right. The bullets had chipped a line of pockmarks in the barbette of turret 2. He looked aft to determine the source. What he saw was a Japanese dive bomber descending on the north end of Battleship Row. He could clearly see the red balls on its wings. Until that moment, it had never occurred to him that the assailants might be Japanese.

He saw a bomb drop, watching its trajectory as the plane pulled out of its dive. Moments later there was a volcanic explosion and an enormous fireball erupted into the sky. Because of its enormity, he was sure the bomb had hit a powder magazine. With *Oklahoma* having entered the harbor with *Arizona* and *Nevada* just two days before, he knew that both were moored at the north end of the row, but from his vantage, he couldn't determine which of the two had been hit.

Now that he realized the ships were under aerial assault, he naturally assumed the explosions he'd felt earlier were the result of bombs. As he had come out from beneath the turret's overhang on the starboard side of the ship, he had no idea that torpedo bombers were assaulting the port side. His first thought was to join an AA crew, his secondary battle station. Aware that the gun's firing locks had been stowed for Monday's inspection, he decided against it. His second thought was to flood the powder magazines. If it could be done, it would mitigate the sort of devastation he had just witnessed. At the very least, if they could flood the starboard magazine, they could coun-terbalance the list, which he guessed was about ten degrees. He has-tened to get below. There were others doing the same.

He located Silva and offered his suggestion. The answer was no. Once again, he was told to return to the gunroom, which was difficult to do now because the ship was listing. Climbing from the emergency battery room to the gunroom, he found himself using the ladder's corners instead of the rungs. By the time he reached the gunroom, he had counted six explosions. Though he still didn't know they had resulted from torpedo hits, he had no doubt that they had caused con-siderable damage. He had glimpsed the *Maryland* when he'd been above. He hadn't seen any damage. If he could get to her, he might be able to join an AA crew to fight back. Believing that the order to abandon ship would have been given if there were someone there to issue it, he decided to take the initiative. He assessed the situation with Gunner's Mate Second Class John C. Carlson and Gunner's Mate Second Class Edgar E. Dishman, and the trio decided to transfer to the *Maryland*. Kolb followed them out through the overhang.

Looking to port, he saw that the outer portion of the teakwood deck was already under water. The ship was going down. It never occurred to him that it would capsize.

Suddenly he realized he'd left his fiancée's engagement ring in his locker on the shell deck. He had purchased it in Honolulu a couple of weeks earlier. It had cost him two hundred dollars, a sum it had taken him 5½ years to save. He was about to go below to retrieve it when he recalled the biblical story of Lot and his escape from Sodom and Gomorrah, a city that God was destroying because it was evil. Because Lot was good, God had commanded him to leave with his wife, with instructions that they should never look back. Concerned for her jewelry, Lot's wife disobeyed, turning instantly into a pillar of salt.

Kolb took the story's message to heart. Had he gone back, he most likely would have died. The two *Oklahoma* sailors who received the Congressional Medal of Honor posthumously, Ensign Francis C. Flaherty and Seaman First Class James R. Ward, both died in the bow-els of turret 1.

Seaman Second Class Melvin L. Vaughn was standing opposite the refrigerators on the third deck when the first torpedo hit. The con-cussion ruptured a refrigerant conduit and tweaked the doorframes.

The doors sagged open, inundating the compartment with ammonia fumes.[1]

Coxswain Chester G. Shacklett moonlighted as a moneylender. His standard loan was five for six: he'd lend five dollars with six dollars due the next payday. Quite successful, he had three hundred dollars stowed in his locker on the morning of December 7, quite a sum when the average seaman made only twenty-one dollars a month. Though he raced to man his AA battle station when the general alarm sounded, it was a different story when word was passed to transfer to the *Maryland.* Finding the nearest ladder, he raced below to retrieve the money from his locker. Following a torpedo explosion, he came across an ensign whose head had become wedged in the framework of a bunk. Shacklett freed him, then swam to the *Maryland,* the money tucked deeply in his pocket.

Ensign Paul H. Backus was the *Oklahoma*'s signal officer, quite an accomplishment for a man who had been on the ship for only five months and out of college for only ten. He shared a second deck cabin with Ensign Lewis Bailey Pride, Jr., a classmate from the Naval Academy.

Backus spent Saturday night aboard ship, retiring shortly after midnight. Pride spent the evening in Honolulu, celebrating a gunnery award with fellow officers from the 5-inch/51-caliber broadside battery. Because their revelry had stretched well into the evening, they'd missed the liberty boat to the ship and had spent the night in their cars. Pride had been in his bunk only a couple of hours when Rommel's warning resounded over the PA. Still semi-inebriated, Pride never heard it.

The general alarm awakened the deep-sleeping Backus, but he only half comprehended its meaning. He was still in his bunk when he heard Rommel's warning. Backus knew Rommel; he was not the type to swear even casually, much less over the ship's PA. Then he heard the announcement that all personnel not engaged in repelling the air attack should take shelter below the armored deck. It spurned Backus to his feet. Pride never stirred. The alarm sounded again as Backus tried to shake him awake. It took a considerable effort, but he finally got him up. Still in a stupor, Pride began to dress. The task, difficult to begin with, became even harder when the cabin started shaking, the result of the first torpedo hit. Because their cabin was on the opposite side of the ship, Backus didn't hear the explosion, but he knew, thanks to Rommel, that they were under attack and surmised that the tremor was related. Discussing their amazement that an enemy could reach the harbor undetected, they quickly finished dressing.

Pride dashed out the door first, followed by Backus a few seconds later. Backus was rounding the barbette of turret 1 when he ran into Lieutenant Lawrence H. Birthisel, Jr., Pride's division officer. Birthisel had come to find Pride because the two had been out together the night before. Somewhat in a daze, he asked Backus to find out where he was. He was infinitely relieved when Backus told him that Pride was awake and en route to his battle station.[2] When the two men parted, Backus started aft along the port side. Passing the barbette of turret 2, he encountered Second Lieutenant Henry H. Gaver, Jr., a marine who lived across the passageway from him. Gaver was attempting to close a trunk hatch, despite the sailors trying to climb through it from the deck below. The general alarm required that the hatch be sealed. It was Gaver's duty to see that it was done. He had no idea they would never get out.

Continuing aft, Backus stepped through a bulkhead hatch to another passageway, then started up a ladder toward the signal bridge. On the way up, he saw a sailor on the deck of the damage control office gathering papers scattered roughshod across the deck. Guessing that the torpedo had struck directly below, Backus continued moving, climbing two decks to the captain's cabin. One of his duties as a communications officer was to remove the crypto material from the captain's safe, secure it in a weighted watertight canister, and toss it overboard. Because the captain had gone ashore earlier, Backus was unable to perform the task; the safe was locked and too large to move. Frustrated, he left.

Exiting the cabin by the No. 3 5-inch/25-caliber AA gun, he stopped to ask a gunner why the gun wasn't firing. In disgust, the sailor retorted that the ammunition was locked up, there was no compressed air to operate the gun's rammers, and the firing locks were in the armory. Backus's frustration mounting, he scaled a starboard-side stairway to his battle station on the signal bridge. He arrived to find no one there. He was angry until he saw flags on the halyard. His men had been there and had done their duty. For the first time that morning, Backus had something to feel good about. But the feeling disappeared when he saw the *Arizona* explode. A moment later, he heard the word to abandon ship on the ship's PA.

After descending from the bridge on the starboard side, Backus passed through the lifelines, then slid down the side of the hull to the water. Swimming for the bow of the *Maryland,* he saw a whaleboat secured to the starboard anchor chain. He angled toward it, pulled himself aboard, and discovered that two other *Oklahoma* survivors already occupied it. Shortly thereafter, they were joined by a fourth.

Backus attempted to start the engine but couldn't locate the starter switch. One of the others finally found it and started the engine. Assuming the position of engineer, Backus ordered one of the men to act as coxswain and the others to position themselves amidships to pick people out of the water. One of them disobeyed, jumping over the side to swim to Ford Island.

Moving slowly between the two ships, the three of them began pulling people aboard, many of them covered with oil. One was the *Oklahoma*'s doctor, Commander Fred Rohow. Fifty years old, he probably would have drowned were it not for a young marine who had held his head above water until the boat could pull alongside him.

They circled to the channel side of the ship, which by now had flipped over, and were cruising along the starboard side when suddenly a steward popped up, having escaped through one of the portholes. After disembarking him with the others near the gas dock on Ford Island, they headed out again. When they couldn't find anyone else in the water, they saw an ensign and two enlisted men standing on *Oklahoma*'s overturned stern. All three were attired in their navy whites. Pulling alongside them, Backus told them to board so that he could take them ashore. The ensign took one look at the boat's filthy interior and told them to shove off, because the boat was too dirty. In disbelief, Backus left. Coincidentally, he would spend the night alongside the same officer on the floor of the Ford Island bachelor's officers' quarters (BOQ).

When Ship's Cook Third Class George A. Brown's mother wrote a letter to Captain Foy complaining that she wasn't receiving any mail from her son, the young cook was reprimanded and ordered to write her once a week. After composing a letter Saturday night, Brown awakened early Sunday morning to finish his duties in the spud locker, planning to address the envelope when his work was completed. He was in the process of doing just that when the general alarm sounded. Dropping the envelope, he hustled to the nearest deck hatch, climbed down through the armored deck, and raced for his third deck battle station, alongside the portside 5-inch AA conveyor belt. By the time he arrived, three torpedoes had hit. Throwing on his headphones, he reported that his station was manned and ready. But there was no reply. Then a fourth torpedo hit, gashing a hole in the port bulkhead some twenty feet away. As water exploded through the void, Brown and others were swept down the passageway into an adjacent crew space. Though they were able to close the passageway door to prevent the space from flooding, this left only a single avenue of escape, an overhead hatch that had been wedged open by one of the explosions. The opening was narrow, but Brown was slim and was able to pull himself through it. Unfortunately, only a few of the others were slight enough to follow him.

After exiting onto the main deck, they had just started aft when the lights went out. They lowered themselves to the deck and continued aft on their hands and knees. A short time later, one of them located a ladder, and one by one, they scaled it to the quarterdeck. Brown was one of the first ones out. After exiting through a portside hatch just forward of turret 3, he slid into the water. Though Brown had little difficulty pushing his way through the myriad flotsam alongside the ship—such as cases of apples, oranges, and potatoes—it was a different matter with the bodies he encountered, of which there were many. Swimming toward the channel, he pushed them aside as reverently as possible. After a brief respite alongside one of the jettisoned floatplanes, he continued into the channel, where he was eventually rescued by a whaleboat.

Hearing the word to abandon ship, Pharmacist's Mate First Class D. L. Westfall joined a line of men passing wounded along the portside passageway to a ladder by the dental office. Once there, they were hoisted upward to the second deck. The passageway was thick with the smell of fuel oil. Standing alongside him was Ensign W. M. McLellon, who said he felt faint, then suddenly collapsed. Stooping to pick him up, Westfall became dizzy. Soon others were falling. Finding it difficult to breathe, Westfall managed to drag himself to the ladder before collapsing and passing out. Incredibly, both men would survive.

Fireman Second Class Arthur M. Grand Pre and Fireman First Class John D. Grand Pre were brothers. Though different in age, they looked like twins. Both would make it into the water on the morning of December 7. After swimming to the *Maryland,* John was informed that Art had boarded a few minutes earlier. Relieved, he was assigned to a battle station, where he fought until the attack was over. Though he would spend the ensuing hours trying to locate Art, he never found him. Two days later, he would learn the horrible truth. While swimming to the *Maryland,* Art had been killed by strafing. The man seen boarding had actually been John.

Yeoman Third Class Raymond L. Richmond's battle station was at the No. 5 broadside gun. His living compartment was on the second deck, starboard side. Known throughout the ship for his charcoal sketches, Richmond spent his off-duty hours on the fantail sketching portraits, charging three dollars apiece. The extra income came in handy on liberties, where Richmond spent it freely with Seaman Second Class Jesse C. Foglesong, a baker in the officer's galley. To reciprocate, Foglesong kept Richmond supplied with fresh donuts.

Rating liberty on Sunday, Richmond awakened early to prepare to go ashore. Believing that the starboard washroom closest to his area would be full, he crossed the center of the ship to the portside washroom. Surprised to find it packed, he retreated to the starboard side. He found an empty stall in the amidships washroom, showered, and was shaving when the first torpedo hit. Though it exploded on the opposite side of the ship, it felt as if someone had "picked up the ship, shook it up, then dropped it back down." Immediately thereafter, he heard the general alarm. Then the second torpedo hit. By the time he had gathered his gear, two more had hit.

He hastened aft toward his living space. He had just stowed his gear when the lights went out. Deciding there was no time to dress, he grabbed a railing in the galley passageway and pulled himself forward to the nearest ladder. After scaling it to the main deck, he climbed another to the upper deck.

Aided by the light from portholes, he saw a group of sailors clustered beneath a deck hatch. Extending down through the hatch were two pairs of hands. Slowed by the clutter of gear aligning the bulkhead, the group had already been pulled aloft when he reached the hatch. Richmond gazed up and extended his hands. To his surprise, the

hands reaching down to meet him belonged to Commander
Kenworthy and Lieutenant Commander Hobby. Because Richmond
was too short, their hands wouldn't meet. They suggested he go out
through the casemate.

Turning to starboard, Richmond crawled up the sloping deck to
the No. 5 5-inch/51-caliber broadside gun, his normal battle station,
and then crawled out through the gun port. Moving across the cat-
walk to the lifelines, he looked down toward the water. Though it was
less than a twenty-foot drop to the water's surface, he realized he'd
have to jump outward to clear the blister ledge because the ship was
canted over. After stepping through the lifelines, he steadied himself,
then jumped outward as far as he could. It wasn't far enough. His legs
cleared the blister but his buttocks didn't, and his tailbone smacked
hard against the outer corner of the ledge. Unable to feel his legs, he
scooted down the remainder of the hull on his hands. Because it was
constructed of overlapping plates, his knuckles were bloodied when
he reached the water.

With only his arms to propel himself, he started swimming toward
the *Maryland*. Directly ahead was a pool of oil. He dove beneath it and
swam until his breath gave out. Raising his hands upward into the oil,
he shook them rigorously to clear an opening. He rose up through
the void, gulped some air, and then went under again. By the time he'd
made it across, he was nauseated. Fighting to keep his chin above water,
he threw up. He remembers the content distinctly—waffles.

Drained of his strength, he was beginning to sink when someone
grabbed him by the hair. It was Foglesong. He heaved him from the
water and then held him until Richmond could get a toehold on a
rope ladder. Grasping it with his hands, he scaled it to the blister ledge.
While Foglesong helped someone else, Richmond staggered to his
feet, and then hobbled to a boarding ladder. On the main deck, he
was directed to join an AA crew. He would fight alongside them for
nearly two hours. When the attack ended, he collapsed. Deprived of
the adrenaline that had sustained him through his injuries, he was
overwhelmed by the sudden onslaught of pain. Unable to walk, he
was secured to a board and carried from the ship.[3]

Seaman First Class Gene Byers was listening to a record when the
first torpedo hit. The resulting tremor caused the needle to skip.
Oblivious to the cause, he repositioned the needle, and Bing Crosby

continued his rendition of "Clementine." It wasn't until the needle skipped two more times that Byers heard the general alarm. He scaled a ladder to the main deck, but his attempt to use an overland route to get to his battle station in turret 1 ended in a hail of bullets from a strafing torpedo plane. He retreated through two lower decks to access the turret from below, where he eventually escaped through the hatch in the overhang.

Fireman First Class Francis R. Parkinson hastened to his battle station at the No. 6 boiler, only to be informed that the boiler room had already flooded. While congregated with other crewmembers in boiler control, he was ordered aloft to seal the hatch in the overhead, because efforts to seal it from below had been fruitless. Though he and two others would climb up through the hatch and secure it from above, they would be unable to reopen it when word was passed to abandon ship a short time later. The order to seal the hatch, which they had perceived as sending them back into harm's way, would instead save their lives, dooming the others they had unwittingly trapped below.

Ensign Joseph C. Spitler was the assistant division officer in turret 4. As such, he was the assistant to Ensign Rommel, the division officer. On Sunday morning, he'd worked the four-to-eight watch as the junior officer of the deck. Relieved at 7:45 he returned to his stateroom in the junior officers' country on the second deck.

After removing his blouse and white service uniform, he'd gone to the junior officers' washroom, the ship's most forward compartment, and was seated on the toilet when he heard Rommel's warning, followed immediately by the general alarm. Departing as quickly as he could, he called out the alarm as he raced through the junior officers' country, repeating it again as he continued aft into the warrant officer's country. Able to move through both areas quickly, he hit a juggernaut when he reached the portside passageway. It was cluttered with some two hundred sailors and marines, many running toward him instead of aft, contrary to the convention that portside traffic be directed aft. Dodging through them, Spitler was about a third of the way aft when the first two torpedoes hit, the first one almost directly below him, lifting the deck a foot.

He was in the crew space alongside the turret 3 barbette when the third and fourth torpedoes hit. With the ship at a pronounced list, he hastened into the adjacent compartment, where he descended a ladder alongside turret 4. After arriving at the carpenter's shop, he descended another ladder to the lower handling room, on the first platform deck. By the time he entered the turret, two more torpedoes had hit, and the lights were out.

Because the lower handling room was his battle station, he would normally have remained there. Informed that Ensign Rommel was not at his battle station in the turret officer's booth, Spitler assumed that Rommel was the acting officer of the deck, because he'd issued the warning, and as such had been needed elsewhere. As Rommel's assistant, Spitler's duty was to act in his absence, so he immediately started up to the turret officer's booth.

Climbing through the turret's five levels, Spitler was shocked to find that the turret was nearly empty. Not having heard the order to abandon ship (and obviously the men in the lower handling room hadn't either), he could only assume that the men had left of their own volition, which he found perplexing. After enduring two more torpedo hits while he climbed, he finally reached the turret officer's booth. Unable to make telephone contact with main battery control, he decided to exit the turret to assess the situation himself. He propelled himself feet first through the escape hatch in the overhang, then dropped to the deck below, only to have his feet slide out from under him the instant he hit it. Due to a combination of sinking and listing, the port half of the quarterdeck, the lowest of the ship's three weather decks, was now underwater. Moments later, he was joined in the water by two sailors who had exited the turret the same way.

Realizing the seriousness of the situation, Spitler felt compelled to return to the turret to order the others out, but it was impossible to get back in. Because the ship was holding steady at a forty-five-degree angle, he surmised that it was already on the bottom, and that the men could eventually climb out on their own accord. Consoled by this belief, which he would soon realize was wrong, he turned his attention to the others who were with him.

Glancing behind him, he saw two more who were clinging to the coaming of a deck hatch. Though the hatch was submerged, it was one of the few handholds available. Looking beyond them, Spitler surveyed the southeast loch. Though he heard rampant gunfire, he didn't see any planes. It wasn't until he looked up that he realized where the fire was directed. Approaching Battleship Row from the southwest was a formation of high-level bombers. Flying in V-shaped groups of five, the formation extended as far as he could see. Realizing the lead group would soon be overhead, he ordered the other men to start swimming because he felt certain the ship would be targeted, and he knew that they could be killed by the concussive impact of any bombs that struck the water.

After they left, the ship started turning. Horrified by the realization that it could capsize, Spitler suddenly became aware of a gangplank dangling precariously above him. Though it was secured with hawsers, it could crush them if the ship continued moving and the hawsers parted. Pushing off with his feet, he began swimming frantically, never daring to look back. But the danger was not in the gangplank, which remained secured; the danger was in the deck. Gaining momentum from the rotation of the superstructure, the deck, which was now inverted, was dropping toward the water at an accelerated rate. He'd have to swim more than forty feet to clear it. He'd gone nearly fifty when it crashed into the water behind him.

After escaping from the overhang of turret 4, Boatswain's Mate Second Class Westley F. Potts swam to the floatplane that had been atop turret 3. It was floating upright in the water amidships. Though he didn't know how to fly, he was determined to try. After tearing the canvas cover off the canopy, he climbed into the cockpit and started manipulating switches. When he couldn't start the engine, he climbed into the back to look for a machine gun. Unfortunately, the gun had been removed. When he saw that the ship was turning over, and that the mainmast was falling toward him, he dove into the water and started swimming. Moments later, the floatplane was crushed by the mainmast.

Shipfitter Second Class Wayne Vickrey was running down a third deck passageway when he saw a group of sailors who had stopped to pray. Attempting to snap them out of their apparent shock, he yelled, "Pray later. Get your asses off the boat!"

With the ship nearly on its side, Fireman Second Class Robert Bromm attempted to escape by crawling through a ventilation shaft in the overhead of the third deck machine shop. By the time he'd reached the outlet, the ship was nearly horizontal, and the shaft was filling with water. Though he was able to pull one other man out, the shaft filled immediately thereafter, trapping some twenty men in the machine shop behind them.

When the attack began, Seaman First Class Donald A. Lester was in the carpenter's shop visiting a friend. Assigned to the No. 5 gun in the 5-inch/25-caliber AA battery, he hastened to starboard when he heard the general alarm. While he was en route, the first torpedo hit. By the time he'd reached the striker's hatch ladder (a ladder generally used by apprentice seamen) on the starboard side of turret 4, two more had hit, and the ship was listing. Guarding the ladder was Boatswain's Mate Second Class William M. Washam. In his belt was a .45-caliber pistol. His words were specific: no one was going up. When Lester told him he was assigned to the AA battery, Washam assured him he wouldn't be needed and ordered him to stand firm. Frustrated, he simply stood there as the ship endured another hit. Below him, he could hear the sound of rushing water. Soon the deck was listing severely. Finally, the word was passed to abandon ship.[4]

Lester turned toward the ladder, which was on its side, so he had to shimmy along the railing instead of using the rungs. Some fifteen feet long, the ladder went up through the second deck to the main deck aft. Fortunately, the deck hatch was open. By the time Lester reached it, the water was pouring in.

Pulling himself through the hatch, Lester glanced up. He saw that the deck was descending. Terrified, he began to swim. Still wearing his shoes and clothes, he had to struggle to make any headway. He'd have to swim more than twenty feet to clear the deck's trajectory. He made it but couldn't escape the ensuing vortex. As the deck disappeared beneath the water, the resulting suction pulled him under.

In describing the event more than sixty years later, Lester said his descent was so rapid that he could literally feel the hair standing up on top of his head. He also experienced a change in temperature in his lower extremities. He didn't know if this was from going through a thermocline or because his legs had become impaled in the mud at the bottom of the harbor. He survived because of the blowback when the ship hit bottom. It was so powerful, it rocketed him upward through forty feet of water. Amazed that he was still alive, he began to swim.

Nearby was a floatplane. At the beginning of the attack, it had been on the quarterdeck. Thrown off when the ship went over, it was floating upside down some thirty feet from the hull. A dozen sailors were already clinging to the pontoon. Lester swam over to it only to find that it was sinking. Grasping hold of it anyway, he'd barely caught his breath when the floatplane was strafed. Realizing that it made an inviting target, he abandoned it after the strafing ceased.

Swimming a short distance he saw a torpedo plane zooming in, this one so low he could see the pilot's face. It was headed for the *West Virginia*. When he saw the torpedo drop, he turned away. He'd seen enough. He heard the explosion and moments later felt the concussion. Though his strength was waning, he continued to swim. It was over six hundred yards to the other side of the channel. Were it not for the sudden appearance of Boatswain's Mate Second Class Westley F. Potts, it's doubtful he would have survived. After escaping from turret 4, Potts had found two wooden planks in the water. With one under each arm, he was swimming toward Lester when he noticed he was struggling. Without a word, he passed one of the planks over to him, and then continued on.

Deciding that Ford Island would provide a quicker safe haven than crossing the channel, Lester turned around. He'd made it halfway back when he saw an officer's launch filled with survivors explode. Horrified by the sight of flying body parts, he turned around again. Starting across the channel, he saw another launch. Though potentially a target too, it wasn't near the battleships, and it was moving slowly.

When he felt he was close enough for the crew to see him, he treaded water to conserve his energy. Incredibly, the launch passed without stopping. Believing he was doomed again, he was about to give up when he saw it was trailing a rope. Summoning his final vestiges of strength, he struggled toward it, more lunging than swimming. In a final burst of energy, he lashed out, grabbed hold of it, and twisted it around his wrist. Rotating his body so he was facing upward to breathe, he ignored the pain in his wrist and simply held on. By the time they had spotted him and stopped, the turbulence had torn his clothes off.

Eventually taken to the submarine base, Lester ran into the ship's former skipper, Captain Foy. Recognizing Lester from his numerous captain's mast appearances, Foy instructed him to muster all the *Oklahoma* survivors he could find so that Foy could address them that evening. In the process, Lester found the *Oklahoma*'s mail orderly working trancelike beneath a tree. Having rushed to the main post office after escaping the ship, the man was fighting back the only way he knew. He was sorting the ship's mail. After taking a few minutes to sit and console him, Lester continued on.

By 6:00 P.M., several survivors were congregated at the submarine base to hear the captain speak. Consoling them as much by his presence as he did with his words, Foy told them that he would get another command and that he would do his best to have them assigned to it. He also gave many of them money.

Though Lester greatly appreciated the captain's intent, he lacked the patience to benefit from it. Anxious to fight back, he volunteered for destroyer duty four hours later. Joining the crew of the destroyer *Phelps*, he would be patrolling the mouth of the harbor by daybreak.[5]

The blowback that Lester experienced would also save the life of Machinist's Mate Second Class Walter Becker. After escaping from the starboard side pump room through a ventilator shaft in the machine shop, Becker entered the water on the port side. Looking up, he saw the overturning ship lurching directly above him. Suddenly something fell on top of him, and he went under. He had no idea what it was, or how big. All he knew was that he had to get out from under it or drown. He swam underwater as far as he could but never found the end. Exhausted and out of breath, he finally gave up. As he sank, he found it odd that his acknowledgment of death could be so peaceful. The next thing he knew, he was in a boat alongside the ship with people screaming at him. The blowback had rocketed him to the surface, and he'd landed in a boat filled with wounded.

Seaman First Class Nelson W. Glidewell was hustling down a portside passageway on the second deck when the first torpedo exploded several decks below. After falling when the deck buckled beneath his feet, he was knocked unconscious. When he regained his senses, he got up and started running, finally arriving at the battle signal station, where he awaited orders from the signal bridge. Though the ship was listing and water was gushing in through nearby portholes, he refused to abandon his battle station, believing he'd be shot if he did. Taking solace at the sight of an unsealed overhead hatch nearby, he decided to wait for the order to abandon ship, then use it for his escape. But when he saw two sailors preparing to seal it from above, his fear was overwhelmed by his instinct to survive. Screaming at them to stop, he waded through knee-deep water to the ladder, then scaled it to the deck above.

Quartermaster Second Class Robert J. McMahon was at central station on the first platform deck when smoke began pouring out the conning tower tube. Hustling to the C Division living compartment, he used an ax to chop open a box containing gas masks. Starting back toward central station, he glanced through a grate to the engine room below. It was nearly inundated with water and oil. To his horror, he saw a large number of floating bodies.

Chief Petty Officer Howard C. French was sitting in the Fifth Division living quarters reading a newspaper when he heard the general alarm, followed immediately by a call to man the AA batteries. Though his primary battle station was the No. 8 broadside gun, which was useless against aircraft, his secondary battle station was in the AA ammunition supply room on the third deck. The room was only one deck below, but he had difficulty getting there because the nearest deck hatch was clogged with sailors. He was waiting his turn in line when the first torpedo hit. When he finally joined his crew in the supply room, four more had hit, and the ship was listing significantly.

French had been aboard the ship since 1932, and his experience told him the ship was going to capsize. Throwing on a headset, he waited for the call to abandon ship. When it wasn't forthcoming, he ordered his men topside. Despite his command, a few were unwilling to leave. Whether their reluctance stemmed from guilt or from fear of what waited above, French didn't know. Nor did he ask. He chased them out, following in their footsteps a short time later.

By the time he reached a ladder, the third deck passageway was empty. Believing he was the last man out, he climbed the ladder to the second deck, and then took another to the main deck messing compartment. With the ship tilted to port, all matter of tables, chairs, and assorted service apparatus were entwined in a heap against the portside bulkhead. Other items were sliding across the deck. French made his way aft through the obstacles, finally reaching a ladder that ascended to the deck above. Seeing that the overhead hatch was closed but unsealed, he scaled the first few rungs. With one hand secured around the side railing, he reached upward with the other to push the hatch open. It wouldn't budge. Guessing something had fallen on top of it, he climbed down and continued aft.

Though it was dark in the immediate area, he could see light in the galley ahead of him. He covered the remaining distance without incident, then exited through a door in the aft bulkhead, shielding his eyes against the sudden brightness. He looked aft across the quarterdeck to the *West Virginia*. She too was listing. But her AA guns were firing, as were those on the *Tennessee,* moored alongside her. Though he didn't see any planes, he could hear the distinctive whine of their engines. In stark contrast, the *Oklahoma* was silent, both her guns and her men. It wasn't until that moment that he realized he was alone. There wasn't a sailor anywhere. Nor could he hear anything from the boat deck, just one level up and directly behind him. It was eerie. There had been more than a thousand sailors aboard when the attack began.

He started aft, passing the boat crane and a 3-inch/50-caliber AA gun. A moment later, he was flat on his back, pummeled by a wall of water from a bomb blast alongside the ship. Though unhurt, he was dazed and found it difficult to get up. Pushing himself upright, he decided he needed a life jacket.

Returning in the direction he'd come, he climbed the casemate of the No. 7 5-inch/51-caliber broadside gun to the boat deck. After clambering over the side, he was greeted by Boatswain's Mate First Class Winfield "Smokey" Struthers. One of his favorite shipmates, Struthers was the only person French saw on the boat deck, and he didn't see him long.

French said, "How you doing, Winfield?" to which Struthers responded, "OK, Howard," after which he made a running start, then jumped over the side of the ship.

Managing a grin, French shuffled down the deck to a motor launch. Reaching over the gunwale, he grabbed a life jacket. He put it on and then returned to the main deck. Stepping through the lifelines, he started down the side of the ship. With the ship rolling toward him in the opposing direction, he had to move fast to make any headway. Glancing left, he saw dozens of sailors streaming down the side with him, many having emerged from the casemates housing the broadside guns, the remainder emerging from starboard portholes. He made it across the majority of the ship's side with relative ease. Once he reached the original waterline, he had to be careful because the hull was coated with slime. Moving slowly, he stepped past the turn of the hull, and then began walking across the bottom, the ship's list having already eclipsed ninety degrees.

Suddenly he heard the sound of machine-gun fire and the *ping* of ricocheting bullets. He had no idea where the bullets were coming from. Seeing a docking keel just ahead, a two-foot-high steel plate welded perpendicularly to the hull, he dove behind it. When the *pinging* stopped, he looked forward along the length of the ship and saw about thirty or forty others doing exactly the same thing.

He saw a launch that had been dragged up the side of the ship and started toward it. While he was en route, Commander Kenworthy appeared. French pointed to the boat and told the commander he'd find some men to push it into the water. Kenworthy's face was ashen, and his response was a feeble mumble. French wasn't sure what he had said and didn't ask him to repeat it. The commander was obviously finding it difficult to accept what had happened. French left him to his thoughts and went to gather some men. He found about thirty. Together they rocked the boat into the water, only to find that the battery was dead. They let it ride with the southerly current, eventually ending up at the gas dock.[6]

Ensigns Edward E. Vezey, Jr., and Francis C. Flaherty shared a berthing compartment in the officer's country. Vezey was in charge of the 3-inch/50-caliber AA battery. Flaherty was the assistant division officer for turret 1. The two were close friends. Hearing the call to "man the antiaircraft batteries," Vezey prepared to go topside while Flaherty prepared to go below. Prior to departing, Flaherty joked that he'd be up later to scrub Vezey's remains from the deck. Both laughed as they departed. Ironically, it was Vezey who survived. While Flaherty made it to his battle station in the bowels of turret 1, he would perish while holding a flashlight to allow his men to escape up a ladder as the ship began to overturn. Flaherty was posthumously awarded the Congressional Medal of Honor.[7]

CHAPTER 11

Twelve-Inch Portholes

*The main deck had forty-seven twelve-inch-diameter portholes and three eight-
een-inch portholes per side; the second deck had sixty-three twelve-inch portholes
and eight eighteen-inch portholes per side; and the third deck had eight twelve-
inch portholes per side, all of which were in the stern.*

When the attack began, Fire Controlman First Class George L.
Coburn was in the plotting room on the first platform deck. A member of the AA battery, he was testing the circuits on the ship's starboard director in preparation for Monday's inspection. While working,
he heard a hiss on the overhead speaker of the PA system, as if someone had pressed the key on the microphone but wasn't talking. The
hissing continued for several seconds. Finally, he heard a voice.

"All hands man your battle station! All hands man your battle station!"

Not sure what to make of it, he hustled into central station, where
he found an electrician. "What the hell's going on?" Coburn exclaimed.
Before the man could respond, Rommel's warning sounded over the
PA. They stared at one another in disbelief.

"Sounds like some drunk," Coburn expounded. When the general
alarm followed, he realized that he wasn't wearing a shirt. Knowing
that it was against regulations to be on deck without one, he scurried
up the nearest ladder to the third deck, and then raced forward to the
fire-control living compartment where his locker was located.

He was on the way back when the first torpedo hit. Though the deck
was shaking, he continued moving, hastening for the nearest up ladder on the starboard side. When he reached it, he was startled to find
that the overhead hatch had already been sealed. Because it was a double hatch (with two ladders), he knew he'd never be able to open it

by himself. Aware there was another ladder in the adjacent ammunition passageway, he entered it, heading aft alongside a waist-high conveyor belt.

Others were approaching the ladder from the opposite direction. It was a strange sight. In the flickering lights, their movements were almost kaleidoscopic, like an old movie. Continuing aft, Coburn reached the ladder just in time to see the overhead hatch slam shut. His shipmates on the second deck were doing exactly what they'd been trained to do. He was joined by the others, and they were conversing when two more torpedoes hit.

Then the lights went out. One of the other men produced a flashlight. While he pointed it at the hatch cover, they heard the sound of rushing water from the deck below. Before long, it was a torrent. Realizing there was nowhere to go but up, two of them scaled the ladder to work on the hatch. The others waited below, grabbing hold of whatever they could to remain upright.

Coburn was alongside the conveyor when he realized he was standing in oil. He didn't know where it was coming from, but he could see in the shadowy light that it was abundant. With the deck on an incline, it was pooling against the portside bulkheads.

When a fifth torpedo hit rocked the ship, men began losing their handholds. Several went sliding across the deck, slamming hard against the bulkheads. Banged up and immersed in oil, one of them started yelling for his mother. His pleas were petrifying.

When the shaking subsided, the sailors on the ladder resumed their work on the hatch. Finally, they opened the last dog. They'd barely opened the hatch when the ladder started moving. Rushing to get out, the others reached the ladder simultaneously. Because it was canted sideways and was not secured to the deck, their momentum and combined weight sheared the outboard steel pin securing the ladder to the coaming. When it rotated around the inboard pin, several of them fell. Realizing that none would escape if the second pin broke, they placed their emotions in check and ascended the ladder one at a time.

Having witnessed the mayhem from the relative safety of the conveyor belt, Coburn was one of the last to go. Scaling the ladder to the second deck, he finally saw some natural light, because the deck had portholes. Heading aft with the others, he quickly ascended the nearest ladder. Climbing into a sleeping compartment on the main deck,

Coburn looked aft. Congregated at the doorway exiting to the quarterdeck was a large group of sailors, none of whom was moving. Deciding he could exit quicker through one of the starboard portholes, Coburn turned to his left. In his path were lockers and five rows of triple-stacked bunks. Aligned parallel to the ship's centerline, the bunks were attached to both the deck and the overhead. Because the lockers were freestanding, they had fallen over on their sides. Climbing over them, Coburn used the bunk's vertical supports as handholds to pull himself up the deck.

After reaching the third row of bunks, he crossed an aisle to a bunk positioned lengthwise on a transverse bulkhead. Though the aisle was cluttered with gear, he was able to step over it as he pulled himself upward along the bunk's length as well as that of the bunk abutting it, which was adjacent to a porthole. Fortunately, the porthole was large, allowing him to pull himself through without much difficulty. Climbing out onto the side of the ship, he remained at the porthole to help six others escape. By the time the last man had exited, the ship was on its side.

Moving starboard, they hastened to the turn of the ship, where they slid down the bottom of the hull to the water. Lumped together, they swam a circuitous route through the patches of oil. There were bullet splashes everywhere. Finally reaching the *Maryland,* they had problems getting out of the water. The only available means were the parted hawsers draped down her side. But the hawsers were covered with sailors, and there were others waiting in the water, most of them struggling to remain afloat. Coburn was an excellent swimmer and could have swum to Ford Island. Concerned for the others, he decided to stay.

Up above, he saw *Maryland* sailors watching from the lifelines. Livid, he started screaming at them to toss some lines. They must have assumed he had rank because lines began dropping moments later. Finally arriving on deck, he joined an AA ammunition detail.

Shipfitter Second Class John H. Birnel was in his living compartment on the third deck aft, port side, when the attack began. He was preparing to go ashore on liberty when he heard the general alarm. The nearest ladder was forward, so he headed for it immediately, despite the convention requiring him to go up and forward on the starboard side, down and aft on the port side. Entering the B-100 passageway, he ran forward along a waist-high conveyor belt, bumping into mess attendants who were manning their battle stations at designated locations along its length. Passing the damage control locker, he reached a "down" ladder from the second deck. With more mess attendants descending it, he stepped aside to let them pass. Then the first torpedo hit, followed moments later by a second one.

Desperate to get to his battle station, he went up the ladder sideways, doing his best to avoid the attendants racing downward. After exiting onto the second deck, he took another ladder to his battle station on the main deck. He was assigned to repair station I, and as he attempted to close a porthole on the port side, two more hits occurred in rapid succession. The resulting explosions shot a deluge of water through the unsealed openings, drenching him to the skin. Moments later, the ship began to list.

With a pronounced sense of urgency, he realized he had the keys to the damage control locker. In the locker were the keys to central flood control. Per damage control protocol, Shipfitter First Class Irvin F. Rice would normally open the locker for Shipfitter Third Class Patrick L. Chess, who would then take the keys to central flood control. Birnel had seen neither when he passed the damage control locker, nor had he seen them on the ladders. Knowing they would have to counter-flood the starboard voids to prevent the ship from capsizing, he decided to get the keys himself.

Running to a nearby double hatch, he looked down at the second deck. It was flooding. Getting to the damage control locker would be impossible. Because battle station protocol dictated that the hatch be sealed, he solicited the help of a nearby sailor to close it. While they tightened the dogs, word was sounded over the PA to abandon ship.

Looking aft, Birnel saw a large group of men in the aft sleeping compartment waiting to exit a door to the quarterdeck. Because the line they were in was long, Birnel decided he'd have a better chance of survival going to starboard. He moved down a passageway, then entered the ship's laundry. When he stepped inside, he slipped on the ceramic tile floor, sliding beneath a washing machine. Despite his efforts, he couldn't get out until he secured a handhold on the surrounding coaming and finally pulled himself free.

Though the overhead lights were out, enough light was coming through the portholes for him to see. All types of machinery had broken loose, shelving had fallen down, and carts and assorted equipment were moving about. He worked his way up the sloping deck to the Dutch doors separating the laundry room from the issuing compartment. A cabinet had fallen against the upper door, sealing it shut. Fortunately, a laundry bag had fallen between the lower door and the bulkhead, allowing just enough room for him to crawl out.

Though the ship had been rolling steadily, it paused as he entered the adjacent berthing compartment. He looked across the compartment to the starboard side of the ship. There were portholes lining the bulkhead, maybe five or six of them, with sailors in front of each one. Though the bulkhead was less than thirty feet away, he'd have to crawl through four rows of bunks to reach it. As the ship resumed its roll, he pulled himself across the compartment by grabbing hold of successive bunk stanchions. Finally, he was able to join the others.

When the ship reached ninety degrees, the rolling stopped again. Birnel waited while a man pulled himself through a porthole, which was now directly overhead. When the man disappeared, Birnel latched onto the coaming, secured his feet on a stanchion, then chinned himself up. Because he had a halyard snap full of keys on his belt, he was unable to pull himself through. Dropping back down, he threw them on the floor, then tried again. This time he succeeded.

He could feel the ship beginning to move again. He looked around. No more than a handful of sailors were on the entire ship. He started up the side, which was beginning to rise toward him as the ship resumed its roll. Beyond it he could see the masts and upper decks of the *Maryland* and could hear the reports of her AA guns.

Glancing skyward, he saw five high-altitude bombers approaching from the south. The roar of AA fire rose to a crescendo. He saw the shells bursting behind the formation. He cursed in frustration. Moments later, he saw five black dots descending on Battleship Row. He felt certain they were headed straight toward him. Birnel was a good Christian and believed the Lord was with him wherever he went. When the bombs missed the ship, he felt certain that the hand of God had reached up to alter their trajectory. Picked up by a boat a short time later, he was taken to Ford Island, where he went ashore near the gas dock.

After finishing chow, Pharmacist's Mate Third Class William E. Duncan hustled to the dental office to complete his preparations for Monday's inspection. At 7:55 A.M. he was startled by the sound of the general alarm. He was startled again when he heard a voice booming over the PA—without the bugle call and boatswain's pipe that generally preceded it.

"All hands man your battle stations. This is a real attack with real bombs and real torpedoes. No shit. Now, goddamn it, get going!"

He immediately dropped his work and hustled forward to a ladder on the starboard side. His battle station was located amidships on the deck below. Running past sickbay, he saw Pharmacist's Mate First Class J. H. Schoonover and Pharmacist's Mate Third Class K. M. Dean carrying a Stokes stretcher with a patient aboard. The patient, Seaman Second Class William F. Pask, had just had his appendix removed two days prior. A second later, Duncan felt a jar and heard an explosion.

Though the explosion was on the opposite side of the ship, the resulting jolt knocked over lockers and mess tables and shattered a number of light bulbs behind him. When the melee was over Duncan hastened into sickbay to lend a hand with the stretcher. Unable to fit the stretcher through the deck hatch, Duncan hoisted Pask into his arms, then descended sideways down the staircase, Pask's incision pressed tightly against his body. When they arrived at the dressing station, it was nearly full. Duncan had just found a vacant spot when two more torpedoes hit in rapid succession.

When the ship settled, he scanned the compartment for Lieutenant Commander Hugh R. Alexander, the ship's dentist. Alexander was in charge of the midships battle dressing station and should have been in the compartment with them. Duncan knew that the officer normally came aft along the port side and wondered if the torpedoes had forced him to seek another course. When he didn't arrive, Duncan waited for the order to abandon ship, doing his best to console Pask. When it finally sounded, the compartment and adjacent passageway were already filling with water, and the ship had a substantial list. In immediate compliance, the men began crowding for the door.

Then another torpedo hit.

When the aftereffects subsided, Duncan yelled at the others to clear the way so that he could carry Pask through. They quickly formed a corridor to allow him passage. Cradling Pask in his arms, Duncan waded to the door, then out into the darkened passageway. With one foot on the bulkhead and the other on the deck, he shuffled through the water. Reaching a ladder, he hoisted Pask as high as he could while yelling for someone to grab him from above. A crewman responded and pulled him through. Though Duncan attempted to follow him, it was difficult because the ladder was swinging by its top pins. When he finally made it through the hatch, Pask was gone. Deciding not to join some crewmen who were attempting to scale a ladder to the main deck, Duncan started toward the operating room, which he knew had portholes.

As he opened the door, the operating table and an instrument cabinet came sliding down the tiled floor toward him. They barely missed him, slamming against the bulkhead. Followed by Dean, Duncan used the side of the table, the water sterilizer, and the water pipes to pull himself upward along the sloping deck. The portholes were now almost directly overhead. He couldn't open them because they were tightly secured. Moving to his right, he opened the door to the adjacent sickbay compartment. Though both he and Dean were able to get through, their passage was difficult because the door, which was hinged on the starboard side of the bulkhead, kept closing on them.

Once inside, Duncan instructed Dean to exit the porthole, saying that he would help by pushing him through. Dean pulled himself through with relative ease. Duncan followed, but he was larger and barely got his shoulders through. Wedged in at the hips, it would require the efforts of both Dean and a nearby boatswain's mate to pull him out.

The three of them decided to wait until the ship was on its side before slipping into the water on the port side. Due to a sudden strafing, they jumped off the starboard side instead. As they swam toward the *Maryland,* they heard a tremendous explosion. Looking down the void between the *Tennessee* and the *West Virginia,* Duncan saw the *Arizona* engulfed in flames. He also saw bodies being hurled through the air.

Though shocked, they managed to swim to a nearby whaleboat and climb aboard. Unfortunately, the engine was inoperable. Hitching a tow from several boats, they finally arrived at the 1010 dock.

Seaman Second Class Duane H. Reyelts was asleep when the general alarm sounded. Leaping from his third deck bunk, he was trying to clear his mind when a thunderous explosion brought him to his senses. Clad in his undershorts, he raced down a portside passageway toward his battle station, pushing and dodging among other crewmen who were racing to theirs. As he passed through the doors of the various compartments, men were yelling to "keep moving!" as the doors were sealed behind them.

When he reached an up ladder to the second deck, another torpedo tore into the ship near the area he had just vacated. The ship seemed to rise out of the water by the bow. Reeling and twisting, the unexpected motion sent him swinging around the ladder. When the ship settled, he scurried up the ladder then raced for his battle station at the after flag bag. His supervisor, Signalman Third Class Andrew P. Sauer, had already arrived, as had several others. They exchanged glances, then rolled the cover off the flag bag. Hearing the sound of guns, Reyelts wondered what it was like outside. He could see light through the halyard scuttle in the overhead but nothing else.

Then another torpedo hit. The explosion was ear shattering. Again the ship rose, the twisting metal making an eerie sound as it strained against the rivets. It settled gently, listing farther to port. Water was gushing in the deck below. It sounded like a waterfall. Moments later, they were instructed to get below the third deck, which was armored.

Turning for the nearest hatch, Reyelts stopped dead in his tracks. Standing in front of him was Seaman First Class Robert V. Young. His clothing was soaked with blood. Having made it to his battle station, he would collapse and die a few moments later.[1]

As ordered, Reyelts and the others hurried below. Descending a ladder to the third deck, he had difficulty maintaining his grasp on the ladder's rungs because the ladder was at an angle. The compartment was already crowded with sailors, each clinging to whatever he could find to remain on the high side of the slanting deck. Water and oil were gushing in through a porthole. It was exceptionally quiet, the men seemingly awaiting further orders. The only sound was the steady hammering of AA fire outside. But the stillness was soon shattered.

With an agonizing yell, a man lost his grip and went sliding into the darkness of oil and water. Soon there was another yell, and then another. The men still clinging to something, or someone, were beginning to panic.

Reyelts glanced at Sauer. When their eyes met, their fear showed through, and without a word, they realized that it was time to leave. With a slight push, Sauer gestured him to the ladder. "Now!" he said. They both started up, followed by a throng of others who had reached the same conclusion.

The ship was nearly on its side when Reyelts was pushed through the hatch opening onto the second deck. Unable to get his footing, he was knocked backward against the bulkhead. Trapped because of the men stampeding past him, he waited until the last one had gone.

With hysteria filling the air, the men dispersed in the general direction of the stern, yelling at one another and inducing others to follow them. It was mayhem. Men fell, bouncing off the bulkheads. When Reyelts couldn't locate Sauer, he headed for the nearest hatch.[2] He found one, but the ladder had broken away.

"This way!" someone yelled. Reyelts joined him and they hastened for the starboard side. Unable to keep up with him, Reyelts found himself alone. Clinging to anything that protruded from the bulkhead, he groped his way along the darkened passageway. He recalled there were portholes in the sickbay. It was just up ahead. He gritted his teeth. Half crawling, he clutched the pipes and wiring along the bulkhead, pulling his way toward the sickbay. When he reached it, the ship was on its side. He eased his way inside. There was a porthole, but it was twenty feet above him (the width of the compartment). He lay back against the bulkhead to figure out how to get to it. There were three rows of anchored bunks that he could scale to get himself within ten feet, and then a cabinet he could climb to gain another two. Though the porthole was slightly removed from the end of the cabinet, angle irons at the top of the bulkhead were situated between the two. If he could hang on to the angle irons with one hand, he could reach out with the other to grab hold of the porthole's rim. But if his hand slipped, he would fall through the doorway and then go crashing into the bulkhead of the next compartment. He was scared and tired, but he also felt a surge of adrenaline.

He rose to his feet and scaled the three bunks without incident. Then he climbed atop the cabinet. He took a breath and steadied himself for the final obstacle. Gripping the angle iron, he reached out for the porthole, extending his arm to its fullest length. He touched the porthole. Leaning as much as he dared, he twisted his fingertips around the rim. He released the angle iron, swung out beneath the opening, and then immediately grasped the rim with his other hand. Mustering his strength, he chinned himself upward. He got his head through, and then a shoulder. Rotating his shoulders toward his sternum, he was able to leverage his other shoulder through by pushing against the hull's exterior with his elbow. Continuing to push while he wiggled upward, he finally got his other arm through. Laying the palms of his hands on the hull, he pushed until his hips were out. Exhausted, he slipped his knees and feet out, then collapsed on his stomach.

An eternity later, he glanced at the porthole. Seeing a rope nearby that was secured at one end, he grabbed it and tossed the other end into the porthole, hoping it would be of use to someone else. Slowly he pushed himself upright. Walking up the ship's side, he stared at the surrounding devastation. There seemed to be smoke billowing everywhere. A thousand feet astern, the *Arizona* was an inferno. In the water below him, men were swimming in desperation toward a motor launch.

Believing the attack was over because of the absence of gunfire, he stopped to consider his options. He could either remain aboard the ship, which could either sink or explode, or he could jump into the water and swim to either the launch or the *Maryland*. Fearful of the long drop, he sat down to think it over.

Glancing at the *Maryland,* he noticed that her AA crews were elevating their guns. Assuming that the attack was about to resume, and that the *Oklahoma* would be targeted again, he slid off the hull feet first. Dropping some fifty feet, his knees buckled as his feet hit the water, which unfortunately did little to slow his descent. He went deep beneath the surface. Though certain that his lungs would explode first, he somehow managed to claw his way back.

By the time he'd regained his breath, his options had diminished by one. Overloaded with sailors, the launch had sunk. He started for the *Maryland*. Though it was only about fifty feet away, he wasn't sure he could make it. His fight to regain the surface had taken its toll. He was utterly exhausted. But he also wanted desperately to live. With each kick and stroke seemingly more desperate than the one before, he made it across to the *Maryland*'s port side. Latching onto a rope, he was hauled aboard by a group of her sailors.

Seaman First Class Schuyler C. "Bob" Burns, Jr., headed aft along the *Oklahoma*'s starboard passageway after making his way to the second deck from the lower powder-handling room of turret 1. As he passed an outboard compartment, a man yelled out to him. It was Lieutenant (j. g.) Aloysius H. Schmitt, the ship's chaplain. Burns was an altar boy and knew Father Al well. Along with Chief Watertender

Francis D. Day and the ship's dentist, Lieutenant Commander Alexander, Father Al was helping smaller crewmen escape through a porthole.

While Burns waded toward him, he watched the chaplain push another man through. Burns was somewhat larger than the man and wondered if he would fit through the twelve-inch hole. Father Al saw the doubt in his eyes and said with finality, "Burns, we are going to get you out! There are two strong guys up there, and one is a big marine!" He then told him to stick one arm through first and then follow it with the other. Burns did as he was told and got his shoulders through as well. But his hips were too wide. With Father Al pushing, and the marine pulling, he finally popped out, his waist covered with blood.[3]

Fireman Second Class James J. Saul was reading a newspaper in the engineer's compartment on the second deck when the general alarm sounded. Immediately, he descended two decks to his battle station in the fire room pump room. He had only been there a few minutes when the first torpedo hit, shaking the deck plates loose. After several more hits, the root steam line to the fuel oil pump snapped. Live steam permeated the compartment. Moments later, someone passed the word to abandon ship. Knowing that the overhead deck hatch had been secured, Saul grabbed a hammer and started up a ladder to work it open. Because there were no lights, he had to use his hands to locate the dogs. Pounding their handles with the hammer, he opened them all except two. Because the adjacent bulkhead had been bent inward against both of them, he was unable to get a good striking angle with the hammer. Mustering his strength, he opened them with his bare hands. Placing his back against the hatch, he forced it open and crawled through. A number of others followed him. Finding another ladder in the darkness, Saul held it while the others climbed. When the last man was gone, he scaled it into a third deck living compartment.

The compartment was a shambles. Bunks and lockers had fallen from the bulkhead, pinning several men against the bulkhead on the opposite side. But there was no time to help them, even if they were alive. As the ship started to capsize, he jumped through the nearest hatch. When the superstructure settled into the bottom, he was in the engineer's washroom on the second deck. The compartment was upside down, and water was pouring in. There were about twenty crewmen with him. They tried to close the door against the water, but it wasn't watertight. The water continued to pour through, rising steadily. The only way Saul could rise above it was by standing on an inverted sink. In the darkness, he could hear some of the others praying.

Knowing there were portholes beside the sink, he ducked underneath the water to feel along the bulkhead. He found one but couldn't find a wrench to loosen the dogs. He finally loosened one with his hands but had to resurface for air. Time and again, he went under until finally they all were loose. He opened the cover, yelling at the others that he'd found a way out.

Stripping down to his shorts, he tried to force his way through the opening. He tried twice without success. Rising for air, he began to skim oil from the water's surface to lubricate his body, then he tried again. Placing both hands on the outside of the ship, he finally pulled himself through. Immediately, he started swimming toward the surface. He gasped as he neared it, swallowing both saltwater and oil. Finally, he broke through.

Rubbing the oil from his eyes, he turned toward the ship. Suddenly there was a terrific explosion. An instant later, he felt a pain in his right leg just below the knee. He went under again. When he regained the surface, he raised his leg. It was bleeding. With no way of stopping it, he started swimming toward a floatplane that was upside down in the water. He reached it, but his hands were so oily that he couldn't pull himself onto the pontoon. Instead, he started swimming across the channel. En route he found a seat cushion from a motor launch. Crawling on top of it, he started paddling. Seeing three others in the water ahead of him, he angled toward them and hauled them aboard. Later the four of them were picked up by a launch and taken to a beach near the submarine base. Hearing strafing, Saul hastened for the nearest building. It was filled with torpedoes, so he quickly left. After hitching a ride to the submarine base, he drew a gun from the armory and then waited for the invasion that everyone was certain was forthcoming. It would be late in the afternoon before his wound was tended to.

After the ship capsized, Ensign Adolph D. Mortensen was propelled into the ship's medical dispensary by a surge of rushing water. Finally broaching the surface, he found himself trapped with four others, one of them the ship's carpenter, John A. Austin. Mortensen, finding a porthole with his feet, reached down and removed the knobs securing the port to its frame. Holding it open, he ushered two of the men through. The third man was a steward, reluctant to go. Mortensen pushed him under and then out. All that remained were Mortensen and Austin. Weighing two hundred pounds, Austin knew he couldn't make it through a twelve-inch porthole. Without a word, he held it open for Mortensen.[4]

Hospital Assistant First Class Gene R. Dick began his morning routine by checking the vital signs of a sailor who'd had his appendix removed at 4:00 that morning. He then checked the status of two other patients, both with minor illnesses. He was new to the ship and went about his work quietly, trying to avoid the ire of his boss, who was sleeping. They were the only two on duty in the ship's sickbay, which was located on the second deck.

Suddenly, the stillness exploded with the blare of a bugle over the ship's PA system, followed by "Battle stations! Battle stations! All hands, battle stations! This is no drill!"

The first class flew from his bunk, screaming, "Get the patients below the armored deck!"

Dick hustled the patients out and then forward along a passageway to a ladder descending to the third deck. Once they were situated, he hastened to the midships battle dressing station, which was also on the third deck. He'd barely arrived when the first torpedo struck.

The explosion was close, the ship rising beneath his feet. The concussion tore a hole in the interior bulkhead, forging a path for a deluge of water and oil. Though both he and the first class were drenched, they escaped the compartment. They hustled up a ladder to the second deck, then back along the passageway to the sickbay where they'd started. Though Dick was content to remain there, the first class thought otherwise.

"Come on, let's get out of here!" he barked.

They rushed out of sickbay, then up a ladder to a sleeping compartment on the main deck. At the rear of the compartment was a door that opened onto the quarterdeck. The compartment was full of sailors waiting to exit. Dick and the first class took their place at the end of the line, winding their way through the bunks as the line snaked forward.

With only two men ahead of Dick, a wall of water came gushing through the opened door. He was knocked off his feet. He began tumbling, the water carrying him away, jamming him against bunks and bulkheads. He struggled to keep his head above water. Suddenly, there was darkness and a deafening silence. The water was up to his shoulders. Panic stricken, he fought hard to regain his composure, the air foul with the stench of fuel oil.

Moments later, he heard voices from an adjacent compartment. Then he saw a light. He swam toward it, relieved that he wasn't alone. Soon others began to appear. In the eerie illumination, he could see their heads above the blackened water. He could also see bodies.

They talked until someone found a porthole. It was small, only twelve inches across, and under water. Though it gave them hope, it also posed a problem. Because no one knew which compartment they were in, they had no idea where it led. There were portholes in the interior of the ship as well as in the hull. If it was an interior porthole, it could open into a compartment that was fully flooded.

There was a great deal of anxiety as they discussed the pros and cons. Some were sure that the porthole offered escape; others were just as sure that it didn't. As the moments waned, the choice became obvious. With only a limited amount of air, they would have to try it or suffocate. Gathering stoically around the porthole, a sailor took several deep breaths, then disappeared beneath the surface. Squirming and twisting, he made it through the narrow opening.

Dick waited his turn. Finally, the man ahead of him went under, but he got stuck as he tried to squirm through. Dick grabbed the man's legs and pushed. The impetus was all that was needed. The man cleared the orifice.

Now it was Dick's turn. He slid his legs into the porthole but then realized that he couldn't get through with his shorts on. He resurfaced. Believing he'd have a problem with his shoulders, he asked the others if he could make another attempt going headfirst. He took a deep breath, descended two feet to the porthole, and tested his width. To his surprise, he found that he fit. Surfacing again, he told the others he could make it, and he removed his shorts.

Positioning himself in front of the porthole again, he took several deep breaths, then reached down and grabbed the rim. He pulled himself underwater, then thrust his head and one arm through the opening. Pushing himself partway through, he twisted his other arm and shoulder through. But his hips became stuck. Panicked, he reached back and pushed against the bulkhead as hard as he could. It worked. He was out, and free.

He started swimming upward. He could see light above but was running out of breath. He kicked harder and harder, his outstretched arms sweeping down his body in giant swathes. It seemed like an eternity, but the light was getting closer. Suddenly his head broke the surface. He took huge gulps of air. He was sick to his stomach and dizzy. He treaded water while waiting for a nearby whaleboat. When it finally arrived and the men had pulled him in, he was struck by an incredible chill, and his teeth began chattering. A sailor found a foul-weather jacket and wrapped it around him. Consoled by his newfound warmth, Dick stared at the devastation around the harbor.

Seaman First Class Daniel Weissman also escaped after the ship had overturned. But instead of swimming out a submerged porthole, he swam downward through a trunk space, exiting the ship at the bottom of the harbor. After pulling himself clear of the trunk's deck hatch, he swam forty-five feet beneath the inverted deck, cleared the lifelines, and then swam another thirty feet to the water's surface. Including the trunk space, he'd swum more than ninety feet, most of it in total darkness.

Though Seaman Second Class William E. Ward, Jr., made it to the relative safety of the *Maryland,* he couldn't help but look back at the *Oklahoma.* As it rolled over on its side, he saw the head of a man he knew sticking up through one of the portholes. It was a terrifying and haunting experience. Because the man was large, Ward knew he was trapped and most certainly would die.

CHAPTER 12

Trapped!

Many Oklahoma *crewmen had battle stations below the third deck, in particular the ship's "black gang" (men assigned to boiler room and engineering spaces). Once they had descended through the deck, the hatches were sealed behind them. Despite the hatches being spring loaded, it was extremely difficult to open them from below. Because the third deck was at water level, there were no portholes in the decks below it.*

At the start of the attack, Seaman First Class Thomas F. Hannon was mess striking (aiding the ship's cook as a food-service attendant) in the No. 6 5-inch/51-caliber casemate. Deciding to take a break when he heard planes over Ford Island, he climbed through the gun port to watch them. He didn't realize they were combative until he saw smoke billowing above the seaplane hanger. Looking forward, he saw a torpedo plane flying low across the water toward the 1010 dock. He saw it launch its torpedo and continued to watch until the torpedo exploded alongside the double-berthed *Oglala* and *Helena*. Moments later, he heard the general alarm, followed by the call to "Man your battle stations!"

He had just reentered the casemate when *Oklahoma* was hit. Racing to get below, he was alongside the gedunk stand on the second deck when the second torpedo hit. The resulting explosion knocked him against the soda fountain. Drenched by a shower of water that exploded through a grate in the overhead, he joined up with Seaman First Class Raymond A. Cymerman, and they raced below to their battle station in radio IV, located on the first platform deck.

When they arrived, Radioman Third Class Merton R. Smith, Seaman First Class Norman O. Roberts, Seaman First Class George J. Thatcher, and Seaman First Class Harold S. Roiland had already manned the compartment. Roiland had the battle phones on. While he awaited instructions, the others sealed the compartment.

Following several more explosions, the lights went out. When the battle lamps came on, Roiland yelled that the battle phones were dead. Roberts tried the telephone. Hannon tried the sound-powered phone. Their efforts were unsuccessful. Everything was dead. If the order had been given to abandon ship, they had no way of knowing it.

When the sloping deck was too steep for them to stand, they decided to try to go topside. They opened a door and crossed the cobbler's shop compartment, then tried to open another door to an adjacent passageway. But it had been sealed from the other side. Trapped, they returned to radio IV. With the ship at a heavy list, they had to crawl up the deck to get there. A short time later, the battle lamps went out. For a moment it was still, the silence almost tranquil. Then all hell broke loose as the ship started going over. In a multitude of tones, both dull and metallic, objects began falling on the linoleum-covered deck, others slamming against the steel bulkheads.

There was a short pause, and then the rolling resumed. Immediately the men started tumbling, landing first along the bulkhead, and then along the overhead, which had now become the floor. Miraculously no one was hurt, but water was pouring in from a ventilator in the cobbler shop. There was also gas, though they couldn't determine the source. They began to cough and choke. Suddenly, the gas cleared, and a beam of light appeared in the cobbler shop.

It was a group of sailors from steering aft. They had left their compartment to find an escape route. Roiland slid down into the cobbler shop to talk with them. Concluding that they were trapped, the group returned to steering aft while Roiland attempted to return to radio IV.

Disoriented by the darkness, he lost his way. Lighting matches while he yelled, he was eventually guided back by the others. After pulling him back into the compartment, they attempted to seal the door behind him, but the dogs were on the opposite side of the door, so it was difficult to seat them. If the door was not secured, the rising water in the cobbler's shop would eventually enter radio IV.

While the others worked to close it, Hannon maneuvered his way through the darkness to the opposite side of the compartment. Feeling a bulkhead in front of him, he raised his hands to locate the overhead.

Instead, he found a metal tabletop. Attached to what had previously been the deck, it was now suspended from the ceiling. Locating an edge, he grasped it and chinned himself upward, locked a foot behind one of the legs, and leveraged himself aboard. After repositioning his body so that he was seated, he located an escape hatch on the overhead. Running his hands around the perimeter, he found a dog wrench.

When he informed the others, Cymerman hurried over to help him. Lighting a piece of paper with a match, Cymerman held it aloft so that Hannon could see the door. Hannon removed the dogs with the wrench but was unable to open the hatch because of the air pressure. Blowing out the torch, Cymerman climbed up to help him. Despite their combined efforts, they couldn't pull it open.

On the other side of the compartment, the others were still trying to seal the door against the rapidly rising water. It was secured except for one dog. Roiland knocked the heel off his shoe trying to kick it closed, but to no avail. It would be dangerous to undog the entire hatch to set the remaining dog because the water in the cobbler's shop would gush in before they could close it. They decided to leave it as it was.

Eventually Hannon became dizzy from the lack of air and climbed down from the table. Sitting on the floor below, he heard SOS's being tapped. The tapping diminished over time, until all they could hear were two, one of them from steering aft. They sat or lay down in the most comfortable positions they could find and waited. Hannon heard firing outside, an occasional explosion, and some gurgling water in the compartments below.

At times the air became so foul that his tongue would swell. On occasion, he found himself panting. The effort made him drowsy. In rare moments, the air would freshen, and with it their spirits. They seldom talked. When they did, it was only for a word or two. Though Roberts had a watch, he was unable to read it because the darkness was thick and solid. It was growing cold, and the bulkheads were sweating.

Hannon was lying alongside the aft bulkhead when he heard voices on the other side. He knocked. A man responded. He said his name was Stephen Young and that there were ten other men with him in the lucky bag (the naval version of a lost and found). They talked for a short time and then quit as the air seemed to thicken.

Sometime later, Hannon heard drilling on the hull up forward. Wanting to pass the word, he stumbled to the rear of the compartment and yelled to the sailors in steering aft. A sailor named Beal answered. He said he'd heard a rescue party working on the hull but added nothing further.

Soon the drilling drew nearer. It was intermittent, starting and stopping at irregular intervals. Hannon held his breath whenever it stopped, not daring to breathe until it resumed. Suddenly, there was a loud hiss, and the water started rising. The compartment had been penetrated, they didn't know where, and the hissing was the sound of escaping air. Thinking that the loss of pressure might allow them to open the escape hatch, Thatcher and Roiland climbed aboard the table to make another attempt. Suddenly, it flew open.

Above it was a man with a light.[1]

Low on funds, Seaman First Class Russell M. Davenport decided to forego liberty on Saturday night. Instead, he remained aboard to watch a movie. Awakening early Sunday morning, he went directly to breakfast, returning afterward to shower and shave. By 7:50 he was at his duty station aboard the No. 2 motor launch, wiping the morning dew off the seats. The fifty-foot launch, which was tethered to a boat boom on the port quarter of the ship, was one of the designated duty boats and as such would have to be ready to take on passengers at 8:00. Similar preparations were being made in the No. 3 launch, which was tethered alongside.

As the time approached 7:55, Davenport heard airplanes approaching. Then suddenly he heard an explosion on Ford Island. Seeing the smoke that followed, he had no doubt that they were under attack. He immediately dropped what he was doing, scurried up a Jacob's ladder to the boom pole, then shuffled across it to the side of the ship. After jumping over a lifeboat, he raced across the deck to the Fourth Division deck hatch. Looking to his left as he started down the south-facing staircase, he saw low-flying planes zooming across the channel toward him. One after the other, they augured upward above the void between *Oklahoma*'s fantail and *West Virginia*'s bow.

He hadn't yet reached the bottom of the stairs when the first torpedo hit. Because it hit well forward, and on the opposite side of the ship, the effect was little more than a jarring bump, but it was enough to cause him to fall off the ladder.

He was racing through the Fourth Division's living compartment when the second torpedo hit. Exploding much closer than the first one, it knocked him off his feet. After getting up, he hastened to a ladder, then descended to the carpenter's shop on the third deck. Then the third torpedo hit. He continued moving, descending another ladder to the first platform deck, where he immediately headed aft.

By the time he'd reached his battle station in the lower handling room of turret 4, another torpedo had hit and the ship had a severe list. Moments later, he heard the word to abandon ship. Nine sailors would depart ahead of him.

They all climbed up a ladder through the turret and were in the shell-handling room, two levels above, when the ship began to roll. Secured to the perimeter bulkheads were dozens of five-foot-long, 14-inch-diameter, 1,400-pound projectiles. Standing upright, they were secured against the bulkhead with a half-inch-diameter cord. As the ship's list increased, the cord broke, and the projectiles began rolling across the compartment, killing all nine of them. Davenport witnessed the carnage from the top of the ladder. Seeing a man pinned against the bulkhead with his tongue and eyes popping out, he retreated to the lower handling room. A short time later, the ship went completely over.

When it settled, he was standing in a foot of water on the compartment's overhead. After exiting through an upside-down doorway, he found a deck hatch in the adjacent compartment. Realizing there was no way out if he went up toward the bottom of the hull, he descended through the hatch to the carpenter's shop on the third deck, which was now filled with water. Completely immersed, he began swimming through the adjacent compartments. When he reached a dead end, he returned to the carpenter's shop, where he ran into Seaman Second Class Frank Wood. After speaking with him for several moments, Davenport heard other voices farther aft. Wanting to find out who they were, he asked Wood to go along with him. Wood declined, saying that he was too tired. Davenport proceeded aft, alone.[2]

Following the voices to the lucky bag, Davenport discovered eleven others. Fortunately, the compartment was dry. After comparing their attempts to escape, they settled in to wait.

Hours later, several attempted to swim out through the bottom of the ship, a route that necessitated swimming down through a trunk hatch to the main deck, across the deck to the starboard side, and then up to the surface, a distance of about ninety feet. Davenport would be one of them. Though he made several attempts, he was never able to get beyond the point where the trunk hatch exited onto the deck.

Deciding that they could conserve air by pulling themselves through the trunk hatch instead of swimming, Davenport and Seaman First Class Frank H. Scott tore their clothing into strips to make a rope. After swimming down the trunk to tie one end to the hatch, they took turns trying to swim out. Unfortunately, each trip was unsuccessful because the knots kept coming loose.

Abandoning the rope, Davenport made one last attempt. Reaching the hatch, he found there was very little space remaining between the coaming and the bottom of the harbor. Returning to the lucky bag, he told the others that if anyone was going to try again, they needed to do it soon, because the ship was sinking into the mud. With one exception, the idea was abandoned.

Coxswain Howard E. Roberts, who had tried before, decided to give it one more chance. He left and never returned. Assuming he had made it, Davenport and Scott were considering another attempt themselves when they suddenly heard cutting up above.[3]

Musician First Class Robert D. West was a clarinet player in the *Oklahoma*'s band. On the morning of December 7, the band mustered on the quarterdeck at 7:45. They had just finished warming up when West saw a line of planes descending on Ford Island. Seeing the lead plane go into a dive, he watched in amazement as an object descended from its belly. At that moment the bugler sounded first call on the PA. The time was exactly 7:55.

Distracted by the bugle, West didn't follow the bomb's trajectory. Because it landed in the water, he didn't hear an explosion either. Perhaps it was another drill. Yet he couldn't recall seeing so many planes above the island at one time.

At the conclusion of first call, the band marched aft toward the fantail. Ahead was the ship's Marine Color Guard. Assembled in front of the flagstaff on the stern, they were making final preparations to raise the flag at 8:00. Suddenly there was an explosion at the 1010 dock. Glancing over his right shoulder, West saw the *Oglala* squeezed in like an accordion, with a huge waterspout rising upward along her port quarter. A moment later, he heard the general alarm, and then Rommel's warning.

The band dispersed immediately. After racing forward to a deck hatch on the port side, West hustled down a staircase to the second deck. Realizing he wouldn't need his instrument, he tossed it down the passageway and then descended another flight of stairs to the third deck. Arriving at his battle station in the carpenter's shop, he positioned himself alongside the door because it was his job to secure it when everyone had arrived.[4]

Informed by the last man to enter that a torpedo was headed straight for the ship, West closed the door. While dogging it down, he heard a thud, followed by a large explosion. It was a task he would never finish because the explosion from the second torpedo sprung the hinges.

With the ship listing heavily following two more hits, he tried to make his way across the compartment to the starboard side. Due to the slanting deck, he was unable to make any headway. A sailor, perched along the starboard bulkhead, saw he was in trouble and tossed him a line. West grabbed it and pulled himself upward.

Nearing the bulkhead, he told the sailor that if the ship took another hit, it was going to capsize. His words were prophetic. Hit again, the ship started to roll, and water began gushing into the compartment. Overwhelmed by the sudden deluge, five sailors were swept into adjacent compartments, and another five would drown. West would be trapped in the compartment with Yeoman Second Class Bert W. Crenshaw, Fireman Second Class Horace W. Harrelson, Seaman Second Class Delbert L. Pittman, and Seaman First Class George E. Russell. Soon, only a foot of air space remained. Though the lamps and battle lanterns were out, there was some light from the phosphorescence being stirred up by the incoming water. It wasn't much, but it was enough for them to see one another's silhouettes. Realizing that the compartment would soon be filled, they swam to the starboard side of the turret 4 barbette, where they located a doorway to an adjacent compartment. They dove beneath the water, swam through the opening, and surfaced in the shipfitter's shop. A search of the compartment yielded a ladder. They gathered around it to discuss their options. Though the ladder led to a hatch, they decided not to open it until they'd consumed the air where they were. Instead, they simply climbed up the ladder to dry out. A while later, they saw a beam of light on the opposite side of the compartment. It was a sailor holding a flashlight above his head. Spotting the five men on the ladder, he swam over to talk with them. He said he knew a way out and asked if they wanted to come along. All five declined. At least on the ladder they were dry.

With the passing of hours, it became increasingly unlikely that they would be rescued. Unwilling to wait any longer, one man tried to kill himself by holding his head underwater. West tried to console another who was sobbing beside him. There was little he could say to help; he didn't think they'd survive either.

Rising steadily, the water was chasing them up the ladder.

When the compartment was nearly filled, they opened the hatch on the overhead. Climbing through it, they took another ladder to the second platform deck where the ladder ended. All that remained above was the hold and the inner bottom. There was no way of getting to either one.

Finding a locked door in the bulkhead, they pounded on it with a wrench until the lock broke. It took nearly ten minutes. Entering the compartment, they realized that they were in an ammunition magazine; the floor was strewn with 5-inch/25-caliber AA shells. Fortunately, it was dry.

Clearing a space on the floor, West took a seat alongside Bert Crenshaw. There was nothing to do but talk. They were terribly thirsty and discussed the perils of drinking the water, talked about how good a milkshake would taste, and talked of home. Nobody was hungry. There was little complaining. Every once in a while, they would count off to be sure that everyone was still alive. On occasion, they would pound on the bulkhead with the wrench.

Finally, there was a response.

Seaman First Class James C. Bounds was a quartermaster striker in the N Division. His living space was in steering aft. Located on the first platform deck, the deck directly below the armored deck, the compartment's floor was approximately eight feet below the waterline. Because it was located in the converging section of the hull, the thirty-eight-foot-long compartment was tapered: sixty-five feet wide along the forward bulkhead, forty feet wide aft. It contained fifteen bunks and lockers, an assortment of hardware kept in bins, and an array of weight-lifting equipment for the ship's wrestling team. Positioned atop vertical supports that ran the length of the compartment was the ship's primary steering shaft. Starboard of the shaft was an auxiliary shaft surrounded by four wooden steering wheels. Six feet in diameter, the spindled wheels, similar in appearance to the type on old sailing ships, were used to steer the ship by hand in the event that electricity was lost.

Bounds spent most of Saturday policing the compartment as a favor to another quartermaster who was away on leave. By the end of the day, most of the work had been completed. Planning to spend Sunday on the beach at Waikiki, Bounds awoke early to finish. Deciding he would eat ashore, he skipped breakfast and went directly to the carpenter's shop for a swab and bucket, then descended to steering aft. He had just filled the bucket with soap and water when he heard the general alarm. Moments later, he heard Rommel's warning and then the sound of a closing deck hatch as the hatch into the carpenter's shop was sealed from above.

When the first torpedo hit, the explosion knocked him off his feet. It also knocked the bucket over, sending a wave of soapy water across the linoleum deck. Seaman First Class Willard A. Beal never saw it. Racing into steering aft, he slipped and went skimming across the deck on his rear end, slamming hard into a bulkhead.

Bounds had returned to his feet when the second torpedo hit. He went down again, hard. Somewhat dazed, he considered remaining there. Then the lights went out. Following a short silence, he heard movement and voices from within the compartment. Though he couldn't see them, there were six other men in the compartment with him. Moments later, there would be seven as Electrician's Mate First Class Irving H. Thesman appeared from an adjacent passageway. Arriving with his tool bag and a flashlight, he was the last one in. When the watertight door was sealed behind him, he would find himself in the company of seven quartermasters: Bounds, Beal, Seaman First Class Albert L. Ellis, Jr., Seaman First Class Richard L. Artley, Seaman First Class George F. Jones, Seaman First Class Herbert S. Kennedy, and Seaman Second Class George A. DeLong. They would all share a common fate. With the deck hatches and watertight doors dogged shut, they had effectively sealed themselves in.

In an effort to determine the status of the ship, Bounds went to the booth in the forward part of the space to listen on the sound-powered phones. The booths were located all over the ship. He could hear men talking, some from the engine room, others from the bridge. Some were hollering, trying to locate people. They weren't on the phone, but he could hear them. He listened until the voices grew quiet.

Following three more hits, the ship started turning. Bounds watched in horror as spare-part boxes broke loose from their fittings and objects began careening across the floor. Knowing there would be more to come as the list increased, he realized that the only place he would be safe was against the starboard bulkhead. He'd have to climb over the steering shaft to get there. Grasping the top of a six-foot-high locker, he used it as a pivot point to swing his legs upward to get a foothold on the shaft. As the deck continued to rise, an adjacent locker slid against the one he was holding, pinning his thumb in between. Incredibly, he was able to separate the two with his other hand and jump to the starboard side of the shaft. Moments later the lights went out and the ship rolled over.

Miraculously, no one was hurt. In subdued silence, the eight men clambered to their feet. Thesman turned on his flashlight. Hearing gushing water, he centered the beam on an air-conditioning vent on the bottom of the compartment, which had been the overhead. The square-shaped vent, which extended three feet above the floor, led to a mushroom vent on the quarterdeck. Though it should have been closed during general quarters, it hadn't been, and water was gushing into it from the bottom of the harbor. In desperation they began stuffing clothing and blankets into the opening, but the pressure driving the water was too powerful to overcome. Whatever they put in it was blown back out. They grabbed a mattress from one of the bunks, rolled it tightly, then jammed it into the opening. To hold it in place, Beal, who was the heaviest, climbed on top. Though it slowed the inflow, water was still seeping in at the corners. Then the flashlight went out.

Removing the bulb and batteries from the canister, they were able to get sporadic flashes of light by holding the batteries end to end, and then rubbing the metal end of the bulb against the positive pole of the top battery. During one of the flashes, they saw an acey-deucey board floating on the water. Fortuitously, it was the same shape as the vent opening. Beckoning Beal from his perch, they removed the mattress and replaced it with the board. They found a length of rope and crisscrossed it over the board, then secured it into place by cinching the rope to some plumbing on the floor. When the final knot was tied, only three inches of rope remained. The water slowed to a trickle, eventually stopping when the air in the compartment was sufficiently compressed to hold it back completely. By then the water was waist high.

Though the floor was underwater, its angle, approximately thirty degrees from horizontal, resulted in shallower water on the high end. They would take refuge there for more than twenty hours. But when the air became stale, they had to move or perish. There was a water-tight door in the bulkhead that accessed the tiller room. If they opened it, and it was dry, they'd have a fresh source of air. If it were flooded, they'd be sealing their own doom.

They held a vote and decided to open it. Leaning against it, they loosened the dogs. When no water came through, they rushed in, quickly sealing the hatch behind them. They found a dry space where they could lie down, then settled in to wait for whatever lay in store. The only noise was the sound of their breathing. But there was water in the compartment, and it was rising steadily. After a while, they were forced to stand.

On occasion they would pound on the bulkhead with wrenches. Finally, there was an answer. After pounding several more times to confirm, the rescuers started communicating in Morse code. Fortunately, both Beal and DeLong were familiar with the code and were able to respond. When asked where they were located, they responded with "Stg aft." Told, "Your aid is coming soon," they were instructed to stop sending. All they had to do now was wait. Standing in waist-high water, they could only hope there was enough time. An eternal optimist, Bounds was certain there was.

Carpenter's Mate Second Class Walter F. Staff was replacing the canvas backing on his "movie-watching" chair in the carpenter's shop, third deck aft, when he heard the general alarm. When he heard Rommel's warning a few moments later, he started forward on the starboard side. Because his battle station was located in the bow, he'd have to run the length of a football field to get there. He hadn't gone far when the first torpedo hit. Though it hit forward on the opposite side of the ship, the effects were sufficient to knock him off his feet.

By the time he'd run the length of the forward ammunition pas-sageway leading to repair II, the ship had been hit again. Putting on a set of headphones to establish communications, he attempted to grab a flashlight from a nearby locker. Finding the locker secured, and no information forthcoming on the headphones, he continued forward into the bow. Arriving at a ladder near the turret 1 barbette, he descended to the first platform deck, then took another ladder to his battle station in the A-28 air-compressor room on the second platform deck.

Following battle station protocol, he shimmied through a crawl space to turn off the freshwater pump in the adjacent compartment, a measure designed to prevent fresh water from being pumped into the ship's assorted compartments in the event of a pipeline rupture. When he reemerged, Motor Machinist's Mate First Class Jackson P. Centers had entered A-28 along with Electrician's Mate Third Class Charles H. Harris and Fireman Third Class Clarence A. Blaylock.

Moments later, the explosion from a third torpedo shattered the compartment's lights, leaving the four of them in complete darkness. Fortunately, one of them had a cigarette lighter. In the dimness of its light, they located a ladder to the deck above.

"Let's get the hell out of here!" Staff commanded.

They raced up the ladder and exited into the windlass machinery room on the first platform deck. With the ship at a substantial list, they were attempting to scale another ladder to the third deck when a torrent of water exploded through the hatch in the overhead. Knocked off the ladder, they were consumed by the ensuing deluge of oil-laden water. When the onslaught was over, only Staff and Centers resurfaced. Unable to see, they attempted to locate the others by voice. When their calls went unanswered, they could only assume that Harris and Blaylock had either drowned or been carried away.[5]

Bent on their own salvation, they waded around the large pitch-black compartment in search of the ladder. Finally discovering one, they scaled it to the deck above. Exiting into another darkened compartment, Staff noticed a circular luminescence on one of the bulkheads. Moving toward it, he realized it was a phone dial. Moving even closer, he saw that it was upside down. It wasn't until then that he realized the ship had capsized and that they were in the same compartment they had left, the forward air-compressor room.

At least they were familiar with it. Though they were obviously trapped, Staff still had a sense of humor. "I found a phone," he exclaimed to Centers. "I'll call the OD to have him come and get us out of here." Centers retorted it was no time for jokes. He would find it even less humorous when Staff informed him that the ship was upside down.

Knowing that the aft bulkhead was solid, and that the overhead compartment was in the ship's hold, with only the hull directly above it, they decided to access the linen compartment, which was forward. Though it would be a dead end as well, at least they'd have something to lie on. With a wrench they found on top of the compressor, they beat the lock off the door. Despite their efforts, which consumed several hours, they were unable to enter the room because something was wedged against the door on the other side. With that avenue blocked, they attempted to access the overhead compartment, but that effort ended in failure as well because they were unable to get into a position to beat the lock off.

With water rising from the deck below, they moved to the high side of the compartment, taking refuge in a dry corner. Knowing that the remaining air would eventually be depleted, they resolved themselves to the fact that their situation was hopeless. Ultimately, they would simply fall asleep and expire. Remaining silent to conserve what air they had, they were left to their own thoughts and prayers for more than thirty hours.

Late Monday evening, they heard pounding on the hull directly above them. Having abandoned the larger wrench earlier, Staff scoured the submerged floor for something to respond with. Finding a small open-end wrench, he tapped on the overhead as hard as he could. Hearing a response, he tapped again, twice. When his taps were mimicked, he knew that they were in direct communication. The tapping continued in intervals for more than an hour.

Suddenly, they heard voices directly above and the whine of a drill motor. A short time later a hole appeared, followed immediately by the shrill of escaping air. Initially exuberant, they were stunned into silence by the rising water, which was rapidly approaching their necks. Because the ship was on a slight angle, there was a dry space between the drill hole and the uppermost corner of the compartment. Realizing that the rising water would soon reach the hole, they moved laterally to the dry space, tilting their heads backward for the final vestiges of air. Hearing a sudden commotion above, they guessed that the water had penetrated the hole and was spewing through the overhead. The commotion ended rather abruptly. Then there was silence.

They had been so close, so very close.

Believing the rescuers were still in the vicinity, Staff decided to try to access the linen compartment again. Moving sideways to the bulkhead, he reached below the water and pushed. Whatever had wedged it shut before was gone because it opened with relative ease. He knew the linen compartment was wider than the one they were in, so he assumed there would be a larger pocket of air on the high side. Positioning himself in front of the opening, he told Centers to follow him. They both entered, sealing the hatch behind them. A short time later, they heard voices.

They had not been abandoned.

CHAPTER 13

Thirty-Two Came Back

The efforts to rescue *Oklahoma*'s trapped crewmen began while the attack was still under way. Though most of the torpedo planes had departed the harbor by 8:10, a second wave of fighters and dive bombers resumed the attack around 8:50. Captain Bode boarded the *Maryland* a few minutes later, but he was ordered to the Lauluai Ammunition Depot by Rear Admiral Walter S. Anderson to oversee the replenishment of ammunition.

Lieutenant Commander Hobby, *Oklahoma*'s damage control officer, boarded the overturned hull at 9:15 to direct the rescue efforts. Unfortunately, the only equipment at his disposal was a twenty-four-foot whaleboat from the *Oklahoma* and a twenty-six-foot motor launch from the *Argonne*. The launch had diving equipment for only one diver. Informed that a survivor, who had escaped the ship by swimming down a trunk hatch near frame 117, had stated that others were trapped at the top of the trunk, Hobby dispatched the diver to investigate.

Hobby then met with Commander Edgar Kranzfelder, the combat-ships materiel officer who had arrived a few minutes earlier. They agreed that pumping equipment, cutting equipment, and additional diving equipment would be required to facilitate any further rescue attempts.

Around 9:30 Lieutenant Commander Herbert Pfingstag crossed over from the navy yard. After surveying the situation, he departed for the *Maryland* to confer with Commander Kranzfelder. Together they compiled a list of equipment and then dispatched a boat to the yard to obtain it. In the interim, *Oklahoma* ensign Joe Spitler was sent to the navy yard for a set of plans, and a sound-powered phone line was run from the *Maryland* to *Oklahoma*'s hull so that there would be direct communication with the battle fleet staff. Shortly thereafter, a boat arrived from the *Rigel* with cutting torches and assorted fire and rescue gear. Boats also arrived from the *Maryland,* the *Solace,* and the submarine base. The boat from the base, fully equipped for diving, was sent to the area around frame 117. Although the diver that Hobby had dispatched had released a buoy into the trunk, there had been no response from within.[1]

Meanwhile Hobby directed others to start tapping on the hull with hammers. There were responses in the vicinities of frames 131, 116, 78, and 22. In addition, voice contact was made via a sea suction line with two men trapped in an evaporator pump room. Fittingly, the contact would be initiated through the efforts of two *Oklahoma* survivors, Fireman Second Class Robert Bromm and Fireman Third Class Charles J. Blaisdell, both of whom had swum back to the *Oklahoma* after escaping to the *Maryland.*[2]

After Spitler returned with the blueprints, two entry points were selected near the stern. A third was chosen amidships to access the sailors trapped in the evaporator pump room near frame 78. The entry points had to be specific because most of the compartments aligning the bottom of the hull contained fuel oil, and the rescuers were using cutting torches.

The work was slow due to small fires and the presence of related fumes. Though air hoses were rigged from the *Maryland* to help ventilate the cutting areas, they proved to be inadequate. Despite the warnings of Machinist's Mate Second Class Walt Becker, who knew that the evaporator pump room had a cork lining, the fumes that permeated from the cork as it was cut asphyxiated the two men trapped inside: Machinist's Mate First Class Winfred O. Woods and Machinist's Mate Second Class Ulis C. Steely. It was a horrifying experience for Becker as well as for Bromm and Blaisdell, who had spent more than a dozen hours consoling the two men. The torches were abandoned in favor of pneumatic hammers with cutting tips.

RADIO IV AND THE LUCKY BAG

An hour past midnight, a barge arrived from the shipyard with air compressors and chipping hammers. Aboard was the chipping gang from Shop 11. Comprising twenty men, it was led by Julio DeCastro, a native Hawaiian. Another boat arrived, carrying Joe Bulgo, a Hawaiian renowned for his strength and uncanny endurance. Relieving exhausted workers who were attempting to cut a hole through the lower blister, Bulgo started his gun, continuing where they had stopped. To cool the chipping blade, buckets of water were brought up from the harbor.

Three holes were cut between frames 122 and frame 115. Only one provided access to the ship's interior, a two-foot-square hole at frame 116, at the level of the first platform deck. Bulgo entered the hole in the aft end of the portside antitorpedo blister. Once inside, he cut a hole in the adjacent bulkhead to access a freshwater storage tank. Pumps were brought aboard, and the tank was drained. After widening the hole, Bulgo entered the tank. Using the light from a cage lantern, he found a manhole in the diagonal bulkhead. He cut through it to enter a void space. Hearing a distinct *tap, tap, tap,* he hastened toward a splinter hatch. Kneeling beside it, he tapped on the cover and heard a voice in response. Trapped beneath him in radio IV were Seaman First Class Thomas F. Hannon, Seaman First Class Raymond A. Cymerman, Radioman Third Class Merton R. Smith, Seaman First Class Norman O. Roberts, Seaman First Class George J. Thatcher, and Seaman First Class Harold S. Roiland. Though the dogs had already been opened from below, the cover remained sealed due to the pressurized air pressing it against the hatch's coaming. The only way it could be opened was to reduce the pressure. A drill was lowered into the void space, and within moments, the trapped men could hear the whine of its motor. It would be quite a contrast to the shrill whistling of the drill bit penetrating the deck. As the air shot through the drill hole, however, the reduced pressure in the compartment allowed the water to rise. Fortunately, it did not take long for the air pressure to be reduced to the point where it was no longer sealing the manhole. The cover fell open, and Bulgo scrambled through to the deck below. Because the compartment was nearly seven feet high, he ordered the nearest sailor to climb on his back. Bulgo hoisted the man through the opening, and then the five others.

One of the first to reach the hull, Hannon would return to tell the rescuers that others were trapped in the lucky bag and in steering aft. The word was immediately relayed to Bulgo. Waist deep in water, Bulgo made contact with the sailors in the lucky bag. Telling them to back off, he drilled a hole in the top of the bulkhead. Greeted by the same hissing he had encountered before, he raised his hammer and began chiseling. Informed that the water level was rising inside, Bulgo cut a horizontal line across the top of the bulkhead, and then two vertical lines, one at either end of the horizontal line. Realizing there was not enough time to cut a complete square, he used a sledgehammer to pound the top of the cutout area backward. When it was wide enough for a man to pass through, water started shifting out along the bottom. He told the men to start coming out. The first two to emerge were Seaman First Class Michael Savarese and Seaman First Class Stephen B. Young.[3]

With water up to their chests, they made their way across the compartment to the same hatch that the men from radio IV had used. Behind them were Seaman First Class Selden Goins, Seaman Second Class Garlen W. Eslick, Electrician's Mate Second Class Rogers L. Tillman, Boatswain's Mate First Class Howard Aldridge, Seaman First Class William P. Schauf, Seaman First Class Frank H. Scott, Seaman First Class Russell M. Davenport, Seaman Second Class Wilbur T. Hinsperger, and Musician First Class John K. Engen.[4]

By the time Bulgo escaped radio IV, it was completely flooded. The rescuers would have to find a different route into steering aft, which abutted radio IV's aft bulkhead. Time was running short. It was 8:00 Monday morning.

AMIDSHIPS

Another rescue crew was already at work amidships, where additional tapping had been heard. A hole cut between frames 100 and 101 resulted in a dead end. Deciding on a different course of action, they reentered the hull through the hole used to access the evaporator pump room. Entering the transverse cofferdam between frames 76 and 77, they cut through the forward bulkhead to gain access to a reserve freshwater storage tank. After cutting through the floor, they descended into a portside fire room. Cutting through one bulkhead after another, they made their way aft through the evaporator pump room and the starboard engine room, traveling nearly eighty-five feet in the process. Entering the shaft alley that abutted the engine room, they cut through the floor to access the 5-inch/25-caliber handling

room. Inside were Musician First Class Robert D. West, Yeoman Second Class Bert W. Crenshaw, Fireman Second Class Horace W. Harrelson, Seaman Second Class George E. Russell, and Seaman Second Class Delbert L. Pittman. Aided by a torch, they were pulled from the compartment then escorted back through the ship. It was 2:00 P.M. Monday when they finally emerged from the hull. They had been trapped for thirty hours.[5]

STEERING AFT

Meanwhile, Joe Bulgo and his men were attempting to reach the men who had been heard in the vicinity of frame 131. After hitting deadwood in the two holes rescuers cut between frames 129 and 134, they returned to the hole they had cut at frame 116 to access radio IV and the lucky bag. Reentering the freshwater storage tank, they cut into an emergency fuel oil tank. From there, they cut into an adjacent void space, where they found a manhole in the floor. Cutting a hole alongside it, they reached through the hole to remove the nuts from the bolts securing the manhole cover. They then removed the cover and slipped through the manhole to the deck below. They were now in steering aft. The compartment contained a great deal of water but no men, because the survivors had already moved aft into the tiller room. Pumps were brought aboard to lower the water level so that the rescuers could work. Finally, the compartment was dewatered to the point where they could wade across it. Arriving at the tiller room door, they discussed the situation with the men inside. Informed that the door's dogs had already been opened but that the air pressure was sealing it, they told the men inside to remove the cap from a nearby air test plug.[6]

Seaman First Class Albert L. Ellis, Jr., immediately acknowledged the instruction and removed the cap. The moment he did, the water level started climbing. When the air pressure equalized, the door came open. Because he was closest to it, Ellis immediately began pushing men out. One by one, they emerged then waded from hole to hole. Each hole had been lined with rags to cover the ragged edges, and a rescuer was stationed alongside each one to help the survivors through.

By 4:00 P.M. Monday, Ellis, Seaman First Class Richard L. Artley, Seaman First Class James C. Bounds, Seaman First Class Willard A.

Beal, Seaman Second Class George A. DeLong, Seaman First Class George F. Jones, Seaman First Class Herbert S. Kennedy, and Electrician's Mate First Class Irving H. Thesman were breathing fresh Hawaiian air for the first time in nearly thirty-two hours.

LINEN STORAGE

While the aforementioned rescues occurred in the rear portion of the ship, the final rescue occurred in the bow. Accessing the hull in the vicinity of frame 22, a hole was cut into a compartment in the ship's inner hull, and then another was cut to access a storage compartment in the hold. On the bottom of the compartment was a manhole. The rescuers tapped on the cover and received a response from the compartment below. When asked if the compartment was dry, Carpenter's Mate Second Class Walter F. Staff responded in the affirmative—even though it was not. The rescuers told him to stand clear, and then they beat the dogs open with a hammer. When the cover dropped, only two men emerged: Staff and Motor Machinist's Mate First Class Jackson P. Centers. Escorted back to the hull, Walt Staff would be the last "cut-out" to escape from the *Oklahoma*. The time was 2:30 A.M. It was Tuesday, December 9. Staff and Centers had been trapped inside for more than forty-two hours.

Because of the determined efforts of the twenty-one men from Shop 11, thirty-two men would be saved. Though cutting continued into spaces where others might still be trapped, and a listening watch was posted throughout the above-water areas of the ship, no one else was located. The rescue efforts ended at 9:00 A.M. on December 11.[7]

CHAPTER 14

Resurrection

In the weeks following the attack, surveys were conducted to determine if any of the five sunken battleships could be salvaged. Preliminary results indicated that *Nevada, California,* and *West Virginia* could be resurrected, but additional studies would be required to make a determination on *Arizona* and *Oklahoma.*

When an underwater examination of *Arizona*'s hull in early 1942 indicated her back had been broken, it was decided to remove her superstructure and salvage her guns. The hull would remain where it lay, as the final resting place for the sailors and marines who had perished aboard her on the morning of December 7. A similar study of *Oklahoma* indicated that she could be raised but that the cost of restoration was prohibitive. Because she had rolled into the harbor's main channel, she posed a navigational hazard. Thus preservation as a memorial was not an option, and the remains of her 429 fallen crewmen would be removed for burial after she was raised.

The study revealed the following: The ship was resting in forty feet of water at an angle of 151 degrees from vertical. Soundings indicated that the masts, superstructure, and turrets were entirely submerged in mud. The upper decks of the port side of the ship were embedded in nearly twenty-five feet of mud, and the two tripod masts were either broken or badly bent. Structural damage on the port side extended over a distance of 260 feet. Additionally, the rear two-thirds of the ship rested on solid soil, while the forward third was floating in mud. Fortunately, the ship's center of gravity was located on solid soil.

Because raising an overturned battleship had never been attempted before, the *Oklahoma* project required much provocative thought and creative engineering. The final plan consisted of five basic stages:

1. Remove as much of the remaining fuel oil as possible to decrease the overall weight. (*Oklahoma*'s bunkers contained 1,185,000 gallons of fuel oil when she sank.)
2. Seal the hull and create an air bubble within it to increase buoyancy.
3. Rotate the ship to an upright position using hauling winches installed on Ford Island.
4. Install patches to seal the portside torpedo damage.
5. Dewater the hull using pumps.

STAGE ONE

The physical work began on July 12, 1942. A working platform was constructed adjacent to the hull. When the platform was completed, cutting points to obtain access to the fuel bunkers were marked on the hull. Because the portside bunkers were submerged, oil could be removed from the starboard side only. The following day workers began cutting at the indicated points on the hull's outer shell. Because the ship had a double bottom, additional holes had to be cut through the inner hull, the hold, to gain access to the fuel bunkers. The pumping plan required a minimum of fifteen access locations.

Because the fuel bunkers were a series of compartments, another network of holes had to be cut through the bulkheads between the compartments to allow oil to drain from one compartment to the other. The oil would eventually be routed to a centralized compartment, where it would be pumped into oil barges. It would take five days to cut the required access holes and another thirty-nine to remove the oil. When the oil removal phase concluded on August 26, the intake hoses were removed, and steel plates were welded over the access holes. Approximately 350,000 gallons of fuel oil had been removed.

STAGE TWO

To create an air bubble, the ship was divided into seven transverse sections, and the bulkheads that formed the forward and aft boundaries of each section were sealed to make them airtight. To allow air to be pumped into the ship to force the water out through the torpedo holes on the port side, divers closed the deck and bulkhead hatches on the decks above the waterline, then closed the hatches on the decks below it.

However, there was a concern that the air pockets would be lost when the ship was righted to ninety degrees. With the ship lying on its side, it was possible that the compressed air would leak out through undetected holes in the compartments and then travel along the ship's passageways to the fire-room uptakes, below the ship's smokestack. To prevent this, the uptakes had to be sealed.

The fire room uptake opening was approximately thirty feet square. To seal it would require the construction of a concrete patch. Since the opening was submerged, the patch would have to be constructed underwater and in total darkness. In addition, the room contained a high concentration of odorless hydrogen sulfide gas, requiring the divers to wear facemasks. The masks made the work cumbersome because air was supplied through a hose, the location of which required constant monitoring, and because hand signals were the only means of communication. Building the patch required that a massive thirty-foot-square box be constructed to form a mold for the concrete.

Once the necessary access openings were cut through the hull, timber was lowered into the ship and transported manually to the fire room. The room contained four feet of water, so the timbers were floated to predetermined locations above the uptake opening. Separating the uptake from the smokestack was an armored steel grill. The timbers were floated into position around the perimeter of the grill, weighted with sandbags, and then wired to the grillwork with steel cable. Once the timber perimeter was fixed in place, metal plating was attached to the grill to form the base of the mold. Finally, a fine wire-mesh screening was overlaid on the plating to prevent the cement from leaching out. Once the forms were in place, underwater concrete was pumped in.

The final step in sealing the hull was the installation of an air lock chamber above each access hole. The chambers were cylindrical compartments approximately eight feet in diameter and ten feet long. Each contained two separate interior compartments. A total of seven were constructed off site and then transported to the *Oklahoma* in boats. They were then attached to the hull over each of the seven access holes.

A diver would enter the chamber through an exterior door and then seal it behind him. He could then open the interior door (located in the bulkhead separating the compartments) without the loss of air pressure. Air was pumped into the interior chamber via an airtight nozzle that was threaded into the cylinder's exterior wall. Once inside the pressurized portion of the chamber, the diver could descend into the ship through the access hole in the hull.

The airlock chambers were temporary; their sole function was to allow divers access to the interior of the ship so that they could seal it to facilitate the creation of air bubbles. Once the bubbles were formed, the divers exited the ship, the access holes were welded shut, and the chambers were removed and taken ashore.

To control the pressure in each air-bubble section during righting, an exterior piping network was installed along the outer portion of the hull. With valve-controlled venting and intake pipes attached to each section, the pressure within the sections could be independently monitored and adjusted. If the air pressure was decreasing due to leakage, additional air could be pumped in. Conversely, a section could be vented if it was rising too quickly relative to the others. The ability to vent the sections was important, because it was feared that the ship would slide forward into the lagoon (turning basin) if the stern came up faster than the bow. To control the airflow, a barge was positioned at the stern to control the flow to the three air-bubble sections aft, while a second barge was stationed at the bow to control the middle and forward sections. As a further deterrent to sliding, 4,500 tons of coral soil was deposited in front of the bow.

Upon completion of the air-pumping stage, the water level in the interior of the ship was twenty-five feet lower than the outside level. The air bubbles had attained their desired goal. Their creation had forced the exit of nearly twenty thousand tons of water through the portside torpedo holes.

STAGE THREE

A plan was devised to pull the ship upright using electric winches and wire-hauling cables. Following the removal of a block of enlisted men's quarters on Ford Island, twenty-one concrete pedestals were constructed along the shoreline. The pedestals were positioned in two parallel rows: eight abutting the shore, the remaining thirteen directly behind them. An electric winch was then mounted atop each of the pedestals.

To increase the pulling momentum, twenty-one timber A-frames were attached to *Oklahoma*'s starboard keel at sixteen-foot intervals. To achieve the necessary leverage, the A-frames extended forty-eight feet above the mean low-water level. Once the A-frames were in place, lights were placed atop each one so that they could be seen at night by approaching airplanes.

Using a block-and-tackle arrangement, wire cables were slung from the winches on Ford Island to the A-frames on the ship. Strain gauges were attached to each set of cables to monitor the pull. This was a necessary precaution because the ship might slide instead of rotate if the pull was not uniform. If required, adjusting the speed of the winch could modify the pull. Because the height of the two concrete quays posed a hindrance to the cables as the ship rotated upward, it was necessary to remove the upper ten feet of each quay. As a final measure, the starboard propeller was removed as well as the blades of the port propeller, and a bridle was attached to the rudder to prevent it from moving. No ammunition and only a limited amount of machinery was removed prior to righting. Floodlights were installed on the beach so that operations could continue at night.

The righting began on March 8, 1943. Pulling the ship upright at a rate of 1.4 degrees per hour, the initial righting took eleven days, including a brief delay for divers to dredge the displaced mud from the shoreward side of the ship. By daybreak of March 19, the ship was lying on its side. The initial righting ceased some ten hours later, with the ship at an angle of sixty-eight degrees from vertical. At this point, the A-frames had rotated nearly eighty-three degrees. Whereas the rear member of each frame had been close to vertical when the pulling began, they were now nearly horizontal, with their tops directed toward the shore. Though the hauling cables remained in tension, they were no longer in contact with the pulley atop the A-frame. Because the A-frames had lost their leverage, they were removed.

On March 20 there was a final pull with the cables still attached to their original positions on the starboard blister and docking keel. When the ship was righted to forty degrees from vertical, the cables were removed then repositioned at higher elevations for better leverage. With the cables looped around the four turret barbettes, the conning tower, and the starboard king post, pulling resumed on March 29. The pulling would continue until April 20, when it was terminated due to excessive loading on the winches. In an effort to reduce the load, deep-well pumps were used to dewater the portions of the ship both forward and aft of the torpedo-damaged areas. The dewatering was a success, reducing the load by nearly 3,500 tons.

Another pull brought the ship to an angle of four degrees from vertical, but this effort would also be terminated due to winch overload. Because more weight would have to be removed, divers were sent below to cut away wreckage and remove the soil that had been scooped into the ship's interior as the hull had rotated across the bottom of the harbor. Soil was also removed from the exterior of the starboard side to allow the ship to settle more evenly, and measurements were taken for the construction of patches.

There was one final pull on June 16. When it ended, the bottom of the ship was resting solidly on the harbor floor, with a portside list of two degrees. Subsequently, five of the twenty-one righting cables were removed. As the tensions decreased with continued dewatering, the number of cables was decreased to ten. On July 8 the ship was moored with two anchors forward and two anchors aft. Three days later, the preservation of her 14-inch main guns began.

The righting had taken more than three months.

STAGE FOUR

The initial phase of the refloating required the construction and installation of patches along the port side. A concrete patch, extending from the upper deck to the second deck, was constructed between frames 31 and 43. Then a series of five concrete-sealed truss patches were installed between frames 43 and 75, a distance of 132 feet. These massive steel and timber truss patches were fifty-six feet tall and extended from above the upper deck to a position beneath the turn of the bilge. Two concrete patches were installed between the main and second decks from frame 75 to 96, and a third was installed between the first platform deck and the second platform deck between frames 85 and 96. Finally, a three-foot-high concrete patch was constructed along the level of the third platform deck between frames 76 and 86. The patching was completed on September 9. However, the hull was not yet watertight.

During the righting operation, witnesses had heard a great deal of grinding and snapping. An underwater inspection revealed that many of the rivets holding the overlapping steel plates in place had snapped, exposing drill holes where water was being sucked inside the hull by submersible pumps. A solution was discovered by one of the navy salvage divers. Positioning themselves beneath the ship, the divers released handfuls of kapok in front of the holes. The kapok was sucked into the holes by the pumps inside, effectively sealing them shut.

STAGE FIVE

Prior to dewatering, a cofferdam was constructed. Basically a four-foot-high wall, the cofferdam extended across the width of the ship just forward of turret 1 and just aft of turret 4, then extended lengthwise along either side. The water confined by the cofferdam was then pumped overboard, allowing a dry working area over most of the ship's length. The cofferdam was completed on October 3.

Calculations indicated that the ship would not float until the interior level of water had been reduced to a level below the third deck. Additionally, the third deck had to be free of water to provide a working level from which to investigate and mitigate the watertight spaces below so that the ship could be ballasted for refloating. By October 15, 1943, this goal had been achieved. However, conditions in the third deck storerooms, which it was necessary to enter to gain access to the compartments below, impeded immediate progress because stores and equipment were blocking most of the hatches. Once the obstructions were removed, the hatches were opened. In the instances where the hatches were dogged shut, access holes had to be cut through the adjacent bulkhead. When access to the lower decks was achieved, divers descended into the liquid darkness. The pumps were then activated and the water level lowered until knee high. Because of the presence of bodies, the water level was monitored the entire time.

More than four hundred sailors had sought refuge beneath the second deck on the morning of December 7, 1941, seeking the protection of its heavy armor. The preservation of their remains was as important as the ship's resurrection, and appropriate measures were undertaken to ensure a thorough and honorable removal. The process of removal was very specific. When a body was located, the skull would be placed in one bag, the remaining bones in another. Both bags would then be marked with the same number. A Marine Honor Guard, similar to the one that guards the Tomb of the Unknown Soldier at Arlington, Virginia, stood at attention on the hull both night and day until every body was located and taken above. The remains in the immediate vicinity of the pumps were placed in canvas bags and taken above. They were then placed in caskets. Each casket was then shrouded with an American flag and taken ashore for burial. The remainder would be removed later when the ship was raised.

Using various submersible pumps, the ship was refloated on the evening of November 3. A week later, the remaining cables were removed. By December 10, four pontoons were secured to the main patch for added buoyancy. On December 19, a six hundred-kilowatt Diesel generator was brought aboard to power the pumps while the ship was towed to dry dock. Prior to towing, roughly a third of the ship's 5-inch/25-caliber AA projectiles and 5-inch/51-caliber broadside gun projectiles were removed. The 14-inch/45-caliber main gun projectiles remained aboard.

Three days after Christmas, two years and three weeks after she had been sunk, *Oklahoma* was again under way. After being towed across the harbor, she entered dry dock at 7:45 A.M. Following the removal of her patches, her port side was reconstructed, and her 14-inch/45-caliber guns were removed.[1] They were gone but not silenced. Transported to her sister *Nevada*, the guns would wreak havoc on the beaches of Normandy, Iwo Jima, and finally, Okinawa.[2]

The *Oklahoma* and *Arizona* were the only U.S. battleships permanently removed from service during World War II. No U.S. battleships were sunk after Pearl Harbor. The three Japanese aircraft carriers whose planes launched torpedoes at *Oklahoma*, the *Akagi, Kaga,* and *Hiryu,* were all sunk at the Battle of Midway in 1942. On October 25, 1944, the Pearl Harbor battleships *Pennsylvania, Maryland, California, Tennessee* and *West Virginia,* joined with the battleship *Mississippi* to sink the Japanese battleships *Fuso* and *Yamashiro* at the Battle of Surigao Strait, numerically avenging the loss of their two sister battleships at Pearl Harbor.[3]

Caskets carrying the remains of ten *Oklahoma* crewmen are taken ashore. Courtesy Oklahoma Historical Society, Solace Collection.

Ship rotated to about ninety degrees, March 1943. Note the twenty-one A-frames secured to the hull and the twenty-one winches positioned along the shore. Courtesy National Archives.

Righting operation, March 1943. Note that the A-frames have been removed. Courtesy National Archives.

View of the starboard side of the superstructure and boat deck. Gun at left is 3-inch/50-caliber antiaircraft. From left to right are the No. 1, No. 3, No. 5, and No. 7 5-inch/25-caliber antiaircraft guns. Above and inboard of the No. 3 gun is the remains of the signal bridge, where Signalman Third Class Paul A. Goodyear was standing when he witnessed the dive-bombing attack on Ford Island. Twisted structure to right of the No. 7 gun is a boat crane. Courtesy National Archives.

View of ship, looking forward from quarterdeck, March 1943. Turret 4 is in the foreground. Courtesy National Archives.

Gun at upper left on the boat deck is the No. 1 5-inch/25-caliber antiaircraft. Gun at center is a 3-inch/50-caliber antiaircraft. Gun at lower center in No. 1 casemate is a 5-inch/51-caliber broadside gun. Courtesy National Archives.

Salvage operation, September 1943. Bow is on left side of picture. Courtesy Naval Historical Center.

Oklahoma entering dry dock on December 28, 1943. Courtesy National Archives.

Oklahoma in dry dock in early 1944. For size reference, note the man standing to the left of the bow. Courtesy National Archives.

BB37   1-7-44   14-44   150-44
STANDING ABOUT FR. 57 & LKG AT PORT SIDE OF
VESSEL

Oklahoma in dry dock with her port side exposed. Note the armor belt plating that extends from the main deck to the third deck. A plate is missing at the left of the picture and the second plate from the left is cracked, both the result of torpedo hits. The antitorpedo blister began at the third deck and extended down to the turn of the hull. A torpedo hit blew off the portion of the blister shown on the left side of the picture. Courtesy National Archives.

Main deck looking forward along port passageway. Bulkhead on the left is the interior bulkhead of the wardroom officer's berthing compartments. Note the ladder with an open deck hatch below it. Courtesy National Archives.

On the main deck looking aft to the outermost port door of bulkhead 85. Note the eight dogs on the bulkhead around the door. These were used to seal the door shut. Courtesy National Archives.

Oklahoma berthed in the west loch with *Wisconsin* outboard, November 1944. Courtesy Naval Historical Center.

Oklahoma at Pearl Harbor in February 1944. Courtesy National Archives.

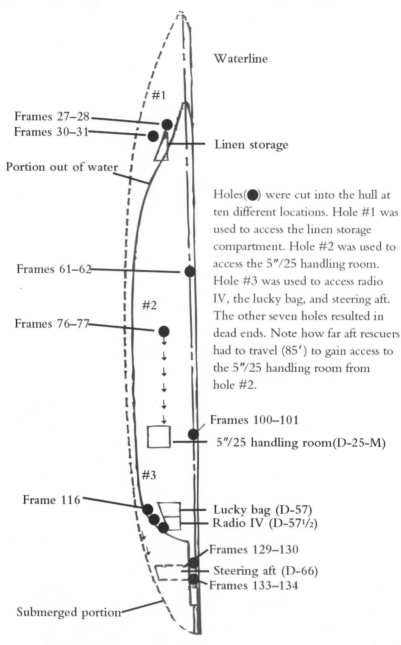

Waterline

#1

Frames 27–28

Frames 30–31

Linen storage

Portion out of water

Holes(●) were cut into the hull at ten different locations. Hole #1 was used to access the linen storage compartment. Hole #2 was used to access the 5″/25 handling room. Hole #3 was used to access radio IV, the lucky bag, and steering aft. The other seven holes resulted in dead ends. Note how far aft rescuers had to travel (85′) to gain access to the 5″/25 handling room from hole #2.

Frames 61–62

#2

Frames 76–77

Frames 100–101

5″/25 handling room(D-25-M)

#3

Frame 116

Lucky bag (D-57)
Radio IV (D-57½)

Frames 129–130

Steering aft (D-66)
Frames 133–134

Submerged portion

NOT TO SCALE

USS *Oklahoma*, rescue schematic (plan view).

CHAPTER 15

She Chose the Sea

The USS *Oklahoma* was decommissioned on September 1, 1944. That same day, she was stricken from the Naval Vessel Register by Secretary of the Navy James V. Forrestal. He was the eighth secretary of the navy she had served under. She had been a commissioned vessel in the United States Navy for 10,348 days.

THE AUCTION

On November 26, 1946, *Oklahoma* was put up for auction at the Brooklyn Naval Yard. The auction was conducted by the Navy Disposal Administration and administered through sealed bids. The navy reserved the right to deny any bid, whether for price or for purpose. The cost of transporting *Oklahoma* from Hawaii to the western seaboard of the United States alone was estimated at seventy-five thousand dollars. If the buyer wanted to rebuild the ship, he or she would need the navy's permission. A foreign country could purchase the ship, though to do so would require an extra layer of scrutiny.

The salvageable items included *Oklahoma*'s two main engines, six boilers, four turbo generators, numerous pumps, and two electric steering units. Because the masts, stack, and most of the superstructure had been removed, the weight of the remaining salvageable steel was estimated at about twenty-four thousand tons. Moore Drydock Company of Oakland, California, submitted the winning bid of $46,127. The vessel was sold "as is, where is."

A short time later, William Rosenthal visited the Pearl Harbor Naval Shipyard on behalf of the buyer. Accompanied by two local consultants, he met with M. W. Douthat of the Design Branch of the shipyard's

Planning Department to discuss the ship's condition. During the course of their meeting, Rosenthal was shown all the unclassified design information that the shipyard had on file. This included a memorandum dated August 19, 1946, that summarized the steps the shipyard deemed necessary to make the ship seaworthy when the navy had considered towing it to the mainland in 1946. When the meeting ended, the ship was inspected. At the inspection's conclusion, W. B. Murray, representing the American Bureau of Shipping, prepared a list of items that needed to be accomplished prior to towing. The work was then contracted. When it was completed, Murray gave his approval to close the vessel. Subsequently, the Puget Sound Tug and Barge Company was hired to make the tow.

Two seagoing tugs would be used, the *Monarch* and the *Hercules*. Each was 117 feet long, had a crew of fourteen, and was powered by a 1,200-horsepower Diesel engine. Commanding the *Monarch* was Captain George O. Anderson. Captain Kelly Sprague commanded the *Hercules*. To supply fuel for the voyage, an eight-thousand-gallon fuel tank was constructed on *Oklahoma*'s deck. The ship would be towed by two thousand-foot-long steel cables, each two inches in diameter, with one attached to each tug. Notified of the scheduled delivery date, Oklahoma governor Roy J. Turner scheduled a trip to San Francisco to pay final tribute to his state's namesake battleship.

GOING HOME

On the morning of May 12, 1947, *Oklahoma* was assisted from Pearl Harbor by navy tugs. After departing the mouth of the harbor, the seagoing tugs shouldered the load, heading east at five knots. All went well for the first seventy-two hours.

In the early morning hours of May 16, a searchlight from *Hercules* revealed that *Oklahoma* was listing to port. When the list had increased to some thirty degrees by the end of the fourth day, the coast guard was contacted. At a point about six hundred miles northeast of Honolulu, the tugs were instructed to turn back. Fearful that *Oklahoma* would founder, Captain Anderson disconnected the magnetic brakes on *Monarch*'s towing winch. Left operative, the magnetic brakes would engage automatically if the cable were strained. Acting in their stead was a hand-operated friction brake that could be disengaged quickly to allow the cable to run out.

Toward the end of the six-to-midnight watch, Anderson saw that *Oklahoma* was going under. As her lights disappeared beneath the ocean's surface, he realized that *Monarch* was being dragged astern. Anderson immediately raced aft to release the brake. By the time he arrived, the stern was taking on water. He glanced at the winch. The cable had entirely played out. In a shower of sparks, it broke free of the spool and whipped through the guides. Seconds later, *Monarch* lurched to a standstill.

The situation on *Hercules* was much more desperate. Because her speed had been slowed when *Oklahoma* started sinking, the pressure of the water against the propeller had reversed its rotation. *Hercules*'s engine was propelling her backward at the same speed that *Oklahoma* was dragging her. With *Oklahoma* heading straight for the bottom, *Hercules* was on the verge of going under when her winch exploded, shearing the cable that would have otherwise pulled her to her doom.

At the request of the coast guard, *Monarch* and *Hercules* remained in the area until daylight, making sure there were no floating remnants to pose a navigational hazard to other ships. When none were found, they returned to Puget Sound.[1]

Oklahoma served her country proudly for twenty-five years, participating in two World Wars. Designed to keep the peace, perhaps it is only fitting that her massive 14-inch main guns were never fired in belligerence. She was a proud lady and a home to thousands. But the ocean was where she lived and where she remains.

Epilogue

Of the 429 sailors and marines who perished aboard the USS *Oklahoma* on December 7, 1941, only twenty-nine were immediately identified. Six others were buried as Unknowns and identified later. All thirty-five were buried at Nuuanu Cemetery (also know as Oahu Cemetery). When *Oklahoma* was raised in 1943, the remains of her recovered crewmen were buried at Halawa Cemetery because Nuuanu had reached its capacity. Dog tags were not common in 1941, so the remains could not be identified; they were buried beneath simple wooden crosses with "Unknown," the date of death, and "USS *Oklahoma*" written on them. When the National Memorial Cemetery of the Pacific (commonly known as the Punchbowl) was constructed near Honolulu in 1949, all but twenty-one of the remains were exhumed and reinterred there. Of the twenty-one, seven were exhumed and reinterred at other national cemeteries, twelve were reinterred in nonmilitary cemeteries, and two remained at Nuuanu.

Unfortunately, the only headstone information transferred to the Punchbowl gravesites was the word "Unknown." It would require the efforts of Hawaii congresswoman Patsy Mink to have the original information restored. The legislation she drafted, a rider to House appropriations bill HR3806, proposed that the grave markers be replaced with new ones, including the date of death and the ship or station to which the man was assigned. In 2001, 74 new markers were laid to replace the USS *Arizona*'s Unknowns. In 2002, an additional 177 markers were replaced, including 45 marking the USS *Oklahoma*'s Unknowns.

In researching casualty records nearly sixty years after the attack, Ray Emory, the official historian of the Pearl Harbor Survivors Association and a survivor himself (USS *Honolulu*), discovered that twenty-seven of the men whose remains had been moved to the Punchbowl had actually been identified in 1941 (in addition to the thirty-five previously mentioned). Because the American Graves Registration Service failed to obtain the signature of a qualified anthropologist prior to the burial date, the remains were buried as Unknowns with no subsequent efforts made to correct. Emory was able to determine the burial locations of the twenty-seven sailors, and with the advent of DNA testing, lobbied the army's Central Identification Laboratory, Hawaii, to exhume the remains to confirm their identities. On April 18, 2003, the believed remains of Ensign Eldon P. Wyman were disinterred along with those of four other *Oklahoma* sailors with whom he shared the grave. The efforts to identify his remains through DNA matching are ongoing.

Two other Unknowns were believed known but were never officially identified until, thanks again to the efforts of Ray Emory, one of them, Fireman Third Class Alfred Eugene Livingston, was finally identified in the summer of 2007. On July 21, 2007, he was reinterred with full military honors at a cemetery in Worthington, Indiana, just footsteps from where his mother and grandparents are buried. An effort is now under way to identify positively the other sailor, Seaman First Class Russell Clyde Roach of Zanesville, Ohio.

Efforts are also under way to gather DNA information to identify other USS *Oklahoma* Unknowns. DNA test kits are being made available to female family members, free of charge, because their DNA markers are more readily traceable than those of male family members. Efforts are also under way to obtain photographs of the Unknowns in hopes that a trace can be made through dental patterns. *Oklahoma* survivor Paul Goodyear has already accumulated 273 of these photographs.

The remains of 380 of *Oklahoma*'s Unknowns (the remains of the thirteen others were never discovered) are currently buried in forty-five different Punchbowl gravesites, which is a difficult situation for visiting family members. It is hoped that the new USS *Oklahoma* Memorial—the fruition of the effort that was formalized when *Oklahoma* sailors Walt Becker, Gene Byers, Paul Goodyear, Gerald Halterman, Chet Jankowski, Wes Potts, and George Smith addressed the Oklahoma Senate on April 15, 2004—will help provide some consolation. Dedicated on December 7, 2007, the memorial is located beside a small grove of banyan trees on Ford Island. Within easy sight of the *Missouri*, now berthed where the *Oklahoma* was moored on

December 7, 1941, the memorial features informative black granite panels and 429 white vertical staffs. Each staff contains the name and rating/rank of individual casualties. Made out of marble mined from the same quarry used for the headstones at Arlington National Cemetery, the seven-foot-high staffs are aligned "shoulder to shoulder" to simulate the "manning the rails" tradition of the U.S. Navy. Designed by Oklahoma City architect Don Beck, the memorial was funded by USS *Oklahoma* survivors, private and corporate donors, and the Oklahoma Centennial Commission. The dramatic black-and-white memorial is a lasting and fitting tribute to the 429 sailors and marines who called the *Oklahoma* their home that fateful Sunday morning.

Listed below are the names and probable hometowns (in 1941) of the twenty-seven casualties identified in 1941 whose names were lost during their reinterment at the Punchbowl in 1949. Any help locating the female descendants of any of these men would be much appreciated. Information can be e-mailed to the webmaster at USSOklahoma.com.

Armstrong, Kenneth Berton (Mldr First Class, USN), National City, CA

Boring, James Bryce (Fireman Second Class, USN), Radcliff, OH

Boxrucker, Lawrence Anton (Fireman Second Class, USN), Dorchester, WI

Carney, Harold Francis (Machinist Mate First Class, USN), Dubuque, IA

Craig, John William (Storekeeper First Class, USN), Monroe, AR

England, John Charles (Ensign, USNR), Alhambra, CA

Finnegan, William Michael (Ensign, USN), San Diego, CA

Goggin, Daryl Henry (Machinist, USN), Los Angeles, CA

Gordon, Duff (Chief Metalsmith, USNR), San Diego, CA

Hayden, Albert Eugene (Chief Electrician's Mate, USN), Mechanicsville, MD

Hittorff, Joseph Parker, Jr. (Ensign, USN), Westmont, NJ

Hoard, Herbert John (Chief Storekeeper, USN), Pevely, MO

Hopkins, Edwin Chester (Fireman Third Class, USN), East Swanzey, NH

Jayne, Kenneth Lyle (Fireman Third Class, USN), Patchogue, NY

Jordan, Julian Bethune (Lieutenant, USN), Easley, SC

Lehman, Gerald George (Fireman Third Class, USN), Hancock, MI

Lindsley, John Herbert (Fireman Third Class, USN), Waukegan, IL

Luke, Vernon Thomas (Machinist Mate First Class, USNR), Turlock, CA

Nash, Paul Andrews (Fireman First Class, USN), Carlisle, IN

Sederstrom, Verdi Delmore (Ensign, USNR), Salem, OR

Stockdale, Louis Stephens (Ensign, USNR), San Francisco, CA

Swanson, Charles Harold (Machinist Mate First Class, USN), Maywood, CA

Thinnes, Arthur Ray (Seaman Second Class, USN), Milwaukee, WI

Thompson, Irving Andrew R. (Ensign, USN), Beaverton, OR

Wagoner, Louis Lowel (Seaman Second Class, USN), Wichita, KS

Welch, William Edward (Seaman First Class, USN), Springfield, OH

Wyman, Eldon Paul Wyman (Ensign, USNR), Portland, OR

USS *Oklahoma* Memorial, December 7, 2007. Note the battleship USS *Missouri* in the background. The *Missouri* is now berthed where the *Oklahoma* was moored on the morning of December 7, 1941. Courtesy of Dick Pryor, OETA, Oklahoma City, Oklahoma.

Commanding Officers and Dates of Service

Captain Roger Welles	May 2, 1916, through June 6, 1917
Rear Admiral Spencer K. Wood	June 6, 1917, through Feb. 1, 1918
Commander Edward T. Costein	Feb. 1, 1918, through Feb. 18, 1918
Commander Mac Gillvray Milne	Feb. 19, 1918, through March 1, 1918
Captain Mark L. Bristol	March 2, 1918, through Oct. 14, 1918
Captain Charles B. McVay, Jr.	Oct. 14, 1918, through July 9, 1919
Captain N. E. Irwin	July 9, 1919, through July 5, 1921
Captain Edwin T. Pollack	July 5, 1921, through Jan. 13, 1922
Captain Stephen V. Graham	Jan. 13, 1922, through July 4, 1923
Captain W. Pitt Scott	July 4, 1923, through June 15, 1925
Captain Willis McDowell	June 15, 1925, through May 5, 1927
Captain T. A. Kearney	May 5, 1927, through Dec. 10, 1928
Captain J. F. Hellweg	Dec. 10, 1928, through May 30, 1930
Captain John D. Wainwright	May 31, 1930, through June 25, 1932
Captain H. D. Cooke	June 25, 1932, through May 1, 1934
Captain W. R. Van Auken	May 1, 1934, through Nov. 1, 1935
Captain William Alden Hall	Nov. 1, 1935, through June 25, 1937
Captain Charles C. Hartigan	June 25, 1937, through Dec. 20, 1938
Captain T. S. McCloy	Dec. 21, 1938, through Jan. 30, 1939
Captain Emmanuel A. Lofquist	Jan. 30, 1939, through June 24, 1940
Captain Edward J. Foy	June 24, 1940, through Oct. 31, 1941
Captain Howard D. Bode	Nov. 1, 1941, through Dec. 7, 1941
Commander Jesse L. Kenworthy, Jr.*	Dec. 7, 1941

*Kenworthy became the active commander when Captain Bode left the ship at approximately 7:30 A.M.

Medal Citations: December 7, 1941

FLAHERTY, FRANCIS C.: MEDAL OF HONOR

Rank and Organization: Ensign, U.S. Naval Reserve
Born: March 15, 1919, Charlotte, Michigan
Accredited to: Michigan
Citation: For conspicuous devotion to duty and extraordinary courage and complete disregard of his own life, above and beyond the call of duty, during the attack on the fleet in Pearl Harbor by Japanese forces on December 7, 1941. When it was seen that the USS *Oklahoma* was going to capsize and the order was given to abandon ship, Ens. Flaherty remained in a turret, holding a flashlight so that the remainder of the turret crew could see to escape, thereby sacrificing his own life.

WARD, JAMES RICHARD: MEDAL OF HONOR

Rank and Organization: Seaman First Class, U.S. Navy
Born: September 10, 1921, Springfield, Ohio
Entered service at: Springfield, Ohio
Citation: For conspicuous devotion to duty, extraordinary courage, and complete disregard of his life, above and beyond the call of duty, during the attack on the fleet in Pearl Harbor by Japanese forces on December 7, 1941. When it was seen that the USS *Oklahoma* was going to capsize and the order was given to abandon ship, Ward remained in a turret holding a flashlight so that the remainder of the turret crew could see to escape, thereby sacrificing his own life.

AUSTIN, JOHN A.: NAVY CROSS

For exceptional service, presence of mind, and devotion to duty during the Japanese attack on the United States Pacific Fleet in Pearl Harbor, Territory of Hawaii, on December 7, 1941. When the USS *Oklahoma* capsized, he and a number of the crew were entrapped in one of the ship's compartments. By his efforts, a porthole under water was located, and he assisted fifteen of the crew to escape. His conduct was in keeping with the highest traditions of the United States Naval Service. He gallantly gave his life in the service of his country.

ALEXANDER, HUGH ROSSMAN: NAVY AND MARINE CORPS MEDAL

For heroic conduct while serving onboard the USS *Oklahoma* during the Japanese attack on Pearl Harbor on December 7, 1941. When his ship capsized and trapped him and numerous crew members in a compartment as the result of damage by the enemy, Lieutenant Commander Alexander selected those men small enough to make their escape through the narrow portholes and continued giving all assistance in his power until the end. His heroic spirit of self-sacrifice and his devotion to the welfare of others were in keeping with the highest traditions of the United States Naval Service. He gallantly gave his life in the service of his country.

DAY, FRANCIS D.: NAVY AND MARINE CORPS MEDAL

For distinguished heroism and intrepidity during the attack by enemy Japanese forces on the United States Pacific Fleet, Pearl Harbor, Territory of Hawaii, on December 7, 1941. When the USS *Oklahoma* capsized, Day, entrapped in one of the ship's compartments with a number of the crew, courageously risked his life in assisting fifteen of the crew to escape through a submerged porthole. His utter disregard for his own personal safety was in keeping with the finest traditions of the United States Naval Service. He gallantly gave his life in the service of his country.

SCHMITT, ALOYSIUS H.: NAVY AND MARINE CORPS MEDAL

For distinguished heroism and sublime devotion to his fellow man while aboard the USS *Oklahoma* during attack on the United States

Pacific Fleet in Pearl Harbor by enemy Japanese forces on December 7, 1941. When the vessel capsized and he became entrapped, along with other members of the crew, in a compartment where only a small porthole provided outlet for escape, Lieutenant (junior grade) Schmitt, with unselfish disregard for his own plight, assisted his shipmates through the aperture. When they, in turn, were in the process of rescuing him and his body became tightly wedged in the narrow opening, he, realizing that other men had come into the compartment looking for a way out, insisted that he be pushed back into the ship so that they might leave. Calmly urging them on with a pronouncement of his blessing, he remained behind while they crawled out to safety. His magnanimous courage and self-sacrifice were in keeping with the highest traditions of the United States Naval Service. He gallantly gave his life in the service of his country.

USS *Oklahoma* Crew Roster: December 7, 1941

Of the 429 sailors and marines who perished aboard the USS *Oklahoma* on December 7, 1941, only 36 have been positively identified. These are listed as Killed in Action (KIA) along with their place of burial. The remaining 394 are listed as Missing in Action (MIA). Of these, 380 are buried at the Punchbowl (National Cemetery of the Pacific, Honolulu, Hawaii) in graves marked Unknown. The remains of the thirteen others were never discovered.

Name	Rank	Status
Adams, George, D.	S2c	USS *Chester*
Adams, John E.	S1c	USS *Louisville*
Adams, Thomas E.	GM2c	USS *Northampton*
Adamson, Wesley G.	S1c	USS *Tennessee*
Adkins, Marvin B.	GM3c	MIA
Aguon, Felix T.	Mat1c	MIA
Albert, Newton J.	S1c	USS *Northampton*
Albin, Milton A.	S1c	Fleet machinegun school
Albitz, Donald J.	S1c	USS *Helena*
Aldridge, Howard	BM1c	Survived: reassignment unknown
Aldridge, Willard H.	S1c	MIA
Alexander, Howard J.	PFC (USMC)	Marine barracks
Alexander, Hugh R.	Lt. Cmdr.	MIA
Allen, Stanley W.	Ensign	MIA
Allison, Hal J.	F2c	MIA

Name	Rank	Status
Anderson, Arvid W.	PhM1c	USS *Enterprise*
Anderson, Caryl C.	S2c	Naval air dispensary
Anderson, Edward A.	Lt. (jg) MC	U.S. Navy Hospital
Anderson, Tomas B.	StM1c	USS *Jarvis*
Anderson, William L.	CTC	USS *Pennsylvania*
Armlin, James F.	CSK	Receiving station
Armstrong, John V.	SK3c	USS *Louisville*
Armstrong, Kenneth B.	M1dr1c	MIA
Armstrong, Terrence J.	SK3c	Receiving station
Armstrong, Thomas E.	SK2c	USS *Louisville*
Arickl, Leon	S1c	MIA
Arrington, Cecil E.	S2c	USS *Louisville*
Arthur, Edwin P.	Ensign, DV-G	USS *Maryland*
Arthurholz, Marley R.	PFC (USMC)	MIA
Artley, Daryl E.	QM2c	MIA
Artley, Richard L.	S1c	USS *Helena*
Aschbrenner, Paul E.	S1c	USS *Louisville*
Ash, Payton C.	PFC (USMC)	Marine barracks
Ashby, Earl B.	Y2c	USS *Pelias*
Athas, Marion H.	S1c	Fleet pooling off. rec. bks.
Atkins, Maury L.	GM1c	USS *Helena*
Augenstein, John A.	S1c	USS *Northampton*
Auld, John C.	S2c	MIA
Austin, John A.	Chief Carpenter	MIA
Avery, Edwin G.	SM2c	Signal tower, Ford Island
Aymond, James J.	WT2c	USS *Northampton*
Backman, Walter H.	RM2c	MIA
Backus, Paul H.	Ensign	CombatWingTwo
Bailey, Donald E.	S2c	Receiving station
Bailey, Gerald J.	S1c	MIA
Bailey, Robert E.	SF3c	MIA
Ballance, Wilbur F.	S1c	MIA
Banks, Layton L.	Cox	MIA
Baran, Stephen B.	EM2c	USS *Northampton*
Barber, Leroy K.	F1c	MIA

Name	Rank	Status
Barber, Malcolm J.	F1c	MIA
Barber, Randolph H.	F2c	MIA
Barclay, Harry A.	S2c	USS *Louisville*
Barker, Alvin F.	S1c	USS *Louisville*
Barkley, Garth L.	S1c	USS *Northampton*
Barlow, Lester E.	S2c	USS *Northampton*
Barncord, Cecil E.	EM3c	MIA
Barrett, Wilbur C.	S2c	MIA
Bartlett, Douglas C.	Y3c	Casualty off. rec. bks.
Bass, Dan C.	S1c	USS *Pelias*
Bates, Harold E.	F1c	MIA
Battles, Ralph C.	F2c	MIA
Bauer, John A.	AMM2c	Naval air station (aviation unit)
Baum, Earl P.	S1c	MIA
Baumgart, Edwin P. (Jr.)	SF2c	USS *Pelias*
Baxley, Marshall E.	S2c	USS *Tennessee*
Baza, Presbeterio A.	Mat1c	USS *Reid*
Beal, Willard A.	S2c	USS *Helena*
Bean, Howard W.	RM3c	MIA
Beasley, Chester	Bkr2c	Naval air station
Beaver, Robert G.	S1c	USS *Helena*
Beck, Edgar B.	GM2c	USS *Louisville*
Becker, Walter	MM2c	USS *Blue*
Belt, Walter S. (Jr.)	F1c	MIA
Bennett, Robert J.	F3c	MIA
Benson, Olney D.	S1c	USS *Worden*
Benson, William L.	Lt. Cmdr.	Submarine base
Bentley, Robert M.	F1c	USS *Blue*
Bergstrom, Royal E.	S2c	USS *Honolulu*
Berkley, Howard J.	F2c	USS *Salt Lake City*
Bernheisel, Deastill S.	Bkr2c	USS *Northampton*
Bernsden, Simon B.	F2c	Survived: reassignment unknown
Berry, James G. (Jr.)	S1c	USS *Northampton*
Bertrand, Donald R.	GM1c	USS *Mahon*

Name	Rank	Status
Bestudick, Paul P.	MM1c	USS *Hull*
Bewley, Bill N.	BM2c	USS *Pennsylvania*
Bickley, Lesley C.	CWT	USS *Enterprise*
Bierman, George B.	Pvt. (USMC)	USS *Indianapolis*
Bill, Robert G.	Ensign	Naval air dispensary
Bird, Harold S.	Mus2c	Yard craft
Birnel, John H.	SF2c	USS *Medusa*
Birthisel, Lawrence H. (Jr.)	Lt.	Shore patrol
Bishop, John L.	Ensign	West loch
Biviano, Lucian S.	SM3c	Signal tower, Ford Island
Black, Jimmy D.	Pvt. (USMC)	USS *Chicago*
Black, Van T.	CBM	Com 14
Black, Waldean	Pvt. (USMC)	MIA
Blackard, Willard D.	RM1c	USS *Chester*
Blackburn, Harding C.	Y3c	MIA
Blaisdell, Charles J.	F3c	USS *Helm*
Blanchard, William E.	Bmker2c	MIA
Blaylock, Clarence A.	F3c	MIA
Blitz, Leo	MM2c	MIA
Blitz, Rudolph	F1c	MIA
Blomstedt, Leonard M.	S1c	USS *Tucker*
Blondin, Claude W.	SC3c	USS *Northampton*
Bobbitt, William S.	S2c	USS *Blue*
Bock, John G. (Jr.)	S2c	MIA
Bode, Howard D.	Captain	Fourteenth Naval District Navy Yard
Boemer, Paul L.	Cox	MIA
Boney, John F.	S1c	USS *Farragut*
Bonham, Roy D.	GM3c	USS *Helena*
Booe, James B.	Bmstr	MIA
Boorman, James A.	Lt. (jg)	Fourteenth Naval District
Boreen, Roy S.	SK2c	Receiving station
Boren, Robert S.	S1c	USS *Dewey*
Boring, James B.	F2c	MIA
Bothne, Adolph M.	Bos'n	USS *Nevada*
Boudreaux, Ralph McH.	StM1c	MIA

Name	Rank	Status
Bounds, James C.	S1c	USS *Helena*
Bowden, Raymond L.	Cox	Com 14
Bowden, Thomas A.	S2c	USS *Louisville*
Boxrucker, Lawrence A.	F2c	MIA
Boyd, Billy D.	GM3c	USS *Lamson*
Boyer, Millard L.	BM1c	USS *Salt Lake City*
Boynton, Raymond D.	S1c	MIA
Bradford, Robert R.	Ensign	Naval hospital
Bradley, Carl M.	F2c	MIA
Brady, Allen E.	S2c	MIA
Bramble, Hubert R.	S1c	USS *Louisville*
Brandt, Orvis V.	S1c	MIA
Brashier, Willard L.	PFC (USMC)	USS *Indianapolis*
Branson, John J.	Lt.	Rec. bks. fleet pooling off.
Bratager, Kermit O.	EM3c	Receiving station
Breedlove, Jack A.	FC3c	MIA
Brender, Bernard W.	Y2c	West loch
Brewer, Randall W.	StM1c	MIA
Brewer, Raymond	PFC (USMC)	USS *Chicago*
Brier, Frank H.	S2c	USS *Louisville*
Brislen, John R.	PFC (USMC)	Marine barracks
Bromm, Robert	F2c	USS *Helm*
Bronson, Charles H.	S2c	USS *Blue*
Brooks, William	S1c	MIA
Brosky, Stanley	S1c	USS *Helena*
Brower, Richard	S1c	USS *Pennsylvania*
Brown, Alvin L.	S1c	USS *Helm*
Brown, Garth G.	GM3c	USS *Helena*
Brown, George A.	SC3c	USS *Worden*
Brown, Leonard W.	Pvt. (USMC)	USS *Indianapolis*
Brown, Maurice M.	CTC	USS *Honolulu*
Brown, Wesley J.	F1c	MIA
Browne, Kingsley F.	MM2c	USS *Hull*
Browne, Wallace B.	CWT	USS *Jarvis*
Bruce, Ray E.	PFC (USMC)	USS *Indianapolis*
Bruesewitz, William G.	S1c	MIA

Name	Rank	Status
Brumback, Robert	S1c	USS *Helena*
Brunmeier, Leopold	S1c	USS *Pennsylvania*
Brunner, Leland H.	S1c	USS *Pennsylvania*
Buchanan, James R.	MM2c	MIA
Buchmeier, Leonard W.	S1c	USS *Hull*
Bucon, Louis F.	F1c	USS *Helm*
Budke, Ralph A.	S1c	USS *Pennsylvania*
Buelow, John F.	Pvt. (USMC)	Marine barracks
Bunch, John W.	EM2c	On leave in States
Bunn, William H.	S1c	USS *Helena*
Burch, Earl G.	Bkr3c	KIA/Punchbowl (C-0763)
Burger, Oliver K.	WT1c	MIA
Burgin, Ervin D.	S2c	Naval air station
Burgin, Mullin D.	EM3c	USS *Blue*
Burk, Millard (Jr.)	S1c	MIA
Burkett, Horace S.	CEM	USS *Pelias*
Burks, James F.	S1c	USS *Louisville*
Burnett, Roscoe L.	S1c	USS *Pennsylvania*
Burns, Charles F.	Cox	USS *Chester*
Burns, Schuyler C. (Jr.)	S1c	USS *Pennsylvania*
Burr, Roland E.	Y3c	Receiving station
Busch, Martin L.	WT2c	USS *Worden*
Butorac, Nicholas J.	QM3c	USS *Enterprise*
Butts, Roger C.	SC1c	MIA
Byers, Eugene	S1c	USS *Dewey*
Cagujas, F.	1stMus	Receiving station
Cain, Carl E.	GM3c	USS *Salt Lake City*
Callahan, Archie (Jr.)	StM2c	MIA
Camery, Raymond R.	F1c	MIA
Campbell, William V.	S2c	MIA
Canady, Cecil F.	S2c	USS *Jarvis*
Cardinal, Lyman E.	F2c	USS *Louisville*
Cargile, Murray R.	S2c	MIA
Carlson, Donald P.	S1c	West loch
Carlson, John C.	GM2c	USS *Selfridge*
Carlson, Robert O.	Mus1c	Yard craft

Name	Rank	Status
Carlstrom, Vernon E.	SK3c	USS *Dobbin*
Carney, Harold F.	MM1c	MIA
Carpenter, William, M.	Ensign	CombatWingTwo
Carrier, William R.	Mus1c	Yard craft
Carroll, Jeremiah F.	WT2c	USS *Indianapolis*
Carroll, Joseph W.	F2c	MIA
Carson, Frank L.	GM3c	USS *Helm*
Carter, Robert M.	AOM1c	Naval air station
Carter, Roy D.	CM2c	USS *Pelias*
Carter, Warren B.	S2c	USS *Jarvis*
Carter, William R.	CM3c	Temporary duty—Camp Andrews
Case, Melvin	Pvt. (USMC)	Marine barracks
Cassinger, Edwin E.	F2c	MIA
Casola, Biacio	S1c	MIA
Casto, Charles R.	F1c	MIA
Casto, Richard E.	F2c	KIA/Punchbowl (P-0668)
Centers, Jackson P.	MoMM1c	Receiving station
Charrier, Roy P.	EM3c	USS *Helm*
Chassereau, Jacob F. (Jr.)	S1c	USS *Louisville*
Cheshire, James T.	CPhM	MIA
Chesney, Roman P.	MM1c	On leave in States
Chess, Patrick L.	SF3c	MIA
Chiger, Harry G.	FC3c	USS *Jarvis*
Christ, Stratis C.	CMM	USS *Enterprise*
Clark, Alto B.	Lt. (jg)	Medusa—Kingfisher Unit
Clark, David (Jr.)	S2c	MIA
Claudmantle, Arthur (Jr.)	BM2c	USS *Salt Lake City*
Clayton, Clarence L.	SM1c	Signal tower, Ford Island
Clayton, Gerald L.	SK2c	MIA
Clement, Hubert P.	FC1c	MIA
Clevenger, William L.	S1c	USS *Louisville*
Clifford, Floyd F.	S1c	MIA
Coburn, George L.	FC1c	USS *Louisville*
Coffman, William K.	S1c	USS *Pennsylvania*
Cohen, Paul J.	Ptr1c	Medusa—Kingfisher Unit

Name	Rank	Status
Coke, George A.	S1c	MIA
Cole, John A. (Jr.)	S1c	USS *Helena*
Cole, Oscar W.	S1c	USS *Helena*
Collier, Walter L.	PFC (USMC)	MIA
Collins, Glen D.	S2c	USS *Pennsylvania*
Collins, James E.	S1c	KIA/Rosedale Cemetery, Pembroke, KY
Combs, Clarence A. (Jr.)	BM2c	USS *Chester*
Comorat, Vincent J.	BM2c	USS *Salt Lake City*
Compton, Harry	CSK	Com 14 (emergency disb. off.)
Connolly, John G.	ChPC1k	MIA
Connolly, Keefe R.	HA1c	MIA
Conrad, Andrew H.	Pvt. (USMC)	USS *Chicago*
Conway, Edward L.	EM1c	MIA
Cook, Grant C. (Jr.)	F1c	MIA
Cook, John B.	Pvt. (USMC)	Marine barracks
Cooper, Claud W.	S1c	USS *Louisville*
Copeland, Louis L.	S1c	USS *Louisville*
Corkern, Carl W.	S1c	USS *Helena*
Corn, Robert L.	FC1c	MIA
Cornwell, Arnold L.	Pvt. (USMC)	USS *Indianapolis*
Corrato, Carmine	F1c	USS *Maury*
Corsette, Ted L.	Ensign	Survived: reassignment unknown
Corzatt, Beoin H.	F1c	MIA
Cotchefer, Gordon, H.	Lt. (jg)	USS *Enterprise*
Cowdry, Paul J.	S1c	USS *Louisville*
Cozart, Robert E.	S2c	USS *Louisville*
Craig, John W.	SK1c	MIA
Cremean, Alva J.	PFC (USMC)	MIA
Crenshaw, Bert W.	Y2c	Detailed at casualty office
Cress, Larkin	S1c	USS *Pennsylvania*
Cress, Lloyd B.	S1c	USS *Helena*
Crim, Warren H.	F3c	MIA
Croghan, William D.	S2c	USS *Helena*

Name	Rank	Status
Crowder, Samuel W.	F1c	MIA
Crunk, James G.	F1c	USS *Blue*
Cruz, Anthony	SF3c	USS *Chester*
Cullins, Thomas O. (Jr.)	Lt. Cmdr.	West loch
Curran, James H. (Jr.)	PFC (USMC)	Marine barracks
Curren, Virgil J.	S2c	USS *Portland*
Currier, Norman L.	GySgt. (USMC)	Marine barracks
Curry, Leonard L. (Jr.)	Y3c	Bishop Point
Curry, William McK.	EM1c	MIA
Curtis, Albert F.	S2c	USS *Helena*
Curtis, Charles R.	S1c	Naval air dispensary
Cushing, Wayne A.	S2c	USS *San Francisco*
Cuzzort, James A.	S2c	USS *Louisville*
Cymerman, Raymond A.	S1c	Receiving station
Cyrlack, Glenn G.	SK2c	MIA
Daigle, George J.	S1c	USS *Pennsylvania*
Daniels, Stewart A.	GM3c	USS *Helena*
Danneels, Francis C.	S2c	USS *Helena*
Darby, Marshall E. (Jr.)	Ensign	KIA/Punchbowl (P-1140)
Darling, Willard D.	PFC (USMC)	Marine barracks
Darulis, Frank	BM1c	USS *Northampton*
Davenport, Irvin, J.	Ensign	CombatWingTwo
Davenport, James W.	F1c	MIA
Davenport, John B.	Ensign	CombatWingTwo
Davenport, Russell M.	S1c	USS *Honolulu*
Davis, George F.	Lt.	ComBaseFour shore patrol
Davis, Lawrence M.	Y2c	Survived: reassignment unknown
Davis, Luther, L.	BM1c	Bishop Point
Davis, Robert S.	FC3c	USS *Patterson*
Day, Francis D.	CWT	MIA
Dean, Kenneth	PhM3c	Naval hospital (duty)
Dean, Nathaniel G.	F1c	USS *Louisville*
DeLeon, Rafael	OC1c	Receiving station
DeLong, George A.	S2c	USS *Helena*
DeMers, Adam W.	Ensign	Naval hospital

Name	Rank	Status
Denny, Arthur E.	GM3	MIA
Denton, Joseph A.	S2c	USS *Louisville*
Derrington, Ralph A.	CMM	MIA
Diaz, Juaquin M.	Mat2c	USS *Jarvis*
Dick, Francis E.	Mus2c	MIA
Dick, Gene R.	HA1c	Naval hospital (duty)
Dill, Leaman R.	EM2c	MIA
Dishman, Edgar E.	GM2c	USS *Balch*
Dittman, Calvin, L.	S2c	Sub base—fleet school
Dobbins, Joseph A.	SC3c	West loch
Dobosz, Jacob	MM1c	USS *Jarvis*
Dobrowolski, Marvin E.	S1c	USS *Pennsylvania*
Doernenburg, Kenneth E.	F1c	MIA
Doherty, Joseph M.	Ensign	Sub base
Doman, George A.	RM1c	Naval air station
Donald, John M.	SF3c	MIA
Donley, Jack L.	SM2c	USS *Helm*
Doore, Lyle W.	GM1c	USS *Porter*
Dorn, Willard McE.	Bkr2c	Naval air station
Dorr, Carl D.	F2c	MIA
Dougherty, Ernest L.	S1c	USS *Helena*
Dougherty, Jerry S.	S2c	USS *Northampton*
Douglass, Gordon E.	Ensign	CINCPAC
Downs, Leo B.	SC1c	Naval air station
Doyle, Bernard V.	S2c	MIA
Drake, Arvel	PFC (USMC)	Marine barracks
Drefahl, Elmer E.	Cpl. (USMC)	MIA
Druktenis, Arthur J.	PFC (USMC)	Marine barracks
Drwall, Stanislaw F.	Pmkr1c	MIA
Duncan, Curtis L.	Y3c	Receiving station
Duncan, William E.	PhM3c	Naval hospital (duty)
Dunn, Arthur R.	S1c	USS *Louisville*
Dunn, Clifford A.	S1c	Signal tower, Ford Island
Dunn, James E.	MM1c	Survived: reassignment unknown
Durbin, Edmund P.	F1c	USS *Louisville*

Name	Rank	Status
Dusset, Cyril I.	StM1c	MIA
Dyer, Buford H.	S2c	MIA
Eakes, Wallace E.	SK3c	MIA
Easley, Herschel	S1c	USS *Jarvis*
Ebberhardt, Eugene K.	MM1c	MIA
Eby, Eugene S. (Jr.)	Pvt. (USMC)	USS *Chicago*
Edmonston, David B.	S2c	MIA
Edwards, John T. (Jr.)	S1c	USS *Dewey*
Eggert, Herman M.	WT1c	USS *Northampton*
Egnatovich, Lewis J.	F1c	USS *Farragut*
Ehlert, James A.	S1c	Naval air dispensary
Ellis, Albert L. (Jr.)	S1c	USS *Helena*
Ellis, Earl M.	RM3c	MIA
Ellison, Bruce H.	RM3c	MIA
Ellsberry, Julius	StM1c	KIA/Grace Hill Cemetery, Birmingham, AL
Engen, John A.	Mus1c	Survived; reassignment unknown
England, John C.	Ensign	MIA
Erwin, Jess L.	S1c	USS *Jarvis*
Eslick, Garlen W.	S2c	Survived: reassignment unknown
Ezzel, Lester W.	GM3c	USS *Worden*
Farfan, Ignacio C.	StM1c	MIA
Farley, Bernard H.	S1c	USS *Helena*
Farley, Paul G.	Ensign	Medusa—Kingfisher Unit
Farmer, Luther J.	MM1c	KIA/New Zion Cemetery, New Zion, KY
Fecho, Lawrence H.	F1c	MIA
Felumlee, Meda W. (Jr.)	S1c	USS *Pennsylvania*
Ferguson, Charleton H.	Mus2c	MIA
Ferguson, Donald L.	S1c	USS *San Francisco*
Ferguson, Frank H.	GM1c	West loch
Ferlet, Warren J.	Cox	USS *Blue*
Fields, Robert A.	EM2c	KIA/Wilmington National Cemetery, Wilmington, NC

Name	Rank	Status
Finch, Kenneth W.	Cpl (USMC)	Marine barracks
Finnegan, William M.	Ensign	MIA
Fitzgerald, Robert D.	S2c	USS *Louisville*
Flaherty, Francis C.	Ensign	MIA
Flanagan, James M.	S2c	MIA
Florese, Felicismo	StM2c	MIA
Foerst, Arthur T.	S2c	USS *Helm*
Fogelsong, Jesse L.	S2c	Com 14
Foley, Walter C.	S1c	MIA
Fomby, William W.	GM1c	Receiving station
Foote, George P.	SK3c	MIA
Ford, George, C.	F2c	MIA
Foreman, Gerald E.	QM2c	On leave in States
Forsyth, Lytle J.	Cox	USS *Helena*
Foster, Hart E.	PhM3c	USS *Enterprise*
Foster, Idell, R.	Y3c	Detailed at casualty office
Fournier, Louis O.	Y2c	Receiving station
Francis, Paul L.	S2c	USS *Louisville*
Francisco, Pedro	OS2c	USS *Helena*
Frazier, Jack R.	S1c	West loch
Freeman, Claude P.	S1c	USS *Worden*
Freeman, Guy R.	S1c	USS *Northampton*
French, Howard C.	CPO	Yard craft office (Com 14)
French, Joy C.	S2c	KIA/Golden Gate National Cemetery, San Bruno, CA
Frey, Emanual H.	Y3c	USS *Saratoga*
Frickman, Robert J.	CWT	USS *Schley*
Fry, Richard G.	Pvt. (USMC)	Marine barracks
Fuller, Darwin L.	PFC (USMC)	Marine barracks
Furr, Ted McK.	CCM	MIA
Galajdik, Michael	F1c	MIA
Galos, Lino	OS1c	Fleet landing
Gara, Martin A.	F2c	MIA
Garcia, Jesus F.	StM2c	MIA
Garrett, Clifford T.	S1c	USS *San Francisco*

Name	Rank	Status
Garris, Eugene	StM2c	KIA/Soldier's Home National Cemetery, Washington, D.C.
Gaskill, Forest R.	Y3c	Detailed at casualty office
Gaver, Harry H. (Jr.)	2nd Lt. (USMC)	MIA
Gebser, Paul H.	MM1c	MIA
Geier, Melvin F.	S1c	MIA
Geller, Leonard R.	F1c	MIA
Genheimer, John W.	BM1c	Receiving station
George, George T.	S2c	MIA
George, William G.	S2c	USS *Northampton*
Gercevic, John W.	QM3c	Receiving station
Gerlach, Frederick H.	F3c	USS *Northampton*
Giambruno, Armando S.	PFC (USMC)	USS *Chicago*
Gibson, George H.	EM3c	MIA
Giesa, George E.	F2c	MIA
Gifford, Quentin, J.	RM2c	MIA
Gilbert, George	FC2c	MIA
Gilbert, Walter H. (Jr.)	Cpl. (USMC)	Marine barracks
Gillett, Alvah G.	Y2c	Detailed at casualty office
Gillette, Warren C.	S1c	MIA
Gilliard, Benjamin E.	StM1c	KIA/Beauford National Cemetery, Beauford, SC
Gilmore, Floyd H.	S1c	USS *Helena*
Gipson, Frank W.	FC2c	Survived: reassignment unknown
Gleason, Harry A.	F2c	USS *Northampton*
Glenn, Arthur	MM1c	MIA
Glidewell, Nelson W.	ACM2c	Signal tower, Ford Island
Gloor, Paul W.	F1c	USS *Blue*
Godfrey, Harris G.	EM1c	USS *Selfridge*
Godwin, Orvill O.	S1c	USS *Northampton*
Goggin, Daryl H.	Mach	MIA
Goins, Selden	S1c	USS *Honolulu*
Goins, Thomas O.	S2c	USS *Blue*
Goldwater, Jack R.	RM3c	MIA

Name	Rank	Status
Gomez, Charles C. (Jr.)	S2c	MIA
Gooch, George M.	EM3c	MIA
Goodwin, Clifford G.	S1c	MIA
Goodwin, Daniel B.	TC1c	Receiving station
Goodwin, Ralph R.	S2c	USS *Helena*
Goodwin, Robert	SC3c	MIA
Goodyear, Paul A.	SM3c	Signal tower, Ford Island
Gordon, Duff	CMsmth	MIA
Gordon, Jack R.	SK3c	USS *Dobbin*
Gowey, Claude O.	F1c	MIA
Graff, Kenneth E.	S2c	USS *Helena*
Graham, Wesley E.	S1c	MIA
Grand Pre, Arthur M.	F2c	KIA/St. John the Baptist Cemetery, Condo, SD
Grand Pre, John D.	F1c	USS *Northampton*
Gray, Eugene L.	Y2c	USS *Dobbin*
Gray, Robert C.	F3c	USS *Jarvis*
Greenaway, William F.	BM1c	USS *Enterprise*
Gregory, Wendell C.	S1c	USS *Pennsylvania*
Griffith, Kenneth	S1c	USS *Hull*
Griffith, Thomas E.	RM3c	MIA
Gross, Edgar D.	WT2c	MIA
Gross, George W.	SC2c	Survived: reassignment unknown
Grow, Vernon N.	S2c	MIA
Grunder, Carl C.	Cox	USS *Northampton*
Grunder, John D.	AS	USS *San Francisco*
Guisinger, Daniel L. (Jr.)	S1c	MIA
Gunning, Everett G.	S2c	USS *San Francisco*
Guoan, John F.	SF3c	USS *Pelias*
Gurganus, William I.	CEM	MIA
Gusie, William F.	FC3c	MIA
Guydry, George	RM1c	USS *Gridley*
Hailey, Thomas E.	Sgt. (USMC)	Marine barracks
Hall, Herbert P.	S2c	MIA
Hall, Ted	Pvt. (USMC)	MIA

Name	Rank	Status
Halterman, Robert E.	S1c	MIA
Ham, Harold W.	MM2c	KIA/Hillside Cemetery, St. Charles, MN
Hamblin, Frank C.	BM2c	Survived: reassignment unknown
Hamilton, Elwood F.	S1c	USS *Mahan*
Hamlin, Dale R.	GM3c	KIA/Galva Cemetery, Galva, Henry County, IL
Hamm, Mann	Lt.	USS *Pennsylvania*
Hammond, John E.	S1c	Receiving station
Hampl, George E.	S1c	USS *Helena*
Hann, Eugene P.	GM3c	KIA/Alliance City Cemetery, Alliance, OH
Hannon, Francis L.	SF3c	MIA
Hannon, John E.	AMM2c	Survived: reassignment unknown
Hannon, Thomas F.	S1c	Receiving station
Hanson, George	MM1c	MIA
Hanson, Harry E.	WT2c	USS *Helena*
Harber, James D.	Pvt. (USMC)	USS *Indianapolis*
Hardy, LeRoy B.	F1c	USS *Blue*
Harkema, Pearson	S1c	USS *Northampton*
Harlen, Robert T.	Pvt. (USMC)	USS *Chicago*
Harne, Kermit L.	BM1c	Bishop Point
Harr, Robert J.	F1c	MIA
Harrelson, Horace W.	F2c	USS *Helena*
Harrelson, Isaac W.	Y3c	Medusa—Kingfisher Unit
Harrington, Frank B.	S2c	USS *Northampton*
Harris, Benjamin F.	S1c	USS *Helena*
Harris, Charles H.	Cox	USS *Northampton*
Harris, Charles H.	EM3c	MIA
Harris, Daniel F.	CFC	MIA
Harris, Harold J.	CM1c	USS *Cummings*
Harris, John W.	S2c	USS *Helena*
Harris, Louis E. (Jr.)	Mus2c	MIA
Hartling, Gerald A.	Mus1c	Yard craft

Name	Rank	Status
Hass, Donald W.	S1c	USS *Helena*
Hatton, Anthony J.	CCStd	Receiving station
Hausladen, Anthony J.	PFC (USMC)	USS *Indianapolis*
Hausman, Eldred E.	SC2c	USS *San Francisco*
Hawkins, H. J.	S2c	Survived: reassignment unknown
Hawkins, John W.	S1c	USS *Helena*
Hayden, Albert E.	CEM	MIA
Hayes, Robert F.	S1c	USS *Phelps*
Head, Harold L.	S2c	MIA
Headington, James	FC3c	USS *Detroit*
Headington, Robert W.	S1c	MIA
Heffernan, Lloyd T.	Cox	USS *Tennessee*
Held, Kenneth G.	S1c	USS *Pennsylvania*
Hellstern, William F.	GM2c	MIA
Helton, Floyd D.	S2c	MIA
Henderson, Harry H.	Lt. Cmdr.	COM 14, ordnance salvage
Henrichsen, Jimmie L.	S2c	MIA
Henry, Otis W.	Pvt. (USMC)	KIA/Kittle Cemetery, West Branch, MI
Henry, Walter F.	FC1c	USS *Mugford*
Hensen, William E. (Jr.)	S2c	KIA/Ashdown Cemetery, Ashdown, TX
Hentschel, Robert K.	AOM3c	Naval air station
Herber, Harvey C.	EM1c	MIA
Herbert, George	GM1c	MIA
Herman, Warren H.	S1c	USS *Jarvis*
Herms, Gunther A.	S1c	USS *Helena*
Heslar, Robert L.	S2c	USS *Mahan*
Hesler, Austin H.	SM3c	MIA
Hicks, Charles C.	GM3c	USS *McCall*
Higday, Gilbert H.	F2c	USS *Chester*
High, John M.	SC1c	On leave in States
Hill, Willis W.	F3c	USS *Helena*
Hilton, Fred T.	BM1c	USS *Enterprise*
Hines, Lloyd A.	Pvt. (USMC)	USS *Indianapolis*

Name	Rank	Status
Hinrichs, Herman J.	F3c	USS *Helena*
Hinsberger, Wilbur T.	S2c	USS *Honolulu*
Hiskett, Denis H.	F1c	MIA
Hittorff, Joseph P. (Jr.)	Ensign	MIA
Hixon, Clyde	S1c	USS *Northampton*
Hoag, Frank S. (Jr.)	RM3c	MIA
Hoard, Herbert J.	CSK	MIA
Hobby, William M. (Jr.)	Lt. Cmdr.	Sub base
Hobson, Tom	Pvt. (USMC)	USS *Chicago*
Hoffman, Joseph W.	Mus1c	MIA
Hoffman, Melvin H.	S2c	USS *Northampton*
Hoffman, Norman C.	Lt. (jg)	COM 14, naval district
Holden, Arnold L.	CWT	USS *Enterprise*
Hollis, Don V.	S1c	USS *Pennsylvania*
Holm, Kenneth L.	F3c	MIA
Holmes, Harry R.	F3c	MIA
Holmes, Lannie, L.	S1c	USS *Northampton*
Holmes, Robert K.	PFC (USMC)	MIA
Holst, Floyd N.	S2c	Naval air dispensary
Holtel, Alphonse B.	BM2c	USS *Louisville*
Holtel, Paul J.	S2c	USS *San Francisco*
Holzhauer, James W.	S1c	MIA
Hopkins, Edwin C.	F3c	MIA
Hord, Chester C.	SK3c	MIA
Hornkohl, Irvin W.	AS	Sub base—fleet school
Hovatter, Branson G.	F1c	On leave in States
Howland, Frank S.	BM1c	Bishop Point
Hryniewicz, Frank A.	S1c	MIA
Hudson, Charles E.	WT1c	MIA
Huey, Dennis L.	RM2c	Survived: reassignment unknown
Huff, Robert L.	Cpl. (USMC)	Marine barracks
Hughes, Vincent E.	CM3c	USS *Pelias*
Hull, Donald L.	PFC (USMC)	USS *Chicago*
Hull, Irvin M.	CM2c	USS *Medusa*
Hultgren, Lorentz E.	MM2c	MIA

Name	Rank	Status
Hunt, Harold F.	S2c	USS *Dewey*
Hunt, Harry M.	S2c	USS *Pennsylvania*
Hunt, Lucian J. (Jr.)	Ensign	West loch
Hunter, Major L.	EM3c	USS *Jarvis*
Hunter, Robert M.	Ensign	KIA/Punchbowl (P-0681)
Husted, Richard C.	S1c	USS *Dewey*
Huston, James A.	S2c	USS *Northampton*
Hutchens, Paul C.	S1c	USS *San Francisco*
Hutchison, Joseph E.	Cpl. (USMC)	Marine barracks
Ingram, Darrell L.	Cox	CINCPAC
Ingram, William T.	Lt. (jg)	Naval air station
Inlow, Roy W.	S1c	CINCPAC
Iszard, Howard E.	S2c	USS *Honolulu*
Iverson, Glaydon I. C.	F3c	MIA
Jackson, Robert B.	S2c	USS *Helena*
Jackson, Robert F.	BM1c	Naval hospital
Jackson, Willie	OC1c	MIA
Jacobs, Charlie B.	PFC (USMC)	Marine barracks
Jacobson, Herbert B.	F3c	MIA
Jaques, Loney	EM3c	USS *Allen*
James, Challis R.	S2c	MIA
Jankowski, Chester F.	F3c	USS *Helena*
Jansen, Ralph N.	S2c	Naval air station (aviation unit)
Jarding, George W.	F3c	KIA/St. Ann's Cemetery, Humbolt, SD
Jayne, Kenneth W.	F3c	MIA
Jennings, Charles R.	Pvt. (USMC)	USS *Indianapolis*
Jensen, Jesse B.	GM3c	KIA/Nuuanu Cemetery, Honolulu, HI
Jensen, Stanley K.	FC3c	USS *Enterprise*
Jensen, Theodore Q.	RM3c	MIA
Johannes, Charles H.	S2c	MIA
Johnson, Billy J.	F1c	MIA
Johnson, Charles A.	SF2c	USS *Medusa*
Johnson, Dwight L.	Lt. (jg)	Yard office

Name	Rank	Status
Johnson, Edward D.	F1c	MIA
Johnson, Hardy N.	PFC (USMC)	USS *Indianapolis*
Johnson, Harold E.	S2c	USS *Worden*
Johnson, Harold O.	S1c	USS *Helena*
Johnson, Joel W.	GM3c	USS *Chester*
Johnson, John V.	S2c	USS *Northampton*
Johnson, Joseph M.	S1c	MIA
Johnson, Kenneth F.	S1c	USS *Hull*
Johnson, Raleigh E.	SK2c	Survived: reassignment unknown
Johnson, Ralph E.	S1c	USS *Northampton*
Johnston, Jim H.	F1c	MIA
Jones, Bobbie G.	F1c	USS *Northampton*
Jones, Charles A.	S2c	MIA
Jones, Fred M.	MM1c	MIA
Jones, George F.	S1c	USS *Helena*
Jones, Herman	GM2c	USS *Porter*
Jones, Howard E.	AMM3c	Naval air station
Jones, Jerry	StM3c	MIA
Jones, Ralph E. (Jr.)	Cox	USS *Northampton*
Jones, Stanton E.	S1c	USS *Helena*
Jordon, Julian B.	Lt.	MIA
Jordon, Wesley V.	S1c	MIA
Ju Aire, Jean J.	F2c	USS *Farragut*
Juanick, Joseph J.	S1c	Survived: reassignment unknown
Jurashen, Charles S.	SF1c	USS *Enterprise*
Jurashen, Thomas V.	S1c	Died December 15, 1941/Mt. Carmel Cemetery, Belleville, St. Clair Co., IL
Jurashen, William M.	F3c	USS *Saratoga*
Kalman, Jesse T.	SC3c	Naval air station
Kaltreider, Daniel R.	BM1c	Receiving station
Kane, Albert U.	F1c	MIA
Karli, John A.	S1c	MIA
Keaton, Vernon P.	Pvt. (USMC)	MIA

Name	Rank	Status
Keefe, William A.	Ensign	USS *Dale*
Keenum, Carl W.	CBM	Receiving station
Keffer, Howard V.	RM3c	MIA
Kegley, Emil W.	F1c	USS *Chester*
Keil, Ralph H.	S1c	MIA
Keller, Donald G.	S1c	MIA
Kelley, Hubert P.	S1c	USS *Northampton*
Kelley, Joe M.	S2c	MIA
Kellogg, Gayle H.	F1c	USS *Louisville*
Kelly, Chester E.	F1c	USS *Hull*
Kelly, Gilbert L.	S2c	USS *Northampton*
Kelly, James	Mat3c	USS *Dale*
Kelly, Joseph L.	S1c	Naval air dispensary
Kempf, Warren J.	RM3c	MIA
Keninger, Leo T.	F1c	MIA
Kennedy, Herbert S.	QM3c	Receiving station
Kennedy, Jesse S.	GM3c	USS *Helena*
Kennedy, William H.	F1c	MIA
Kenworthy, Jesse L. (Jr.)	Cmdr.	West loch
Kenyon, Vern W.	S1c	USS *Helena*
Kerestes, Elmer T.	F1c	MIA
Kesler, David L.	Bkr2c	MIA
Kesler, Gerald L.	S1c	USS *Northampton*
Kiefer, Wilbur E.	GM3c	USS *Louisville*
Kiley, Charles W.	Cox	USS *Saratoga*
Kimmons, Earl F.	S1c	USS *Pennsylvania*
Kinart, Keith N.	S1c	USS *Northampton*
Kinderman, Robert R.	F1c	USS *Hull*
King, Daniel	CTC	USS *Maryland*
King, Edker L.	GM3c	USS *Northampton*
King, James H.	S2c	USS *Helena*
Kirk, Lyle O.	EM2c	USS *Honolulu*
Kirves, Elmer E. C.	CM1c	USS *Oklahoma* post office
Klasing, William A.	EM3c	MIA
Klein, Edward G.	GM3c	Receiving station
Knight, Francis W.	SM3c	Signal tower, Ford Island

Name	Rank	Status
Knight, George S.	S1c	Receiving station
Knights, Richard P.	EM1c	USS *Honolulu*
Knipp, Verne F.	Cox	MIA
Koch, Robert O.	F1c	USS *Chester*
Koester, Melvin L.	S1c	USS *Pennsylvania*
Kolb, Leon C.	GM2c	USS *Balch*
Kolb, William	S1c	USS *San Francisco*
Kolodziej, Jan	EM1c	USS *Pelias*
Kosek, Ben	S1c	USS *San Francisco*
Kotowski, Henry P.	BM2c	USS *Pelias*
Kottong, Harold	F1c	USS *Indianapolis*
Kovein, Donald M.	S1c	USS *Phelps*
Kozlowitz, Robert S.	S2c	USS *San Francisco*
Kozlowski, Stanley J.	FC3c	USS *Northampton*
Krames, Edward C.	S1c	USS *Helena*
Krause, Kenneth R.	S2c	USS *Louisville*
Krause, Lloyd S.	S1c	USS *San Francisco*
Krell, Don F.	S2c	Sub base—fleet school
Krueger, Doran C.	GM3c	West loch
Kuhn, Malvin G.	S1c	USS *Northampton*
Kvalnes, Hans C.	S2c	KIA/Punchbowl (C-1062)
Kvidera, William L.	CM3c	MIA
Kyser, D. T.	S2c	MIA
Laing, Kirk D.	S1c	USS *Northampton*
Lakers, John B.	Y3c	Naval air dispensary
Laman, Charles E. (Jr.)	F1c	MIA
Langford, Alva D.	S1c	USS *Northampton*
Larson, Elliott D.	S1c	MIA
Larson, Harry O.	S1c	USS *Helena*
Latourette, John G.	S1c	Naval air station
Laurie, Johnnie C.	StM1c	MIA
Lawrence, Elmer P.	S1c	MIA
Lawrence, Everett L.	S1c	USS *Helena*
Lawrence, L. R.	Elec.	Survived: reassignment unknown
Lawson, Willard I.	F3c	MIA

Name	Rank	Status
Lawter, Joseph M.	Fmfc	Marine barracks
Lay, Leo M.	PhM1c	USS *Pennsylvania*
Leach, Otis C.	PFC (USMC)	USS *Chicago*
Lehman, Gerald G.	F3c	MIA
Lehman, Lawrence K.	S2c	USS *Louisville*
Lehman, Myron K.	S2c	MIA
Leigh, Miles J.	S2c	USS *Helena*
Lentz, Francis G.	F1c	USS *Blue*
Leomascola, Vincent	S2c	USS *Saratoga*
Leon-Guerrero, Jesus A.	Mat1c	USS *Honolulu*
Leonard, Cecil B.	F3c	USS *Salt Lake City*
Leonardi, Lewis F.	S2c	USS *Hull*
Lescault, Lionel W.	BgMstr2c	MIA
Lester, Don A.	S1c	USS *Phelps*
Letourneau, Marsall J.	CGM	Survived: reassignment unknown
Lett, James H.	WT1c	Survived: reassignment unknown
Levasseur, Julian J.	Lt. Cmdr. (SC)	Supply dept., navy yard
Lewis, Harold L.	Mus1c	Yard craft
Lewis, Robert J.	S2c	USS *San Francisco*
Lindsey, Harold W.	S2c	MIA
Lindsley, John H.	F3c	MIA
Link, William T.	CSF	USS *Medusa*
Linnartz, Luther L.	F3c	MIA
Little, Philip E.	AS	USS *Hull*
Livingston, Alfred E.	F3c	KIA/Worthington Cemetery, Worthington, IN
Lochner, Robert C.	Sc3c	Receiving station
Lockwood, Clarence M.	WT2c	MIA
Loebach, Adolph J.	FC3c	MIA
Logan, Robert L.	ACMM	Naval air station
Loganbuhl, Bernard J.	Bkr2c	USS *Medusa*
Long, Henry A.	RM3c	USS *Schley*
Love, Joseph E.	BM2c	USS *Waters*
Lovrien, Warren G.	Fm (USMC)	Marine barracks

Name	Rank	Status
Lowell, Harold F.	S1c	USS *Helena*
Lowery, Donald B.	Pvt. (USMC)	USS *Chicago*
Lubanski, Frank A.	S2c	USS *Farragut*
Lucas, Carlton C.	Lt.	Medusa—Kingfisher Unit
Luckadoo, Jack H.	S1c	USS *Tennessee*
Luebke, Celestine C.	Cox	USS *Helena*
Luke, Vernon T.	MM1c	MIA
Lusche, Carroll G.	ChCk (USMC)	Marine barracks
Lutenegger, Walter J.	S1c	USS *Tennessee*
Luttrell, Richard N.	S1c	Signal tower, Ford Island
Lynn, Clarence D.	GM1c	USS *Allen*
Mabine, Octavius	StM1c	MIA
Madden, Harold S.	Y2c	USS *Jarvis*
Magers, Howard S.	S2c	MIA
Mahaffey, Jesse A.	S1c	USS *Northampton*
Malek, Michael	S2c	MIA
Malfante, Algeo V.	SF2c	MIA
Mallon, Charles W.	PFC (USMC)	Marine barracks
Manning, Walter B.	EM1c	MIA
Marksman, Paul A.	S1c	USS *Helena*
Marshall, William H.	EM3c	Receiving station
Martinez, Francisco P.	Mat1c	USS *Detroit*
Mason, Harold G.	S2c	USS *Northampton*
Mason, Henry C.	Mus1c	MIA
Mathieson, Harry L.	F1c	Com 14
Mathieson, Louis R.	F1c	USS *Hull*
Matthews, George W. (Jr.)	F1c	USS *Helm*
Matthews, James E.	Bkr3c	USS *Louisville*
Mattingly, Joseph P.	S2c	USS *Northampton*
Maule, Joseph K.	S1c	MIA
Maxon, Robert P.	S1c	USS *Tennessee*
Maxwell, James A.	GM3c	USS *Louisville*
Mayfield, Everett R.	S1c	USS *San Francisco*
McBeth, Charles F.	GM1c	USS *Blue*
McBride, Jack L.	S2c	USS *San Francisco*
McCabe, Edwin B.	WT1c	MIA

Name	Rank	Status
McCleary, Malcolm J.	S2c	USS *San Francisco*
McCloud, Donald R.	FC2c	MIA
McCullough, M. L. (Jr.)	Lt.	Naval air dispensary
McDonald, Douglas G.	S2c	USS *Helena*
McDonald, James O.	F1c	MIA
McDowell, John R.	GM3c	USS *Helena*
McFall, John T.	Ensign	Wounded. Naval air dispensary
McGaffin, Albert A.	S2c	West loch
McGinty, John A.	F2c	USS *Farragut*
McGlynn, James J.	QM2c	On leave in States
McGuire, Charles S.	S2c	USS *Honolulu*
McIver, Edsel V.	S2c	USS *San Francisco*
McKee, Wayne T.	QM3c	USS *Fanning*
McKeenan, Bert E.	F1c	MIA
McKinney, William R.	Ensign	Camp Andrews
McKissack, Hale	S1c	MIA
McKnight, Edward J.	PFC (USMC)	Marine barracks
McLaughlin, James W.	S1c	USS *Northampton*
McLaughlin, Lloyd E.	S2c	MIA
McLellon, Waldron M.	Ensign	Sub base
McMahon, Robert J.	QM2c	USS *Enterprise*
McMeans, Ralph H.	S1c	USS *Louisville*
McMillan, Edward G.	S2c	USS *Portland*
McMillan, John D.	S2c	USS *Northampton*
McNary, Ralph E.	S2c	USS *Northampton*
McNeil, R. H.	S2c	Survived: reassignment unknown
McPherson, Carl R. (Jr.)	Pvt. (USMC)	Marine barracks
McQuay, Clayton W.	TC1c	USS *Helena*
McQuilkin, John M.	S2c	Naval air dispensary
McStay, Hugh F. (Jr.)	CGM	Receiving station
McVey, David G.	S1c	USS *Northampton*
Melton, Earl R.	MM1c	MIA
Melton, Herbert F.	BM2c	KIA/Punchbowl (C-1288)
Meyer, Herbert W.	GM3c	USS *Enterprise*

Name	Rank	Status
Meyer, Louis B.	GM3c	USS *Hull*
Middleswart, John F.	PFC (USMC)	MIA
Mihalka, Alex M.	Cox	USS *Salt Lake City*
Mihalko, Michael P.	S1c	USS *Saratoga*
Milam, A. J. (Jr.)	S2c	Receiving station
Miles, Archie T.	MM2c	MIA
Miller, Curtis E.	F1c	MIA
Miller, Donald H.	S1c	USS *Louisville*
Miller, Jack V.	S1c	Receiving station
Miller, Merle L.	F2c	USS *San Francisco*
Miller, Posey	GM3c	Survived: reassignment unknown
Millman, John P.	PhM2c	Naval hospital (Duty)
Mink, Joe P.	1st Sgt. (USMC)	Marine barracks
Mitchell, Wallace G.	S1c	MIA
Mitschek, Erwin P.	S1c	Receiving station
Mixter, William A.	F1c	USS *Blue*
Moeller, Elmer J	Y2c	West loch
Monoghan, John M. (Jr.)	S2c	USS *Northampton*
Monroe, Leroy L.	S1c	USS *Salt Lake City*
Monseu, Joseph P.	Y2c	Receiving station
Montgomery, Charles A.	RM3c	MIA
Moone, Joseph E.	ARM2c	On leave in States
Moore, Clarence R.	F2c	USS *Chester*
Moorhouse, Marshel	RM3c	Receiving station
Moran, George A.	GM3c	USS *Gridley*
Morey, William R.	Ensign AV (N)	Medusa—Kingfisher Unit
Morris, Marvin L.	Cox	Receiving station
Mortenson, Adolph H.	Ensign	Commander battle force
Moss, George L.	F1c	USS *Blue*
Mueller, Donald R.	GM3c	USS *Allen*
Mulick, John M.	HA1c	MIA
Mullaley, Clarence J.	S1c	USS *Honolulu*
Mullen, Elmer H.	S1c	Signal tower, Ford Island
Muller, William G. (Jr.)	2nd Lt. (USMC)	Marine barracks
Murphy, George D. (Jr.)	S1c	USS *San Francisco*

Name	Rank	Status
Mycock, William F.	GM3c	USS *Worden*
Myers, Ray H.	S2c	MIA
Naegle, George E.	S1c	MIA
Nail, Elmer D.	F1c	MIA
Nance, Rufus F.	BM2c	USS *Enterprise*
Nash, Maurice L.	S2c	USS *Northampton*
Nash, Paul A.	FC1c	MIA
Naugle, Edwin C.	GM3c	USS *Northampton*
Neeser, Henry F.	S1c	Survived: reassignment unknown
Neher, Don O.	EM3c	MIA
Neil, John L.	F2c	USS *Louisville*
Nelms, Lonnie T.	CGM	Receiving station
Nelson, Ervin R.	S1c	USS *Southampton*
Nelson, Everett	S2c	USS *San Francisco*
Nelson, Johnnie H.	S1c	Receiving station
Nelson, Lewis C.	S1c	USS *Louisville*
Nelson, Mervwyn C.	S1c	USS *Blue*
Neuenschwander, Arthur C.	GM1c	MIA
Nevill, Sam D.	Y3c	MIA
Newman, Jacob L.	CTC	Survived: reassignment unknown
Newton, John F.	S2c	Receiving station
Newton, Wilbur F.	S1c	MIA
Nicholes, John C.	WT2c	USS *Schley*
Nichols, Carl	S2c	MIA
Nichols, Harry E.	SK3c	MIA
Niehus, Everild A.	GM3c	USS *Hull*
Nielsen, Arnold M.	BM1c	MIA
Nigg, Edward L.	S2c	USS *Northampton*
Nigg, Herbert G.	S1c	USS *Northampton*
Nigg, Laverne A.	S2c	MIA
Nigg, Robert F.	S2c	USS *Northampton*
Nightengale, Joe R.	S1c	MIA
Niles, Richard M.	Ensign	USS *Maryland*
Nix, Charles E.	SM3c	MIA

Name	Rank	Status
Noe, James W.	S2c	USS *San Francisco*
Noonan, Frank A.	S2c	USS *Helm*
Norman, Donald O.	Pvt. (USMC)	USS *Indianapolis*
Novac, Michael F.	S1c	USS *Helm*
Nuckolis, Francis J.	S2c	Receiving station
O'Dell, Harold E.	CEM	CEM
O'Donnell, Thomas	S2c	USS *Northampton*
O'Donovan, Charles E.	S2c	USS *Northampton*
Ogle, Charles R.	F1c	MIA
Ogrady, Camillus M.	S1c	Survived: reassignment unknown
Oleson, Harald R.	TC1c	USS *Helena*
Ollom, Donald J.	Pvt. (USMC)	Marine barracks
Olsen, Eli	SK3c	MIA
Olsen, Norman A.	S2c	Sub base—fleet school
O'Neill, Francis J.	GM3c	USS *Helena*
Ortmann, Jackson H.	SF2c	USS *Medusa*
Ostberg, Harry H.	CCStd	USS *Grebe*
Osterby, Alvin E.	GM3c	USS *Monaghan*
Outland, Jarvis G.	F1c	MIA
Overley, Lawrence J.	FC2c	MIA
Owsley, Alphard S.	EM3c	MIA
Oxford, William A.	Cox	West loch
Pace, Jesse M.	Cox	Com 14
Pace, Millard C.	F1c	MIA
Padgett, James F.	S1c	Survived: reassignment unknown
Palides, James J.	Mus2c	MIA
Palmer, Calvin H.	S2c	MIA
Palmer, Paul E.	F1c	MIA
Palmer, Roger A.	Fc3c	USS *Jarvis*
Palmer, Wilfred D.	S2c	MIA
Paradis, George L.	PhM3c	MIA
Parker, Isacc	Mat3c	MIA
Parker, Linwood P.	GM3c	Bishops Point
Parker, Norman R.	S1c	USS *Louisville*

Name	Rank	Status
Parkins, Alfred S.	SK3c	USS *Pennsylvania*
Parkins, Ellis J.	GM3c	USS *Selfridge*
Parkinson, Clayton L.	S2c	USS *Jarvis*
Parkinson, Francis R.	F1c	USS *Northampton*
Parks, William G.	S1c	USS *Louisville*
Parnell, Orville E.	S1c	USS *Louisville*
Parnell, Roy C.	S1c	USS *Louisville*
Parris, Harold J.	S1c	USS *Helena*
Pascual, Roman R.	CCk	Survived: reassignment unknown
Pask, William F.	F1c	Survived: reassignment unknown
Patrick, Delbert J.	PltSgt. (USMC)	Marine barracks
Pauly, Thomas S. (Jr.)	SF3c	Survived: reassignment unknown
Peak, Robert H.	Pvt.	KIA/Punchbowl (A-0524)
Pearce, Dale F.	S2c	MIA
Peigler, Frank K.	S1c	USS *Northampton*
Pence, Archibald B.	S2c	USS *Helena*
Pennington, Raymond	Pvt. (USMC)	KIA/Golden Gate National Cemetery, sec. L, 3–5346
Pentico, Walter R.	S2c	MIA
Penwell, Jones C.	GM3c	USS *Flusser*
Pepe, Stephen	WT1c	MIA
Perdok, Michael	Mach.	Com 14
Perdue, Charles F.	SF1c	MIA
Perrett, William A.	EM1c	USS *Medusa*
Peterson, Roy W.	GM3c	USS *Gridley*
Petway, Wiley J.	BM2c	KIA/Hampton National Cemetery, Phoebus area, sec. F-214
Phillips, Charles W.	CMM	CINCPAC
Phillips, Milo E.	WT1c	MIA
Phipps, James N.	S2c	MIA
Pickett, Bernard E.	WT1c	USS *Chester*
Pickins, Robert S.	GM1c	Fleet pooling off. rec. bks.

Name	Rank	Status
Pilgrim, Louis H.	S2c	USS *Louisville*
Pirtle, Gerald H.	F1c	MIA
Pirtle, Grover C. (Jr.)	GM2c	USS *Lawson*
Piskuran, Rudolph V.	S2c	MIA
Pitke, Dale H.	MM2c	On leave in States
Pittman, Delbert L.	S2c	Survived: reassignment unknown
Plumb, Anthony C.	1stMus	Yard craft
Poindexter, Herbert J. (Jr.)	S1c	MIA
Polk, Howard M.	F2c	USS *Salt Lake City*
Polk, Wendell R.	Lt. (jg)	Survived: reassignment unknown
Polk, Woodrow A.	Sgt. (USMC)	Survived: reassignment unknown
Polston, Samuel L.	CM2c	Medusa—Kingfisher Unit
Poole, Julian L.	Y3c	Receiving station
Poplofsky, Isadore K.	S2c	USS *Helena*
Postlethwaite, Ralph E.	BM1c	USS *Salt Lake City*
Potts, Westley F.	BM2c	USS *Worden*
Powell, Thomas O.	S1c	Naval air station
Pray, Oren (Jr.)	S2c	USS *Dewey*
Prewitt, Brady O.	S2c	MIA
Pribble, Robert L.	FC3c	MIA
Price, George F.	F1c	MIA
Price, George G.	Pvt. (USMC)	USS *Chicago*
Price, James H.	S1c	USS *Louisville*
Pride, Lewis B. (Jr.)	Ensign	MIA
Prythero, Norman	S2c	USS *Worden*
Pue, Jasper L. (Jr.)	F3c	MIA
Purcell, James (Jr.)	F3c	USS *Jarvis*
Quatlebaun, Lanie C.	GM1c	Receiving station
Ragland, Norman C. (Jr.)	S2c	USS *Conyngham*
Rahder, Donald W.	BM2c	USS *Saratoga*
Rahlfs, Donald J.	F1c	USS *Rigel*
Raimond, Paul S.	S1c	Survived: reassignment unknown

Name	Rank	Status
Rainey, Frank W.	EM3c	USS *Jarvis*
Ramsey, Elgin D.	F1c	USS *Allen*
Rauch, Edward C.	PFC (USMC)	USS *Indianapolis*
Ray, Eldon C.	SK3c	MIA
Ray, Jennings B.	Gun. (USMC)	Survived: reassignment unknown
Raymond, Glenn H.	S1c	USS *Northampton*
Reagan, Dan E.	F1c	MIA
Redyk, Milton	F1c	USS *Farragut*
Reed, Richard E.	Pvt. (USMC)	Marine barracks
Reese, Pauline G.	CM1c	USS *Pelias*
Regan, Leo B.	WT1c	Survived: reassignment unknown
Reyelts, Duane H.	S2c	USS *Dewey*
Reynolds, Clifford M.	S1c	Naval air station (aviation unit)
Rice, Irvin F.	RM3c	MIA
Rich, Porter L.	WT2c	MIA
Rich, William A.	S1c	USS *Montgomery*
Richmond, Raymond L.	S2c	Receiving station
Ridenour, Clyde (Jr.)	RM3c	MIA
Riggs, Francis E.	Cox	USS *Pennsylvania*
Riley, David J.	S2c	MIA
Risher, Charles M.	Pvt. (USMC)	USS *Indianapolis*
Ritch, Nelson R.	GM3c	Survived: reassignment unknown
Roach, Russell C.	S1c	KIA/Punchbowl (Q-1048), grave marked Unknown
Robb, Samuel E.	S1c	USS *San Francisco*
Roberts, Clyde	CMM	USS *Enterprise*
Roberts, Howard E. (Jr.)	Cox	USS *Tennessee*
Roberts, Howard G.	Lt. (jg) (MC)	Sub base
Roberts, Norman O.	S1c	Receiving station
Roberts, Orville W.	S1c	USS *Louisville*
Robertson, Earl O.	F1c	MIA
Robertson, John B. (Jr.)	Lt.	Commander base force

Name	Rank	Status
Robertson, Joseph N.	S2c	MIA
Robinson, Glenn H.	S1c	USS *San Francisco*
Rochel, Emil H.	BM2c	USS *Enterprise*
Rodina, John A.	Cox	Receiving station
Rodriguez, Richard	Ensign	CINCPAC flag.
Roesch, Harold W.	S1c	MIA
Rogers, Walter B.	F1c	MIA
Rohow, Fred M.	Cmdr. MC	Wounded. Naval hospital, Pearl Harbor
Rohrer, Robert R.	S2c	USS *Worden*
Roiland, Harold S.	S1c	Receiving station
Romans, John J.	S1c	USS *Patterson*
Rommel, Herbert F.	Ensign	Sub base
Ross, George W.	GM2c	USS *Patterson*
Ross, Richard P. (Jr.)	Capt. (USMC)	Marine barracks
Rouse, Joseph C.	S1c	MIA
Roysden, James H.	S2c	USS *Helena*
Ruff, John L.	S1c	USS *Helena*
Rumrill, George F.	S1c	Receiving station
Ruse, Charles L.	Mus2c	KIA/Punchbowl (Q-0582)
Rush, Henry L.	CWT	Receiving station
Russell, David W. (Jr.)	S1c	USS *Mahan*
Russell, Delbert L.	S1c	USS *Northampton*
Russell, George E.	S2c	USS *Mahon*
Russell, Leroy S.	WT2c	USS *Jarvis*
Russell, Thomas H.	CMM	USS *Enterprise*
Russo, Francisco J.	Cox	USS *Pelias*
Ryan, Edmund T.	Y3c	MIA
Ryburn, Robert D.	S1c	Signal tower, Ford Island
Sabo, Eugene	PFC (USMC)	Marine barracks
Sadlowski, Roman W.	EM3c	MIA
Salaski, Arthur A.	SM2c	Signal tower, Ford Island
Salmons, Chester R.	S1c	USS *Northampton*
Salter, Glen K.	PFC	USS *Chicago*
Sammis, Lee M.	Cox	USS *Allen*
Sampson, Kenneth H.	S1c	MIA

Name	Rank	Status
Sandall, Albert F.	Cox	Com 14
Sandall, John A.	S1c	USS *Helena*
Sandberg, Elbert O. T.	S1c	USS *Northampton*
Sanders, Dean S.	CMM	MIA
Sandlin, James E.	S2c	USS *Farragut*
Sands, Leslie K.	Ensign	Sub base
Santos, Miguel S.	StM3c	USS *Saratoga*
Sauer, Andrew P.	SM3c	USS *Blue*
Saul, James J.	F2c	USS *Farragut*
Saunders, Charles L.	S2c	MIA
Savage, Lyle J.	S1c	MIA
Savarese, Michael J.	S1c	USS *Honolulu*
Savich, Stanley G.	S1c	USS *Louisville*
Savidge, John E.	S1c	MIA
Saylor, Paul E.	F1c	MIA
Scamporino, Joseph A.	S1c	USS *Northampton*
Schaid, Charles R. (Jr.)	Mus1c	Yard craft
Schauf, William P.	S2c	USS *Honolulu*
Schempp, John T.	SM1c	Signal tower, Ford Island
Schleiter, Walter F.	F1c	MIA
Schleuter, James V.	Bkr3c	Naval air station
Schlink, Richard A.	PhM2c	Naval hospital (duty)
Schmidt, Herman	GM3c	MIA
Schmitt, Aloysius H.	Lt. (jg) ChC	MIA
Schmitz, Andrew J.	F1c	MIA
Schoonover, John H.	PhM1c	MIA
Schreiner, Dale R.	S2c	USS *Chester*
Schultz, Clyde I.	S1c	USS *Hull*
Schwartz, Robert J.	SK1c	Com 14
Schweizer, Frederick O.	Ensign	Sub base
Scott, A. G.	GM3c	Receiving station
Scott, Bernard O.	StM1c	KIA/Richmond National Cemetery, 1B-5524
Scott, Edward L.	RM3c	USS *Northampton*
Scott, Frank H.	S1c	USS *Honolulu*
Scott, Harry L. (Jr.)	S1c	USS *San Francisco*

Name	Rank	Status
Scott, James W.	F1c	USS *Blue*
Scott, John W.	SK2c	USS *Blue*
Scott, Rodney J.	GM3c	USS *Helm*
Seale, Marlin S.	PFC (USMC)	Marine barracks
Sears, John A.	BM1c	Bishops Point
Seaton, Chester E.	F1c	Survived: reassignment unknown
Sebo, Harold J.	S1c	USS *Helena*
Sederstrom, Verdi D.	Ensign SC	MIA
Seidel, Lawrence S.	S2c	USS *Chester*
Sellers, Leslie A.	SK2c	Receiving station
Sellon, Robert C.	RM3c	USS *Northampton*
Sellon, William L.	S2c	MIA
Severinson, Everett I.	SF1c	KIA/Punchbowl (C-0631)
Shacklett, Chester G. (Jr.)	Cox	USS *Waters*
Shafer, William K.	F2c	MIA
Shanahan, William J. (Jr.)	SM3c	MIA
Shannon, William W.	S1c	Naval air dispensary
Sheldon, Edward J.	FC1c	MIA
Sherman, Gerald A.	WT2c	On leave in States
Sherman, Thomas C.	CWT	USS *Enterprise*
Sherwin, Sidney A. (Jr.)	Ensign	Sub base
Shipman, Thurman J.	GM2c	USS *Tennessee*
Shoemake, Edward C.	S1c	USS *Hull*
Shook, Gordon T.	S1c	USS *Northampton*
Short, Horace C. (Jr.)	S1c	Naval air dispensary
Showalter, Howard A.	S1c	USS *Phelps*
Shrader, Warren H.	S1c	USS *Chester*
Sidener, Donald L.	S2c	USS *Saratoga*
Silva, William G.	GM1c	KIA/9100 Forest Lawn Cemetery, Glendale, CA, sec. Immortality, lot 1320, grave 2
Simmons, George A.	BM2c	USS *Waters*
Simons, Jack W.	Mus2c	Yard craft
Skaggs, Eugene M.	SM1c	MIA

Name	Rank	Status
Skiles, Garold L.	S2c	KIA/Punchbowl (C-0623)
Skinner, Kenneth E.	S2c	USS *Helena*
Skjaret, Jalmer H.	SF1c	USS *Northampton*
Skorzak, Walter A.	RM3c	Survived: reassignment unknown
Slagter, Arthur G.	MM1c	USS *Chester*
Slapikas, Edward F.	S1c	Survived: reassignment unknown
Sleeter, George F.	Y3c	Receiving station
Slusher, Raymond E.	S2c	USS *Chester*
Smith, George A.	S2c	USS *Preble*
Smith, George B.	CY	Detailed casualty office
Smith, George H. (Jr.)	S2c	USS *Helena*
Smith, Harry A.	S1c	Signal tower Ford Island
Smith, Herbert O.	CBM	Com 14
Smith, Joe K.	Cox	USS *Tennessee*
Smith, Leonard F.	Msmth1c	MIA
Smith, Lester A.	S1c	USS *Tennessee*
Smith, Lester F.	F2c	USS *Salt Lake City*
Smith, Marion E.	S1c	USS *Chester*
Smith, Merle A.	EM3c	MIA
Smith, Merton R.	RM3c	CINCPAC
Smith, Norman E.	GM3c	USS *Helena*
Smith, Roland H.	Mus1c	MIA
Smith, Samuel D.	F1c	USS *Louisville*
Smith, Virgil	CGM	Mine depot, west loch
Smith, Walter R.	S1c	USS *Waters*
Snyder, Melvin E.	S2c	USS *Helena*
Sollie, Walter H.	WT1c	MIA
Solomon, James C.	S1c	MIA
Sonntag, William F.	S1c	USS *Hull*
Spangler, Maurice V.	S1c	MIA
Sparks, Victor T.	GM3c	USS *Benham*
Spaulding, Albert B.	Cox	USS *Louisville*
Speights, Ellis D.	AsstCk	Marine barracks
Spence, Arlemando J.	BM2c	USS *Salt Lake City*

Name	Rank	Status
Spence, George T.	S2c	USS *Helena*
Spencer, Frank R.	RM2c	USS *Drayton*
Spencer, John C.	Ensign	Sub base
Spitler, Joseph C.	Ensign	COMDESFLOT one rec. station
Staff, Walter F.	CM2c	USS *Medusa*
Stallings, James E.	S2c	USS *Pruitt*
Standal, Merton O.	S2c	MIA
Stanford, Kenneth E.	GM3c	USS *Helena*
Stangle, Leonard L.	S1c	USS *Maryland*
Stapleton, Christopher G.	S1c	USS *Mahan*
Stapleton, Delbert R.	FC3c	USS *Porter*
Stapleton, Kirby R.	S1c	MIA
Stecz, Michael	QM3c	USS *Salt Lake City*
Steely, Ulis C.	MM2c	MIA
Steen, Harold B.	S2c	USS *Helena*
Steen, Paul T.	F1c	USS *Helm*
Stein, Walter C.	S1c	MIA
Steiner, Samuel C.	F1c	MIA
Steinhauer, Russell F.	WT1c	USS *Enterprise*
Stephens, Ralph W.	S1c	Receiving station (pooling office)
Sterns, Charles M. (Jr.)	Ensign	MIA
Stevens, Charles H.	S2c	Naval air dispensary
Stewart, Everett R.	MM2c	MIA
Stewart, Roy	TC1c	USS *Louisville*
Stien, Clyde V.	WT1c	USS *Enterprise*
Stockdale, Louis S.	Ensign	MIA
Stott, Donald A.	S1c	MIA
Stout, Robert T.	FC2c	MIA
Stouten, James	CBM	KIA/Nuuanu Cemetery, sec 13, 235/114
Stover, William T.	S1c	USS *Phelps*
Stowell, Finch	FC3c	USS *Mugford*
Stretch, James A.	F2c	USS *Louisville*
Strong, Raymond J.	S1c	USS *Helena*

Name	Rank	Status
Struthers, Winfield L.	BM1c	Bishops Point
Stuart, Lenus L.	S1c	USS *Northampton*
Suess, Ernest	F1c	USS *Helena*
Sumrall, Woodrow I.	GM3c	Survived: reassignment unknown
Surlet, Herbert W.	S1c	USS *Blue*
Surratt, Milton R.	S1c	MIA
Sutton, V. E.	APC1k	Supply dept. navy yard
Swain, J. T.	S2c	USS *Helena*
Swain, Lindsay R.	S1c	Sub base (fleet machine gun school)
Swain, Ray B.	Cox	Survived: reassignment unknown
Swanson, Charles H.	MM1c	MIA
Swiderski, Stanley J.	Prtr1c	CINCPAC flag allowance (Temporarily based on USS *Argonne*)
Szewerenko, Joseph V.	S1c	USS *Chester*
Szymanski, Aloysius L.	S1c	USS *Henley*
Tajalle, Vincent S.	Mat2c	USS *Detroit*
Talbert, Edward E.	S1c	MIA
Tanner, Rangner F. (Jr.)	S2c	MIA
Tarbett, Ray L.	S1c	USS *Phelps*
Tarlton, Dennis C.	SC3c	USS *Saratoga*
Tate, Daniel B.	SC2c	Yard craft off., NYD
Tato, John C.	CCStd	Com 14 (yard cafeteria)
Taylor, Charles R.	PFC (USMC)	MIA
Taylor, James E.	S2c	USS *Louisville*
Taylor, Murphy L.	CFC	USS *Chester*
Temple, Monroe	S1c	MIA
Temples, Houston	S1c	MIA
Templeton, Louis C.	BM1c	Bishops Point
Tener, Lewis E.	S1c	USS *Conyngham*
Tengwall, Gordon E.	S1c	USS *Louisville*
Tenorio, Gregorio S.	Mat2c	USS *Cummings*
Terhune, Benjamin C.	F2c	MIA

Name	Rank	Status
Teske, Owen H.	S1c	USS *Louisville*
Tessmer, Irvin G.	S1c	MIA
Thatcher, George J.	S1c	USS *Tennessee*
Thesman, Irvin H.	EM1c	Receiving station
Thinnes, Arthur R.	S2c	MIA
Thomas, C.	S2c	Receiving station
Thomas, Donald H.	S1c	USS *Louisville*
Thomas, John R.	Cox	USS *Enterprise*
Thomas, William S.	S1c	Fleet machine gun school
Thomas, William Stanley	SF1c	USS *Medusa*
Thompson, Charles W	F1c	MIA
Thompson, Clarence	SC1c	MIA
Thompson, Frank E.	RM2c	Survived: reassignment unknown
Thompson, George A.	S2c	MIA
Thompson, Irvin A. R.	Ensign	MIA
Thompson, William M.	Ensign SC	MIA
Thomson, Richard J.	S2c	MIA
Thornton, Cecil H.	S2c	MIA
Thrombley, Robert L.	S2c	KIA/Punchbowl (P-0935)
Tidball, David F.	S1c	MIA
Tillman, Rogers L.	EM2c	Survived: reassignment unknown
Timm, Jack G.	S2c	USS *Louisville*
Timm, Lloyd R.	S2c	MIA
Timmons, Glen J.	S1c	USS *Worden*
Tindall, Lewis F.	F1c	MIA
Tini, Dante S.	RM3c	MIA
Tipton, Henry G.	S1c	MIA
Titterington, Everett C.	F1c	MIA
Todd, Neal K.	F1c	MIA
Todd, Wesley R.	F1c	USS *Blue*
Tomhave, Beatus C.	GM3c	MIA
Tomlinson, John W.	S2c	Sub base—fleet school
Torres, Juan Santos	Mat2c	MIA
Torti, Natale I.	S1c	MIA

Name	Rank	Status
Townsend, Donald S.	Cox	Com 14
Trager, Edward	BM1c	Receiving station
Trammell, Robert L.	S2c	USS *Preble*
Transbarger, Orval A.	S1c	MIA
Trapp, Harold F.	FC2c	MIA
Trapp, William H.	EM3c	MIA
Treadway, Shelby	GM3c	MIA
Trousdale, Jess E.	S1c	USS *Worden*
Truope, Claire M.	FC2c	USS *Jarvis*
Tucker, William D.	F1c	MIA
Tumlinsin, Victor P.	FC3c	MIA
Turner, Billy	S1c	MIA
Turner, Ramon L.	S1c	USS *Louisville*
Turpin, Raymond J.	Pvt. (USMC)	Marine barracks
Tushla, Louis J.	F1c	MIA
Ufford, Russell O.	S2c	MIA
Uhrdahl, Myron	F1c	USS *Chester*
Unpingco, Vincente M.	StM2c	USS *Whitney*
Valentine, Aubrey J.	S1c	USS *Helena*
Valentine, Robert K.	F1c	MIA
Valley, Lowell E.	F2c	MIA
Van Alstine, Carl E.	Pvt. (USMC)	USS *Chicago*
Van Campeleare, August L.	S2c	USS *Chester*
Van Derheide, Charles W.	S2c	USS *Louisville*
Van Ness, Earl E.	WT2c	USS *Jarvis*
Van Slyke, G. L.	ChElec.	MIA
Vaughn, Melvin L.	S2c	USS *Hull*
Venckeleer, Theodore F.	GM1c	USS *Blue*
Vezey, Edward E. (Jr.)	Ensign	West loch
Vickery, V. T.	MM1c	USS *Maryland*
Vickrey, Wayne S.	SF2c	Naval air station (aviation unit)
Vidito, Raymond C.	S1c	Signal tower, Ford Island
Villagomez, Pridencio U.	Mat2c	Naval air dispensary
Volkman, Robert B.	S1c	USS *Mahan*
Vollmer, Walter	GM3c	USS *Blue*

Name	Rank	Status
Vondale, Earl H.	S1c	USS *Helm*
Wade, Durrell	AMM2c	MIA
Wagner, Leonard K.	Cpl. (USMC)	Marine barracks
Wagoner, Louis L.	S2c	MIA
Wakeman, Joseph A.	S1c	USS *Louisville*
Walker, Harry E.	SK1c	MIA
Walker, Robert E.	S2c	USS *Helena*
Walker, Wakefield J.	Cox	USS *Enterprise*
Walker, William M.	BM2c	USS *Enterprise*
Walkowiak, Robert N.	F3c	Survived: reassignment unknown
Wallace, Edward F.	Pvt. (USMC)	Marine barracks
Wallen, Samuel E.	S1c	USS *San Francisco*
Walpole, Eugene A.	S2c	KIA/Punchbowl (M-1177)
Walpole, Raymond O.	S1c	USS *Honolulu*
Walters, Charles E.	S2c	MIA
Walters, Elmer N.	S1c	USS *Montgomery*
Ward, Homer D.	S2c	USS *Louisville*
Ward, James R.	S1c	MIA
Ward, William E. (Jr.)	S2c	USS *Chester*
Ware, David A.	CMM	USS *Salt Lake City*
Warner, Fred M.	FC1c	USS *Jarvis*
Washam, William M.	BM2c	USS *Chester*
Wasielewski, Edward	S1c	MIA
Waters, William W.	S1c	USS *Helena*
Watson, Oliver L	SK3c	USS *Chester*
Watson, Richard L.	S1c	MIA
Waugh, Arlos E.	S2c	USS *Louisville*
Wears, Leo G.	Sgt. (USMC)	Marine barracks
Weary, Noel O.	F2c	West loch
Webb, Frank W.	S1c	Receiving station
Webb, James C.	F1c	MIA
Webb, Wilbur B.	ARM2c	Naval air station (aviation unit)
Weber, Bernard L.	Cox	USS *Northampton*
Weddington, Eugene F.	S1c	USS *Phelps*

Name	Rank	Status
Weidling, John F.	Ensign	West loch
Weier, Othman J.	S2c	USS *Helena*
Weissman, Daniel	S1c	USS *Tucker*
Welch, William E.	S1c	KIA/Punchbowl (Q-177 or P-1003), Grave marked Unknown
Wells, Alfred F.	MM1c	MIA
Wells, Howard R.	SF3c	USS *Selfridge*
Werteen, Edwin L.	S1c	USS *San Francisco*
Wery, Kenneth F.	S1c	USS *Chester*
West, Archie C.	SC1c	USS *Blue*
West, Ernest R.	S1c	MIA
West, Gordon E.	S2c	USS *Honolulu*
West, Robert D.	Mus1c	Yard craft
Westfall, D. L.	PC1k	Survived: reassignment unknown
Whalley, James R.	S1c	Receiving station
Whatley, John R. (Jr.)	F1c	USS *Schley*
Wheeler, John D.	F2c	MIA
Whisenand, Gerald F.	S2c	USS *Helena*
White, Claude	CWT	MIA
White, Jack D.	S1c	MIA
Whiteford, Allan P.	S1c	USS *Blue*
Whitman, Richard F.	GM2c	USS *Helena*
Whitson, Alton W.	EM3c	MIA
Wick, James F.	Cox	USS *Blue*
Wicker, Eugene W.	S1c	MIA
Wickstrand, Eugene V.	Pvt. (USMC)	USS *Chicago*
Widener, Floyd N. (Jr.)	S1c	USS *Louisville*
Wiegand, Lloyd P.	Mus2c	MIA
Wilcox, George J. (Jr.)	S2c	MIA
Wilcox, Mayland H.	F1c	USS *Louisville*
Wiley, Norman E.	S1c	Survived: reassignment unknown
Wilkerson, Charles W.	S1c	Receiving station
Willett, Deava G.	S1c	USS *Blue*

Name	Rank	Status
Willey, Paul E.	S2c	USS *Louisville*
Williams, Albert L.	Mus2c	MIA
Williams, Edward C.	GM3c	USS *Cummings*
Williams, Ira (Jr.)	S1c	USS *Louisville*
Williams, J. R.	S1c	USS *Tennessee*
Williams, James C.	S1c	MIA
Williams, Lester J.	SM1c	USS *Enterprise*
Williams, Wilbur S.	OS2c	MIA
Williamson, Roy F.	S2c	USS *San Francisco*
Wilson, Doyle L.	EM3c	USS *Hull*
Wilson, M. N.	F1c	Receiving station
Wimme, John A.	S1c	MIA
Wimmer, Bernard R.	FC1c	MIA
Winders, Louis M.	S1c	USS *Oklahoma* post office
Windle, Everett G.	S2c	MIA
Winfield, Starring B.	RM3c	MIA
Winters, Doyle E.	S1c	USS *Louisville*
Wise, Rex E.	F1c	MIA
Wittenburg, Arlen J.	S1c	USS *Tennessee*
Wittman, Jacob P.	S2c	Sub base—fleet school
Wood, Frank	S2c	MIA
Wood, Lester R.	QM1c	USS *Honolulu*
Woodford, Frank E.	S2c	USS *Chester*
Woods, Lawrence E.	F1c	MIA
Woods, William F.	S1c	West loch
Woods, Winfred O.	MM1c	Died December 9, 1941/Punchbowl (C-0301)
Woodward, Theodore G.	S1c	USS *Waters*
Woollum, Henry L.	S1c	USS *Phelps*
Workman, Creighton H.	S1c	MIA
Wortham, John L.	GM2c	MIA
Wosick, Raymond L.	S1c	USS *Saratoga*
Wozniak, Frank	S1c	USS *Chester*
Wright, Kenneth W.	SF3c	USS *Pelias*
Wright, Paul R.	CWT	MIA
Wrobel, Joseph	S1c	USS *Chester*

Name	Rank	Status
Wyman, Eldon P.	Ensign	MIA
Wynkoop, Joseph B.	RM3c	Bishops Point
Wyrick, Clifton W.	Mus2c	Survived: reassignment unknown
Yancy, Sam H.	CMM	USS *Enterprise*
Yandell, Carl V.	S2c	USS *Worden*
Yankavich, Edward J.	F3c	USS *Schley*
Yarnall, William K.	Ensign	USS *Pollack*
Ygnacio, Marcelo	Mus1c	Receiving station
Young, Martin D.	S1c	MIA
Young, Raiford O.	S1c	USS *Tennessee*
Young, Robert V.	S1c	MIA
Young, Stephen B.	S1c	USS *Honolulu*
Yurko, Joseph J.	WT1c	KIA/Punchbowl (C-0106)
Zahradka, Joseph (Jr.)	EM3c	Survived: reassignment unknown
Ziemke, Edison	S2c	USS *Cummings*
Ziner, William	RM3c	USS *Blue*
Zony, John J.	RM3c	USS *Blue*
Zulawnick, Stanley W.	BM1c	Receiving station
Zvanski, Thomas	CSM	MIA

Ships Named for
USS *Oklahoma* Crewmen

USS *Austin*	DE-15	Chief Carpenter John A. Austin
USS *Sederstrom*	DE-31	Ensign Verdi D. Sederstrom
USS *Wyman*	DE-38	Ensign Eldon P. Wyman
USS *Flaherty*	DE-135	Ensign Francis C. Flaherty
USS *Barber*	DE-161	Firemen First Class Leroy K. and Malcolm J. Barber and Fireman Second Class Randolph H. Barber
USS *Sterns*	DE-187	Ensign Charles M. Sterns, Jr.
USS *Jordan*	DE-204	Lieutenant Julian B. Jordon
USS *Darby*	DE-218	Ensign Marshall E. Darby, Jr.
USS *Day*	DE-225	Chief Watertender Francis D. Day
USS *Finnegan*	DE-307	Ensign William M. Finnegan
USS *Pride*	DE-323	Ensign Lewis B. Pride, Jr.
USS *Stockdale*	DE-399	Ensign Louis S. Stockdale
USS *Schmitt*	DE-676	Lieutenant (j. g.) Aloysius H. Schmitt

Notes

CHAPTER 1. *OKLAHOMA*'S GENESIS

1. *Annual Reports of the Navy Department for the Fiscal Year 1916*; Hone and Friedman, "Innovation and Administration in the Navy Department."

2. Barton and Stickney, *Naval Reciprocating Engines and Auxiliary Machinery*; Department of Marine Engineering, *Naval Machinery*; Friedman, *U.S. Battleships*; U.S. Department of the Navy, *Ships' Data*; Office of the Chief of Naval Operations, "Cruising Radii of U.S. Naval Vessels."

3. Hone, "The Evolution of Fleet Tactical Doctrine."

CHAPTER 2. LIFE ON THE *OKLAHOMA*

1. *Annual Reports of the Navy Department for the Fiscal Year 1926*, p. 29.

2. *Annual Reports of the Navy Department for the Fiscal Year 1926*.

3. *Our Navy* 10, no. 8 (December 1916): 46.

4. *Our Navy* 29, no. 11 (October 1, 1935): 10.

5. Ibid.

6. *Annual Reports*, 1926, p. 29.

7. *Annual Reports of the Navy Department for the Fiscal Year 1932*, p. 333.

8. See the following issues of *Our Navy*, a magazine published by Our Navy Publishing Company of New York and San Francisco: December 1916; April 1917; April 1918 (for food served aboard ship, pay scales, and athletics); mid-April 1922; mid-September 1933; July 1, 1935 (Iron Man standings); October 1, 1935 (a critical review of fleet athletic competitions); mid-October 1935; mid-November 1935; mid-December 1935; mid-June 1936 (several photographs of *Oklahoma*); September 1, 1936; mid-September 1936 (coverage of *Oklahoma*'s deployment off the coast of Spain), December 1, 1936; and mid-December 1937.

CHAPTER 3. *OKLAHOMA*'s First Mission

1. The five other *Oklahoma* crewmen who succumbed to the flu virus were Fireman Third Class B. Woody, Private Charles L. Nelson (USMC), Seaman

Second Class C. Logadon, Fireman Third Class J. R. Dettlaff, and Gunner's Mate Third Class Fred B. Nation.

CHAPTER 4. THE GREAT CRUISE AND MODERNIZATION

1. The treaty also spawned several aircraft carriers. The U.S. would gain the services of the *Lexington* and the *Saratoga*, laid down as battle cruiser hulls but converted to aircraft carriers as a result of the treaty, and Japan would gain the *Akagi* and the *Kaga*. Originally a battleship destined for the scrap pile, the *Kaga* was resurrected when the *Amagi*, the battle cruiser originally slated for conversion, was wrecked during the Tokyo earthquake of 1923. The *Akagi* was commissioned on March 25, 1927. In 1929 Captain Isoruku Yamamoto became Akagi's new skipper. Twelve years later, Admiral Yamamoto would conceive the attack on Pearl Harbor. On December 7, 1941, planes from the *Akagi* and *Kaga* would spearhead the torpedo assault on Battleship Row.

2. The treaty was heralded worldwide as a diplomatic coup by the U.S. State Department. Special acclaim was given to Secretary Hughes and his seemingly uncanny skills in the high-stakes game of diplomatic poker. Undeniably brilliant, Hughes had been armed with insight; the Japanese diplomatic code had been broken just weeks before the conference by American cryptologist Herbert O. Yardley. Knowing that the Japanese government favored disarmament for economic reasons, and would eventually capitulate to the disproportionate 5:5:3 ratio, Hughes held firm for thirty-nine days, enduring the ridicule of the press for his inability to compromise, while the Japanese delegation maneuvered to up the ratio to placate the demands of Japan's militarists.

3. John McCain, Jr., was commander in chief of U.S. forces in the Pacific during the height of the Vietnam War (1968–1972). His son, John Sidney McCain III, became a POW in October 1967, enduring six years of captivity. He is currently a U.S. senator from Arizona. Vice Admiral John Sidney McCain, Sr., was aboard the USS *Missouri* during the Japanese surrender on September 2, 1945. Four days later, he died of a heart attack at the family home on Coronado Island, California. He was promoted to the rank of admiral posthumously. In 1974, James L. Holloway, Jr., and James L. Holloway III became the second pair of father-son admirals in the U.S. Navy.

CHAPTER 5. EARTHQUAKES, REFUGEES, AND WAR

1. In a storm, two of the *Macon*'s fins were shattered, sending shards of metal through the rear gas cells, causing the 785-foot-long airship to descend.

Two of her eighty-three crewmembers would perish: one man jumping to his death as the airship was going down; another drowning while he attempted to reenter the floating wreckage to retrieve his belongings.

2. Kenworthy became the ship's acting commander when Captain Howard D. Bode went ashore approximately thirty minutes prior to the Japanese attack.

3. Martha gave birth to another son on August 13, 1936. That son, John L. Odom, donated the flag to the Oklahoma Historical Society on November 17, 2005.

CHAPTER 6. COUNTDOWN TO PEARL HARBOR

1. Richardson, *On the Treadmill to Pearl Harbor*, 435.

2. Kimmel, *Admiral Kimmel's Story*, 36.

3. Stark to Kimmel, January 15, 1941, as cited in Kimmel, *Admiral Kimmel's Story*, 18.

4. From a general perspective, the move would prove to be warranted when German submarines attacked U.S. destroyers in fall 1941. *Greer* survived a submarine attack off Iceland in September; *Kearny* was badly damaged, with 11 sailors killed, on October 16; and *Reuben James* was sunk on October 29, with 115 killed, including all her officers.

5. In terms of physical appearance, the battleships could be divided into two distinct groups: those with cage masts and those with tripod masts. The ships with tripod masts were the four oldest: *Nevada, Oklahoma, Pennsylvania,* and *Arizona.* Just as the *Oklahoma* was identical to the *Nevada, Arizona* was identical to the *Pennsylvania.* Of the cage mast battleships, *California* and *Tennessee* were sisters, as were the *Colorado, West Virginia,* and *Maryland.* The cage mast battleships were commonly known as the Big Five.

6. Prange, *At Dawn We Slept*, 159.

7. Kimmel, *Admiral Kimmel's Story*, 20.

8. Admiral Kimmel discussed the intercept at length in his memoirs: "In the volume of intercepted Japanese dispatches . . . about military installations and naval movements, the dispatches concerning Pearl Harbor, on and after September 24, 1941, stand out. . . . No other harbor or base in American territory or possessions was divided into sub-areas by Japan. In no other area was the Japanese government seeking information as to whether two or more vessels were alongside the same wharf. . . . In the period immediately preceding the attack, the Jap consul general in Hawaii was directed by Tokyo to report even when there were no movements of ships in and out of Pearl Harbor. These Japanese instructions and reports pointed to an attack by Japan

upon the ships in Pearl Harbor. . . . Knowledge of these intercepted Japanese dispatches would have radically changed the estimate of the situation made by me and my staff. It would have suggested a re-orientation of our planned operations at the outset of hostilities. . . . Knowledge of a probable Japanese attack on Pearl Harbor would have afforded an opportunity to ambush the Japanese striking force as it ventured to Hawaii." *Admiral Kimmel's Story,* 86–88.

9. Fewer than two hours after *Arizona* berthed alongside the 1010 dock, a diving party inspected her damage. The V-shaped hole was four feet wide and approximately twelve feet long. Were it not for *Oklahoma*'s reciprocating engines, which could go from full forward to full reverse much faster than turbine engines, the damage would likely have been much more severe. *Oklahoma* was the only Pacific Fleet battleship with reciprocating engines.

10. Though no longer in command of the *Oklahoma,* Foy never forgot the men. Following the Japanese attack, Foy and his wife drove around the base in their convertible, distributing assorted foods and toiletries to members of his former crew. Neither Foy nor any of his men were found guilty of misconduct during the collision with *Arizona* on October 22. J.A.G. BB39/A17-24(411119).

11. Named after Seth Porter Ford, who assumed ownership in 1886, Ford Island was appropriated by the army in 1917, when the United States entered World War I. An army airfield constructed on the northwest side of the island was subsequently named Luke Field in honor of Lieutenant Frank Luke, Jr., a World War I aviator who was posthumously awarded the Congressional Medal of Honor. In 1923 a naval air station was commissioned on the island's southeastern side. Though the island would increase in size through the placement of fill material, the continued expansion of both the army and the navy facilities would eventually outstrip its new perimeter. In 1939, the army moved its facilities to Wheeler and Hickam Fields, and the island became the domain of the navy.

12. Until 1941, battleships entering Pearl Harbor would sail directly up the main channel to Battleship Row because the waterway on the northwest side of Ford Island wasn't deep enough to allow for their passage. The battleships would stop with their port side facing the quays and would then be rotated 180 degrees by harbor tugs so that their bows were pointed toward the mouth of the harbor, allowing for a quick exit. The process was called "winding ship." Once dredging operations were completed on the northwest side of the island, the battleships circled Ford Island so that their bows were already exit oriented when they were pushed alongside the quays.

13. Entry in *Oklahoma* deck log, October 26, 1941.

14. Seaman First Class Charles Elijah Swisher would die on December 7, 1941.

15. Fireman First Class Leonard R. Geller would die on December 7, 1941. Following the attack, Bentley wrote a "horrible" letter to Geller's sister, informing her of her loss.

CHAPTER 7. A QUIET SUNDAY MORNING

1. *Enterprise* was returning from Wake Island; *Lexington* was en route to Midway; and *Saratoga* was approaching San Diego.

2. None of the Japanese midgets would survive the attack.

CHAPTER 8. DAMN THE TORPEDOES

1. A series of articles in *Naval History* magazine (December 1999, June 2000, December 2000) claim that an additional torpedo was launched at *Oklahoma* by Japanese midget submarine I-16tou. The supposition is controversial and lacks the support of many Pearl Harbor historians.

2. It is impossible to determine the exact number of torpedoes that struck *Oklahoma*. The salvage report ("Industrial Drafting Room Report") prepared after the ship was raised and moved to dry dock stated eight. However, some torpedoes may have struck in the same area, allowing the possibility for more. Probably the most accurate accounting of aerial torpedo launches was presented by Pearl Harbor historian David Aiken in "Torpedoing Pearl Harbor," the main reference for this text. Aiken's article is based on his interview with Lt. Heita Matsumura, a torpedo-plane pilot who remained over Pearl Harbor during most of the torpedo assault on Battleship Row. The article chronicles eleven aerial launches on the *Oklahoma*: six from *Akagi* planes, two from *Hiryu* planes, and three from *Kaga* planes. If indeed a midget submarine also launched on *Oklahoma*, then a possible twelve were launched. It is highly probable that at least one can be discounted—the plane S1c John A. Cole, Jr., saw flying over the *Oklahoma* with its torpedo still attached (see chapter 9). The plane could have returned for a second launching attempt, but it is doubtful that it would have targeted *Oklahoma* again. There is also a report of a torpedo seen passing behind the stern of the *Maryland* (Scott, "A Star for Each," 104). This would bring the total number of possible hits to ten. Assuming that the preceding launching information is correct, then either two hits went undetected in the salvage report, or two torpedoes are still at the bottom of Pearl Harbor. A detailed analysis presented by John D. Virgilio

in his technical report "Japanese Thunderfish" chronicles nine hits. The Japanese claimed twelve.

3. *Arizona* suffered 1,177 casualties, *Oklahoma* 429, and *Nevada* 57. The combined casualties of the BatDivOne battleships (1,663) thus accounted for 71 percent of the total U.S. military casualties (2,340).

CHAPTER 9. TOPSIDE—7:55 A.M.

1. The exact cause of the explosion that destroyed *Arizona* is unknown. Though it has been universally speculated that the magnitude of the blast was due to fires that ignited her forward powder magazines, it is unclear whether the fires were caused by a delayed detonation of the bomb that Goodyear witnessed, or by an armor-piercing bomb that hit later on the starboard side of turret 2.

2. When ordered off the *Maryland*, Goodyear and several other *Oklahoma* signalmen went ashore to Ford Island. Running into Ensign Paul Backus, their division officer, they were instructed to transfer dependents from the chief's housing to the bachelor officers' quarters (BOQ). After finding a truck, they transported several families, then drove to the seaplane hangars at the southwest end of the island. Despite the wreckage and commotion, they obtained rifles and an unassembled .30-caliber machine gun. They took off driving without a real destination, finally ending up in front of a laundry. Seeing that it had been broken into, they went inside and exchanged their wet, oily seaman's garb for fresh clothing. They spent the night simply wandering around. Because they had no identification, they were refused admittance to the mess hall. Fortunately, they were able to obtain blankets from the BOQ. The next day, one of them remembered a twenty-dollar bill that he'd left in his pants at the laundry. Because none of them had money, they were anxious to retrieve it so that they could buy supplies to write their parents. By the time they returned, however, a marine sentry had been posted. While two of them distracted him, the others went inside. Fortunately, the money was still there. To conserve it, they wrote a letter to one set of parents, instructing them to contact the others. They then proceeded to the Ford Island fire station, where they established a rudimentary signal tower. Because one of the signalmen had been in the army, he was tasked to assemble the machine gun. When he was finished, he loaded it and fired a quick burst— receiving an immediate response from a host of trigger-happy gunners around the harbor. Later the signalmen heard that survivors from the *California* were being admitted to the mess hall using cards with USS *California* written on them as their only identification. The signalmen manufactured

facsimiles and were finally able to eat. They would later take turns impersonating an officer to receive canned goods offloaded from the *California*, which was sitting on the bottom of the harbor. Because the labeling had peeled off, they never knew what they'd be eating until the lids had been removed. Goodyear's first shower after the attack would be aboard the *Indianapolis* on December 15. He would remain at the signal tower on the Ford Island fire station until April 1942.

3. Two days later, Cole was assigned to the light cruiser USS *Helena*. He would be aboard her when she was sunk during a night surface battle in the Kula Gulf, Solomon Islands, July 5, 1943. Cole survived, retiring from the navy as a lieutenant commander.

CHAPTER 10. CHAOS BELOW

1. Vaughn was later strafed while driving a pickup filled with wounded to the Ford Island dispensary. Later in the day, a marine ordered him to carry a box of .30-caliber ammunition up to the roof. After depositing it, Vaughn was given a rifle. Returning to ground level, he saw a low-flying plane coming in on a strafing run. He raised his gun to fire, as did six or seven others. Suddenly the helmet he was wearing snapped down over his face, struck by a bullet from the man behind him, whose rifle had discharged prematurely.

2. Ensign Lewis Bailey Pride, Jr., was killed on December 7, 1941. The destroyer escort USS *Pride* was named in his honor.

3. Richmond would spend eight months recuperating in a navy hospital. It was a difficult period, and his only salvation was his drawing. Every night when the ward had quieted down, a nurse would come sit with him, and he'd sketch her portrait. Word spread quickly, and before long most of the staff had a Ray Richmond original. His physician would prove to be his greatest admirer and, as it turned out, his greatest benefactor. Under the guise of rehabilitation, the doctor arranged for Richmond to be transferred to the navy recruiting office in New York City. There he would find his life's work as a commercial artist. Richmond's sketches would appear on countless navy recruiting posters. The sketch for which he would receive the most acclaim was of a bee toting a machine gun, monkey wrench, and hammer, conceived and drafted for the Navy's construction battalion. It not only became the unit's logo, it also became the basis for the battalion's name: the Seabees.

When the *Oklahoma* was raised in 1943, the navy sent Richmond the contents of his locker: his wallet, a coin purse, a knife his father had owned, and his razor. The contents had been identified through a bank deposit slip in his wallet. The only thing that was ruined was the rubber mouthpiece he'd used for boxing at Friday night smokers. Everything was sent to New York in a big wooden box. The freight cost him a fortune. Later, the Gillette Company offered him a tidy sum for the razor, which Richmond declined. He still has it.

4. Lester and Washam would discuss the event some forty years later when they ran into each other at a bank in San Diego. As it turned out, they had been living within a half-mile of each other for years.

5. Like many sailors, Don Lester had a tattoo, a beautiful girl who happened to be nude. When Foy discovered it during an inspection, he ordered Lester to clean it up. When Foy saw it next, it was a mermaid—or at least half a mermaid. Because Lester didn't have the funds for a full-scale revision, only a tail had been added to the original. Foy grinned and moved on, endearing himself to the young sailor forever. When Lester discovered that the captain's favorite alcoholic beverage was Calvert's Special, he started drinking it himself. He still does.

6. French was at the Ford Island dispensary when a bomb landed in the patio area. Though the impact shook the entire building, the bomb didn't explode. It was discovered later, buried beneath a slab of concrete.

7. Ensign Flaherty's Medal of Honor citation is presented in appendix B. The destroyer escort USS *Flaherty* was named in his honor.

CHAPTER 11. TWELVE-INCH PORTHOLES

1. Seaman First Class Robert V. Young had been sent forward to hoist the Union Jack just moments before the attack began. The cause of his mortal wound was never discerned.

2. After diving off the port side of the ship, Signalman Third Class Andrew P. Sauer was caught in a whirlpool as the ship turned over. Fortunately, he was able to grab hold of a swirling board that was stuck between two navy cork life rings.

3. Lieutenant (j. g.) Aloysius H. Schmitt, Chief Watertender Francis D. Day, and Lieutenant Commander Hugh R. Alexander died December 7, 1941. All three were posthumously awarded the Navy and Marine Corps Medal. The destroyer escort USS *Schmitt* was named in the chaplain's honor. The destroyer escort USS *Day* was named in honor of Chief Watertender Day. It is unknown why Lieutenant Commander Alexander wasn't honored in the same manner. The three men's medal citations are presented in appendix B.

4. Carpenter John A. Austin died on December 7, 1941. He was posthumously award the Navy Cross. The destroyer escort USS *Austin* was named in his honor. His medal citation is presented in appendix B.

CHAPTER 12. TRAPPED!

1. Seaman First Class Thomas F. Hannon was killed in action in a subsequent battle. His account was written just a few days after the attack. According to Seaman First Class Harold S. Roiland, it was the first account committed to paper. I rewrote it in third person.

2. Seaman Second Class Frank Wood died on December 7, 1941.

3. Roberts would survive. Surfacing alongside the ship, he was rescued by a boat. His description of the lucky bag and the men trapped inside would initiate the rescue efforts that would eventually save them.

4. West was happy to be rid of the clarinet. When he had played at a dance in Bremerton, Washington, a drunken officer had fallen into the bandstand and landed on top of it. Broken in two, the instrument had been repaired at the navy yard using a steel splice that extended its length by an inch. The instrument never sounded the same again.

5. Electrician's Mate Third Class Charles H. Harris and Fireman Third Class Clarence A. Blaylock died on December 7, 1941.

CHAPTER 13. THIRTY-TWO CAME BACK

1. The sailors had already moved from the trunk to the lucky bag, where they were eventually rescued.

2. Other *Oklahoma* survivors who returned to help were Lieutenant Commander William L. Benson, Ensign Joseph C. Spitler, Machinist's Mate Second Class Walter Becker, Shipfitter Second Class John H. Birnel, Coxswain Charles F. Burns, Seaman First Class Eugene Byers, Shipfitter First Class William S. Thomas, Carpenter's Mate First Class Harold J. Harris, Chief Boatswain's Mate Carl W. Keenum, and Boatswain Adolph M. Bothne. Burns had two brothers-in-law trapped inside. Neither would be rescued.

3. Seaman First Class Stephen B. Young wrote an excellent account of his USS *Oklahoma* experiences in his book, *Trapped at Pearl Harbor.*

4. Taken to a launch alongside the ship, Musician First Class John K. Engen recalled being greeted by three sailors, one who asked for his service number, a second who gave him a glass of orange juice, and a third who gave him a cigarette. He was reluctant to take the cigarette because it was against regulations to smoke in a launch, but the sailor calmly reassured him: "It's OK today." After arriving at the *Solace*, Engen was cleaned and then ushered into a compartment with a line of coffee mugs on a table. A warrant officer filled one about a third full with coffee and two-thirds with twenty-year-old Golden Wedding Bourbon.

5. After being taken to the hospital ship *Solace,* Seaman Second Class Delbert L. Pittman was given a kerosene sponge bath. He had cut his head severely when the ship rolled over, so a doctor applied some sort of salve to his scalp, stitched him up, and sent him to bed. Pittman would awaken with most of his hair missing.

6. An air test plug was a threaded pipe section that was welded around a drilled hole. Each plug had a threaded cap. They were used to determine if a compartment was airtight and watertight. When a test was being conducted, the cap would be removed, an air hose would be attached to the threaded pipe, and then air would be pumped in. The pressure would then be monitored with a gauge to see if it was diminishing.

7. The twenty-one men from Shop 11 were Joseph Bulgo, Irving C. Carl, Julio DeCastro, J. Walter Drapala, Duncan S. Ellis, Maurice G. Engle, Vasco D. Ferreira, Richard A. Goings, Paul J. Hakanas, Thomas V. Hill, Lawrence V. Jordan, John F. Madura, William K. Mahaiula, Elber F. McCutcheon, Archie R. Pittchette, John K. Rasmussen, Alexander M. Smith, Fred W. Taylor, Frederick C. Twigger, John M. R. Washlick, and Ensign F. M. P. Sexton.

CHAPTER 14. RESURRECTION

1. Most of the information presented in this chapter was obtained from an official report prepared by Captain Francis H. Whitaker (USN), "Salvage of USS *Oklahoma.*"

2. The following list describes the disposition of the other battleships damaged at Pearl Harbor (Friedman, *U.S. Battleships*):

Arizona: Stricken from the navy list Dec. 1, 1942 as a total loss; later recommissioned as a war memorial.

California: Raised at Pearl Harbor in April 1942 and rebuilt at Puget Sound Navy Yard from June 1942 to Jan. 1944.

Nevada: Raised at Pearl Harbor in Feb. 1942 and rebuilt at Puget Sound Navy Yard between April and Dec. 1942.

Pennsylvania: Repaired for service by Jan. 1942. Modernized at the Mare Island Navy Yard between Oct. 1942 and Feb. 1943.

Tennessee: Repaired for service by Jan. 1942. Rebuilt at Puget Sound Navy Yard from Sept. 1942 to May 1943.

Maryland: Repaired for service by Jan. 1942.

West Virginia: Raised in June 1942. Repaired at Pearl Harbor and rebuilt at Puget Sound Navy Yard from May 1943 to July 1944.

3. Of the sixteen U.S. battleships (besides *Oklahoma*) that were in service when Pearl Harbor was attacked, nine were eventually scrapped (*New Mexico, Mississippi, Idaho, Tennessee, California, Colorado, Maryland, West Virginia,* and *Washington*), one was sunk in the 1946 Bikini Bomb Test (*Arkansas*), three survived the test only to be sunk by the U.S. military later (*New York, Nevada, Pennsylvania*), two became museums (*Texas* and *North Carolina*), and one became a National Park Memorial (*Arizona*).

CHAPTER 15. SHE CHOSE THE SEA

1. Though there are no coast guard reports to confirm it, it is believed that the *Oklahoma* sank in about seventeen thousand feet of water, approximately 540 miles northeast of Oahu.

Glossary

AA. Antiaircraft.

aft. Rear portion of the ship. Moving aft means moving toward the stern.

after flag bag. Secondary flag bridge located belowdecks.

amidships. Middle portion of the ship.

barbette. The cylindrical sleeve for the body of the turret.

bilge. The rounded areas that form the transition between the bottom and the sides on the exterior of the hull.

boat boom. A long wooden pole that extended perpendicularly from the side of the ship when the ship was in port. The ship's launches would secure their lines to this pole. When the ship was preparing to go to sea, the boom would be rotated inward and then secured against the side of the ship.

broadside guns. Guns positioned on the side of the ship. Can fire outward, not forward or aft.

bow. Front of the ship.

bulkhead. Wall.

caliber. The length of a gun's barrel divided by the diameter of the gun's bore.

cane fender. A bumper placed between ships moored side by side.

casemate. An enclosure for guns.

coaming. A raised border around an opening in the deck to prevent water from running below.

deck. Floor.

dog wrench. Hollow bar that slides over the handle of the dog so that the user can apply leverage.

dogs. An L-shaped handle with a threaded nut on the short end. Used to secure hatches.

fantail. The rounded portion of the stern.

forecastle. Weatherdeck located at the front of the ship.

forward. Moving forward means moving toward the bow.

gedunk stand. A ship's store, run by marines. It featured ice cream, candy, and a few necessities such as razors and toothpaste.

halyard. A line for hoisting a spar, sail, or flag into position for use.

inboard. Located closest to the center; opposite of outboard.

Jacob's ladder. A hanging ladder made of ropes supporting wooden rungs.

king post. A post that a securing line is wrapped around during docking.

knot. Nautical mile (6,080 feet).

knots. Airspeed or waterspeed (number of nautical miles traveled per hour).

lifelines. Chains strung between metal posts to form a protective fence on the ship's weatherdecks.

lucky bag. The ship's lost-and-found compartment.

outboard. Located farthest from the center; opposite of inboard.

overhead. Ceiling.

port. Left side of the ship as you face the front (bow) of the ship.

quarterdeck. Weatherdeck located at the rear of the ship.

ready boxes. Storage boxes for AA ammunition located close to the AA guns.

scupper. Drainage gutter.

scuttle. A small hatch or port in the deck, side, or bottom of a vessel.

shell deck. Deck in a main turret where fourteen-inch-diameter projectiles are stored.

sounding tubes. Used to measure the level of oil in the fuel-oil tanks.

splinter hatch. Hatch located in the splinter deck, which is directly below the armored deck.

spud locker. Storage facility for potatoes.

starboard. Right side of the ship as you face the front (bow) of the ship.

stern. Rear of the ship.

striker. Apprentice seaman (seaman second class).

waterplane. The horizontal area of a ship when measured at the waterline.

weatherdeck. A deck without an overhead (open to the air, i.e., to the weather).

yeoman. Clerk.

Sources

ARCHIVAL SOURCES

Bromm, Robert. Written statement. USS *Oklahoma* Family, Phoenix, Arizona.

Cole, Jr., John A. Written statement. USS *Oklahoma* Family, Phoenix, Arizona.

Commanding Officer, USS *Oklahoma*. Letter to Commander-in-Chief, U.S. Pacific Fleet, December 18, 1941, RG 38. National Archives and Records Administration, College Park, Maryland.

Curtis, Charles R. Written statement. USS *Oklahoma* Family, Phoenix, Arizona.

Daggett, R. B., Captain (USN). Memorandum for File, May 19, 1947, subject: Ex-USS *Oklahoma* (BB37), Sinking of, RG 19. National Archives and Records Administration, College Park, Maryland.

Davenport, Irving J. Written statement. USS *Oklahoma* Family, Phoenix, Arizona.

Davenport, Russell M. Written statement. Oklahoma Historical Society, Oklahoma City, Oklahoma.

DeCastro, Julio. "General Recall," Dec. 7, 1978, article on file at USS *Oklahoma* Family, Phoenix, Arizona.

Duncan, William E. Written statement. Oklahoma Historical Society, Oklahoma City, Oklahoma.

Gillett, Alvah G. Written statement. USS *Oklahoma* Family, Phoenix, Arizona.

Grand Pre, John D. Written statement. USS *Oklahoma* Family, Phoenix, Arizona.

Hannon, Thomas F. Written statement. USS *Oklahoma* Family, Phoenix, Arizona.

Hobby, Jr., Lieutenant Commander W. M. (USN). Letter to Commander Battleships, Battle Force. December 12, 1941, RG 38, National Archives and Records Administration, College Park, Maryland.

"Industrial Drafting Room Report: Navy Yard, Pearl Harbor, T.H., No. 0930419 (C-BB37/L11–1)." Signed by Frederick H. Otis (Compiler), Franklin Y. Sunn (Squad Leader), and M. W. Douthat (Supervisor). National Archives and Records Administration, College Park, Maryland.

Japanese Raid on Pearl Harbor, December 7, 1941. Report. Box 8, Copies, Feb. 15, 1942, RG 38. National Archives and Records Administration, College Park, Maryland.

Kalman, Jesse T. Written statement. USS *Oklahoma* Family, Phoenix, Arizona.

Kenworthy, Jr., Commander Jesse L. (USN). Letter to Captain H. D. Bode (USN), December 16, 1941, RG 38, National Archives and Records Administration, College Park, Maryland.

Langford, Alva D. Written statement. USS *Oklahoma* Family, Phoenix, Arizona.

McBeth, Charles F. Written statement. USS *Oklahoma* Family, Phoenix, Arizona.

Office of the Chief of Naval Operations, Division of Fleet Training. "Cruising Radii of U.S. Naval Vessels from Actual Steaming Data," FTP 136 (Change No. 2), May 1940, Box 46, Folder F.T.P. 136—Changes 2 & 3. RG 38, Records of the Office of the Chief of Naval Operations), National Archives and Records Administration, Washington, D.C.

PT-27. Deck log, 1941 to present, RG 24. National Archives and Records Administration, College Park, Maryland.

PT-28. Deck log, 1941 to present, RG 24. National Archives and Records Administration, College Park, Maryland.

PT-29. Deck log, 1941 to present, RG 24. National Archives and Records Administration, College Park, Maryland.

PT-30. Deck log, 1941 to present, RG 24. National Archives and Records Administration, College Park, Maryland.

Reyelts, Duane H. Written statement. USS *Oklahoma* Family, Phoenix, Arizona.

Risher, Charles M. Written statement. USS *Oklahoma* Family, Phoenix, Arizona.

Rommel, Herbert F. Written statement. Oklahoma Historical Society, Oklahoma City, Oklahoma.

Sauer, Andrew J. Written statement. USS *Oklahoma* Family, Phoenix, Arizona.

Scott, Jr., Harry L. Written statement. USS *Oklahoma* Family, Phoenix, Arizona.

Sinking of Ex-*Oklahoma*. Letters and enclosures regarding C-AVP 40 thru C-BB62, box 14, HM 1991. RG 19, Records of the Bureau of Ships, Confidential General Correspondence, 1947. National Archives and Records Administration, College Park, Maryland.

Smith, Jr., George H. Written statement. USS *Oklahoma* Family, Phoenix, Arizona.

Vickrey, Wayne S. Written statement. USS *Oklahoma* Family, Phoenix, Arizona.

Ward, Jr., William E. Written statement. USS *Oklahoma* Family, Phoenix, Arizona.

Weissman, Daniel. Written statement. USS *Oklahoma* Family, Phoenix, Arizona.

Westfall, D. L. Written statement. USS *Oklahoma* Family, Phoenix, Arizona.

USS *Antares*. Deck log, 1941 to present, RG 24. National Archives and Records Administration, College Park, Maryland.

USS *Argonne*. Deck log, 1941 to present, RG 24. National Archives and Records Administration, College Park, Maryland.

USS *Arizona*. Deck log, 1941 to present, RG 24. National Archives and Records Administration, College Park, Maryland.

USS *Avocet*. Deck log, 1941 to present, RG 24. National Archives and Records Administration, College Park, Maryland.

USS *Bagley*. Deck log, 1941 to present, RG 24. National Archives and Records Administration, College Park, Maryland.

USS *Blue*. Deck log, 1941 to present, RG 24. National Archives and Records Administration, College Park, Maryland.

USS *Bobolink* (AM-20). Deck log, 1941 to present, RG 24. National Archives and Records Administration, College Park, Maryland.

USS *Breese*. Deck log, 1941 to present, RG 24. National Archives and Records Administration, College Park, Maryland.

USS *California*. Deck log, 1941 to present, RG 24. National Archives and Records Administration, College Park, Maryland.

USS *Castor*. Deck log, 1941 to present, RG 24. National Archives and Records Administration, College Park, Maryland.

USS *Condor*. Deck log, 1941 to present, RG 24. National Archives and Records Administration, College Park, Maryland.

USS *Crossbill*. Deck log, 1941 to present, RG 24. National Archives and Records Administration, College Park, Maryland.

USS *Detroit*. Deck log, 1941 to present, RG 24. National Archives and Records Administration, College Park, Maryland.

USS *Dolphin*. Deck log, 1941 to present, RG 24. National Archives and Records Administration, College Park, Maryland.

USS *Enterprise*. Deck log, 1941 to present, RG 24. National Archives and Records Administration, College Park, Maryland.

USS *Gamble*. Deck log, 1941 to present, RG 24. National Archives and Records Administration, College Park, Maryland.

USS *Grebe*. Deck log, 1941 to present, RG 24. National Archives and Records Administration, College Park, Maryland.

USS *Henley*. Deck log, 1941 to present, RG 24. National Archives and Records Administration, College Park, Maryland.

USS *Honolulu*. Deck log, 1941 to present, RG 24. National Archives and Records Administration, College Park, Maryland.

USS *Hulbert*. Deck log, 1941 to present, RG 24. National Archives and Records Administration, College Park, Maryland.

USS *Jarvis.* Deck log, 1941 to present, RG 24. National Archives and Records Administration, College Park, Maryland.

USS *Keosanqua.* Deck log, 1941 to present, RG 24. National Archives and Records Administration, College Park, Maryland.

USS *Macon* (airship). Deck log, 1941 to present, RG 24. National Archives and Records Administration, College Park, Maryland.

USS *Maryland.* Deck log, 1941 to present, RG 24. National Archives and Records Administration, College Park, Maryland.

USS *Montgomery.* Deck log, 1941 to present, RG 24. National Archives and Records Administration, College Park, Maryland.

USS *Mugford.* Deck log, 1941 to present, RG 24. National Archives and Records Administration, College Park, Maryland.

USS *Narwhal.* Deck log, 1941 to present, RG 24. National Archives and Records Administration, College Park, Maryland.

USS *Neosho.* Deck log, 1941 to present, RG 24. National Archives and Records Administration, College Park, Maryland.

USS *Nevada.* Deck log, 1941 to present, RG 24. National Archives and Records Administration, College Park, Maryland.

USS *New Orleans.* Deck log, 1941 to present, RG 24. National Archives and Records Administration, College Park, Maryland.

USS *Oglala.* Deck log, 1941 to present, RG 24. National Archives and Records Administration, College Park, Maryland.

USS *Oklahoma* (BB-37). Booklet of General Plans. BU. CRR. No. 157370, Sheets 1–5, Records of the Bureau of Ships, RG 19. National Archives and Records Administration, College Park, Maryland.

USS *Oklahoma.* Deck log, 1941 to present, RG 24. National Archives and Records Administration, College Park, Maryland.

USS *Patterson.* Deck log, 1941 to present, RG 24. National Archives and Records Administration, College Park, Maryland.

USS *Pelias.* Deck log, 1941 to present, RG 24. National Archives and Records Administration, College Park, Maryland.

USS *Pennsylvania.* Deck log, 1941 to present, RG 24. National Archives and Records Administration, College Park, Maryland.

USS *Pruitt.* Deck log, 1941 to present, RG 24. National Archives and Records Administration, College Park, Maryland.

USS *Ralph Talbot.* Deck log, 1941 to present, RG 24. National Archives and Records Administration, College Park, Maryland.

USS *Ramapo.* Deck log, 1941 to present, RG 24. National Archives and Records Administration, College Park, Maryland.

USS *Ramsay.* Deck log, 1941 to present, RG 24. National Archives and Records Administration, College Park, Maryland.

USS *Rigel*. Deck log, 1941 to present, RG 24. National Archives and Records Administration, College Park, Maryland.

USS *Sacramento*. Deck log, 1941 to present, RG 24. National Archives and Records Administration, College Park, Maryland.

USS *San Francisco*. Deck log, 1941 to present, RG 24. National Archives and Records Administration, College Park, Maryland.

USS *Schley*. Deck log, 1941 to present, RG 24. National Archives and Records Administration, College Park, Maryland.

USS *Selfridge*. Deck log, 1941 to present, RG 24. National Archives and Records Administration, College Park, Maryland.

USS *Sicard*. Deck log, 1941 to present, RG 24. National Archives and Records Administration, College Park, Maryland.

USS *Solace*. Deck log, 1941 to present, RG 24. National Archives and Records Administration, College Park, Maryland.

USS *St. Louis*. Deck log, 1941 to present, RG 24. National Archives and Records Administration, College Park, Maryland.

USS *Sumner*. Deck log, 1941 to present, RG 24. National Archives and Records Administration, College Park, Maryland.

USS *Sunnadin*. Deck log, 1941 to present, RG 24. National Archives and Records Administration, College Park, Maryland.

USS *Swan*. Deck log, 1941 to present, RG 24. National Archives and Records Administration, College Park, Maryland.

USS *Tautog*. Deck log, 1941 to present, RG 24. National Archives and Records Administration, College Park, Maryland.

USS *Tennessee*. Deck log, 1941 to present, RG 24. National Archives and Records Administration, College Park, Maryland.

USS *Tern*. Deck log, 1941 to present, RG 24. National Archives and Records Administration, College Park, Maryland.

USS *Thornton*. Deck log, 1941 to present, RG 24. National Archives and Records Administration, College Park, Maryland.

USS *Trever*. Deck log, 1941 to present, RG 24. National Archives and Records Administration, College Park, Maryland.

USS *Vestal*. Deck log, 1941 to present, RG 24. National Archives and Records Administration, College Park, Maryland.

USS *Ward*. Deck log, 1941 to present, RG 24. National Archives and Records Administration, College Park, Maryland.

USS *Wasmuth*. Deck log, 1941 to present, RG 24. National Archives and Records Administration, College Park, Maryland.

USS *West Virginia*. Deck log, 1941 to present, RG 24. National Archives and Records Administration, College Park, Maryland.

INTERVIEWS

Backus, Paul H. Interview by U.S. Naval Institute, Oral Histories Division. Transcript. USNI, Annapolis, Maryland.

Becker, Walter. USS *Oklahoma* survivor. Telephone interview by the author. March 2, 2005.

Bentley, R.M. USS *Oklahoma* survivor. Interviews by the author. August 18, 2003, and January 1, 2005.

Birnel, John. USS *Oklahoma* survivor. Interviews by the author. July 20, 2003, and December 26, 2004.

Black, James. USS *Oklahoma* survivor. Telephone interview by the author. January 7, 2005.

Bounds, Jim. USS *Oklahoma* survivor. Interview by the author. June 20, 2003.

Bowden, Ray. USS *Oklahoma* survivor. Telephone interview by the author. February 24, 2005.

Brown, George. USS *Oklahoma* survivor. Telephone interview by the author. December 13, 2005.

Burns, Charles Schuyler "Bob." In *Interviews from USS* Oklahoma*: Remembrance of a Great Lady*. Compiled by Joe L. Todd. Oklahoma City, Okla.: USS *Oklahoma* Association, 1990.

Coburn, George. USS *Oklahoma* survivor. Interviews by the author. August 18, 2003, and January 2, 2005.

Davenport, John. USS *Oklahoma* survivor. Telephone interview by the author. March 11, 2005.

Dick, Gene R. In *Pearl Harbor Survivors*. By Pearl Harbor Survivors Association. Paducah, Ky.: Turner Publishing, 1992.

Ehlert, James. USS *Oklahoma* survivor. Telephone interview by the author. March 3, 2005.

Emory, Ray. Pearl Harbor Survivors Association historian. Telephone interview by the author. May 27, 2005

Engen, John. USS *Oklahoma* survivor. Telephone interview by the author. January 12, 2005.

French, Howard. USS *Oklahoma* survivor. Interviews by the author. August 18, 2003, and January 1, 2005.

Goodyear, Paul. USS *Oklahoma* survivor. Interviews by the author. December 27, 2002, May 7, 2003, and July 19, 2003.

Goto, Jinichi. Interview by Gordon W. Prange. Transcripts of oral interviews conducted by Mr. Prange on file at the University of Maryland, College Park.

Kalman, Jesse. USS *Oklahoma* survivor. Telephone interview by the author. March 11, 2005.

Kitajima, Kazuyoshi. Interview by Gordon W. Prange. Transcripts of oral interviews conducted by Mr. Prange on file at the University of Maryland, College Park.

Kolb, Leon. USS *Oklahoma* survivor. Interview by the author. August 17, 2003.

Koth, Art. Telephone interview by the author. October 21, 2005.

Lester, Don. USS *Oklahoma* survivor. Interview by the author. July 19, 2003.

Matsumura, Heita. Interview by Gordon W. Prange. Transcripts of oral interviews conducted by Mr. Prange on file at the University of Maryland, College Park.

————. Interview by National Park Service, Pearl Harbor. Transcript of oral interview #228.

Parkinson, Francis. USS *Oklahoma* survivor. Interviews by the author. June 19, 2003, and January 2, 2005.

Pittman, Delbert. USS *Oklahoma* survivor. Telephone interview by the author. January 12, 2005.

Richmond, Ray. USS *Oklahoma* survivor. Interview by the author. June 20, 2003.

Saul, James. USS *Oklahoma* survivor. Telephone interview by the author. February 18, 2005.

Sebald, William J. Interview by U.S. Naval Institute, Oral Histories Division. Transcript. USNI, Annapolis, Maryland.

Spitler, Joseph C. USS *Oklahoma* survivor. Telephone interview by the author. March 9, 2005.

Staff, Walter P. USS *Oklahoma* survivor. Interview by National Park Service. Transcript. USS *Arizona* Memorial, Honolulu, Hawaii.

West, Robert D. In *Interviews from USS* Oklahoma*: Remembrance of a Great Lady*. Compiled by Joe L. Todd. Oklahoma City, Okla.: USS *Oklahoma* Association, 1990.

Woodward, Ted. USS *Oklahoma* survivor. Telephone interview by the author. August 31, 2005.

BOOKS, ARTICLES, AND WEBSITES

Aiken, David. "Torpedoing Pearl Harbor." *Military History* (December 2001): 46–53, 82.

Allen, Thomas, B. "Return to Pearl Harbor." *National Geographic* (December 1991): 50–77.

Backer, Steve. "USS *Oklahoma* BB-37: Commanders/Iron Shipwright 1:350 Scale." Review. www.steelnavy.com/ISWOklahoma.htm.

Barry, John M. *The Great Influenza*. New York: Penguin, 2005.

Barton, John K., and H. O. Stickney, Department of Marine Engineering and Naval Construction, U.S. Naval Academy. *Naval Reciprocating Engines and Auxiliary Machinery*. Annapolis, Md.: U.S. Naval Institute, 1914.

Beach, Samuel Wheeler. *The Great Cruise of 1925*. San Francisco: International Printing, 1925.

Boyd, Carl, and Akihiko Yoshida. *The Japanese Submarine Force and World War II*. Annapolis, Md.: Naval Institute Press, 1995.

Burlingame, Burl. *Advance Force Pearl Harbor*. Kailua, Hawaii: Pacific Monograph, 1992.

Byas, Hugh. *Government by Assassination*. New York: Knopf, 1942.

Clark, Blake. "The Rescue." *Remember Pearl Harbor*. New York: Harper and Brothers, 1943. Cohen, Stan. *East Wind Rain*. Missoula, Mont.: Pictorial Histories Publishing, 1981.

Conway's All the World's Fighting Ships, 1906–1921. London: Conway Maritime Press, 1985.

Conway's All the World's Fighting Ships, 1922–1946. London: Conway Maritime Press, 1980.

Costello, John. *The Pacific War, 1941–1945*. New York: Quill, 1982.

De Virgilio, John F. "Japanese Thunderfish." *Naval History* (Winter 1991): 61–68.

Department of Marine Engineering, U.S. Naval Academy. *Naval Machinery*. Annapolis, Md.: U.S. Naval Institute, 1935.

Farago, Latislas. *The Broken Seal: The Story of Operation Magic and the Pearl Harbor Disaster*. New York: Random House, 1967.

Friedman, Norman. *U.S. Battleships: An Illustrated Design History*. Annapolis, Md.: Naval Institute Press, 1985.

Gilbert, Martin. *The Second World War: A Complete History*. New York: Henry Holt, 1989.

Goldstein, Donald, Katherine Dillon, and J. Michael Wenger. *The Way It Was: Pearl Harbor, the Original Photographs*. New York: Brassey's, 1991.

Goodyear, Paul, and Kevin King. USS *Oklahoma* Official Site. www.ussoklahoma.com.

Great White Fleet Organization website. www.greatwhitefleet.org.

Hone, Thomas, and Norman Friedman. "Innovation and Administration in the Navy Department: The Case of the *Nevada* Design." *Military Affairs* (April 1981): 57–62.

Hone, Trent. "The Evolution of Fleet Tactical Doctrine in the U.S. Navy, 1922–1941." *Journal of Military History* 67 (October 2003): 1107–48.

Hoyt, Edwin P. *Yamamoto: The Man Who Planned the Attack on Pearl Harbor*. Guilford, Conn.: Lyons Press, 1990.

Jane's Fighting Ships of World War II. New York: Random House, 1998.

Jones, Jerry W. *U.S. Battleship Operations in World War I.* Annapolis, Md.: Naval Institute Press, 1998.

Kimmel, Husband E. *Admiral Kimmel's Story.* Chicago: Henry Regnery, 1955.

Kimmett, Larry, and Margaret Regis. *The Attack on Pearl Harbor: An Illustrated History.* Seattle, Wash.: Navigator Publishing, 1991.

"List of Warships Scuttled at Scapa Flow." World War I Naval Combat. http://www.worldwar1.co.uk/scapa-flow.html.

Lord, Walter. *Day of Infamy.* New York: Henry Holt, 1985.

Morison, Samuel Eliot. *The Rising Sun in the Pacific, 1931–1942.* Edison, N.J.: Castle Books, 2001.

Pearl Harbor Survivors Association. *Pearl Harbor Survivors.* Paducah, Ky.: Turner Publishing, 1992.

Prange, Gordon W. *At Dawn We Slept: The Untold Story of Pearl Harbor.* New York: Viking Penguin, 1982.

Prange, Gordon W., with Donald M. Goldstein and Katherine V. Dillon. *God's Samurai: Lead Pilot at Pearl Harbor.* McLean, Va.: Brassey's, 1990.

Prange, Gordon W., with Donald M. Goldstein and Katherine V. Dillon. *December 7, 1941: The Day the Japanese Attacked Pearl Harbor.* New York: McGraw-Hill, 1988.

Raymer, Edward C. *Descent into Darkness: Pearl Harbor, 1941: A Navy Diver's Memoir.* Novato, Calif.: Presidio Press, 1996.

Richardson, James O. *On the Treadmill to Pearl Harbor; The Memoirs of Admiral J. O. Richardson.* Washington, D.C.: Naval History Division, Department of the Navy, 1973.

Rodgaard, John, Peter K. Hsu, Carroll L. Lucas, and Andrew Biache, Jr. "Attack from Below." *Naval History* (December 2000): 64–67.

———. "Pearl Harbor—Attack from Below." *Naval History* (December 1999): 16–23.

———. "Update: Attack from Below." *Naval History* (June 2000): 36–37.

Shanks, Sandy. *The Bode Testament.* Lincoln, Neb.: Writers Club Press, 2001.

Shrader, Grahame F. "The *Oklahoma*'s Last Voyage." Copy of article of unknown source, obtained from *Oklahoma* survivor Francis Parkinson.

Simon, Mayo. "No Medals for Joe." *Reader's Digest* (December 1990): 138–43.

Smith, Carl. *Pearl Harbor.* Oxford, UK: Osprey Publishing, 2001.

Smithers, A. J. *Taranto 1940: Prelude to Pearl Harbor.* Annapolis, Md.: Naval Institute Press, 1995.

Stillwell, Paul. *Air Raid Pearl Harbor! Recollections of a Day of Infamy.* Annapolis, Md.: Naval Institute Press, 1981.

———. *Battleship Arizona: An Illustrated History.* Annapolis, Md.: Naval Institute Press, 1991.

———. *Battleships.* New York: MetroBooks, 2001.

Toland, John. *The Rising Sun: The Decline and Fall of the Japanese Empire, 1936–1945*. New York: Modern Library, 2003.

Tomatsu, Haruo, and H. P. Willmott. *A Gathering Darkness: The Coming of War to the Far East and the Pacific, 1921–1942*. Lanham, Md.: SR Books, 2004.

Toppan, Andrew C. Haze Gray & Underway. www.hazegray.org.

U.S. Congress. Proceedings of the Roberts Commission, part 24 of the *Joint Committee on Pearl Harbor Attack Hearings*. 77th Cong., 2d sess., 1942, 1570–1611.

U.S. Department of the Navy. *Annual Reports of the Navy Department for the Fiscal Year 1916*. Washington, D.C.: GPO, 1917.

———. *Annual Reports of the Navy Department for the Fiscal Year 1926*. Washington, D.C.: GPO, 1927.

———. *Annual Reports of the Navy Department for the Fiscal Year 1932*. Washington, D.C.: GPO, 1933.

———. *Ships' Data, U.S. Naval Vessels, January 1, 1914*. Washington, D.C.: GPO, 1915.

U.S. Navy. Naval Historical Center. www.history.navy.mil.

———. U.S. Navy. Office of Information. www.chinfo.navy.mil.

Valley, Robert L. "Punchbowl Cemetery." *Ontonogon Herald*, April 2004.

Wallin, Homer. *Pearl Harbor: Why, How, Fleet Salvage, and Final Appraisal*. Washington, D.C.: Naval History Division, 1968.

Wheeler, Keith. "Robert West's Second Life." *Life* December 16, 1966, 90–100.

Whitaker, Francis. "Salvage of USS *Oklahoma*." *Transactions of the Society of Naval Architects and Marine Engineers* 52 (1944): 133–209.

Yardley, Herbert O. *The American Black Book*. Annapolis, Md.: Naval Institute Press, 1931.

Young, Stephen. *Trapped at Pearl Harbor: Escape from Battleship Oklahoma*. Annapolis, Md.: Naval Institute Press, 1991.

Index